LIVES AND SPEECHES

OF

ABRAHAM LINCOLN

AND

HANNIBAL HAMLIN.

H. Hamlin

A. Lincoln

LIVES AND SPEECHES

OF

ABRAHAM LINCOLN

AND

HANNIBAL HAMLIN.

NEW YORK:
W. A. TOWNSEND & CO.,
COLUMBUS: FOLLETT, FOSTER & CO.
1860.

STEREOTYPED AT THE
FRANKLIN TYPE FOUNDRY,
CINCINNATI.

PRINTED BY
APPLEGATE & CO.,
CINCINNATI.

ILLUSTRATIONS.

INDEX.

LIFE

OF

ABRAHAM LINCOLN.

BY

W. D. HOWELLS.

2

PREFACE.

WHEN one has written a hurried book, one likes to dwell upon the fact, that if the time had not been wanting one could have made it a great deal better.

This fact is of the greatest comfort to the author, and not of the slightest consequence to anybody else.

It is perfectly reasonable, therefore, that every writer should urge it.

A work which seeks only to acquaint people with the personal history of a man for whom they are asked to cast their votes—and whose past ceases to concern them in proportion as his present employs them—will not be numbered with those immortal books which survive the year of their publication. It does not challenge criticism; it fulfills the end of its being if it presents facts and incidents in a manner not altogether barren of interest.

It is believed that the following biographical sketch of ABRAHAM LINCOLN will be found reliable. The information upon which the narrative is based, has been derived chiefly from the remembrance of MR. LINCOLN's old friends, and may, therefore, be considered authentic. It is hardly necessary to add, that no one but the writer is responsible for his manner of treating events and men.

CONTENTS.

CHAPTER I.

CHAPTER II.

CHAPTER III.

CHAPTER IV.

CHAPTER V.

CHAPTER VI.

CHAPTER VII.

CHAPTER VIII.

CHAPTER IX.

LIFE OF ABRAHAM LINCOLN.

CHAPTER I.

It is necessary that every American should have an indisputable grandfather, in order to be represented in the Revolutionary period by actual ancestral service, or connected with it by ancestral reminiscence. Further back than a grandfather few can go with satisfaction. Everything lies wrapt in colonial obscurity and confusion; and you have either to claim that the Smiths came over in the Mayflower, or that the Joneses were originally a Huguenot family of vast wealth and the gentlest blood; or that the Browns are descended from the race of Powhattan in the direct line; or you are left in an extremely embarrassing uncertainty as to the fact of great-grandparents.

We do not find it profitable to travel far into the past in search of Abraham Lincoln's ancestry. There is a dim possibility that he is of the stock of the New England Lincolns, of Plymouth colony; but the noble science of heraldry is almost obsolete in this country, and none of Mr. Lincoln's family seems to have been aware of the preciousness of long pedigrees, so that the records are meagre. The first that is known of his forefathers is that they were Quakers, who may have assisted in those shrewd bargains which honest William Penn drove with the Indians, for we find them settled at an early day in the old county of Berks, in Pennsylvania, where doubtless some of their descendants yet remain. Whether these have fallen away from the calm faith of their ancestors is not a matter of history, but it is certain that the family from which the present Abraham Lincoln derives his lineage, long ago ceased to be Quaker in everything but its devout Scriptural names. His grandfather, (anterior to whom is incertitude, and absolute darkness of names and dates,) was born in Rockingham county, Virginia, whither part of the family had emigrated from Pennsylvania; and had four brothers, patriarchially and apostolically named Isaac, Jacob, John, and Thomas; himself heading the list as Abraham Lincoln.

The descendants of Jacob and John, if any survive, still reside in Virginia; Thomas settled in the Cumberland region, near the adjunction of North Carolina, Tennessee, and Virginia, and very probably his children's children may there be found. Late in the last century, Abraham, with his wife and five children, removed from Rockingham to Kentucky, at a time when the border was the scene of savage warfare between the Indians and the whites, and when frontier life was diversified by continual incursions, repulsions, and reprisals, on one side and on the other. In one of these frequent invasions, Abraham Lincoln was killed by the Indians, who stole upon him while he was at work and shot him. There is historical mention made of an Indian expedition to Hardin county, Kentucky, in 1781, which resulted in the massacre of some of the settlers; but the date of Lincoln's death is fixed some three years later, and there is no other account of it than family tradition.

His wife, his three sons and two daughters survived him; but the dispersion of his family soon took place; the daughters marrying, and the sons seeking their fortunes in different localities. Of the latter, Thomas Lincoln, the father of Abraham Lincoln of to-day, was the youngest, and doubtless felt more severely than the rest the loss which had befallen them. They were poor, even for that rude time and country; and as a child, Thomas made acquaintance only with hardship and privation. He was a wandering, homeless boy, working when he could find work, and enduring when he could not. He grew up without education; his sole accomplishment in chirography being his own clumsy signature. At twenty-eight he married Lucy Hanks, and settled in Hardin county, where, on the 12th of February, 1809, ABRAHAM LINCOLN was born.

Lincoln's mother was, like his father, Virginian; but beyond this, little or nothing is known of her. From both his parents young Lincoln inherited an iron constitution and a decent poverty. From his father came that knack of story-telling, which has made him so delightful among acquaintances, and so irresistible in his stump and forensic drolleries. It is a matter of some regret that the information with regard to Thomas Lincoln and his wife is so meager. The information is, however, not altogether necessary to the present history, and the conjecture to which one is tempted would be as idle as impertinent. It is certain that Lincoln cherished, with just pride, a family repute for native ability, and alluded to it in after life, when he felt the first impulses of ambition, and began in earnest his struggle with the accidents of ignorance and poverty.

A younger brother of Abraham's died in infancy; and a sister, older than himself, married and died many years ago. With her he attended school during his early childhood in Kentucky, and acquired the alphabet, and other rudiments of education. The schooling which Abraham then received from the books and birch of Zachariah Riney and Caleb Hazel, (of pedagogic memory,) and afterward from Azel W. Dorsey,* and one or two others in Indiana, amounted in time to nearly a year, and can not be otherwise computed. It is certain, however, that this brief period limits his scholastic course. Outside of it, his education took place through the rough and wholesome experiences of border

*This gentleman is still living in Schuyler county, Illinois.

life, the promptings of a restless ambition, and a profound love of knowledge for its own sake. Under these influences, he has ripened into a hardy physical manhood, and acquired a wide and thorough intelligence, without the aid of schools or preceptors.

In the autumn of 1816, when Abraham was eight years old, his father determined to quit Kentucky. Already the evil influences of slavery were beginning to be felt by the poor and the non-slaveholders. But the emigration of Thomas Lincoln is, we believe, to be chiefly attributed to the insecurity of the right by which he held his Kentucky land; for, in those days, land-titles were rather more uncertain than other human affairs. Abandoning his old home, and striking through the forests in a northwesterly direction, he fixed his new dwelling-place in the heart of the "forest primeval" of what is now Spencer county, Indiana. The dumb solitude there had never echoed to the ax, and the whole land was a wilderness.

The rude cabin of the settler was hastily erected, and then those struggles and hardships commenced which are the common trials of frontier life, and of which the story has been so often repeated. Abraham was a hardy boy, large for his years, and with his ax did manful service in clearing the land. Indeed, with that implement, he literally hewed out his path to manhood; for, until he was twenty-three, the ax was seldom out of his hand, except in the intervals of labor, or when it was exchanged for the plow, the hoe, or the sickle. His youthful experiences in this forest life did not differ from those familiar to many others. As an adventurous boy, no doubt the wood was full of delight and excitement to him. No doubt he hunted the coon, trapped the turkey, and robbed the nest of the pheasant. As a hunter with the rifle, however, he did not acquire great skill, for he has never excelled an exploit of his eighth year, when he shot the leader of a flock of turkeys which ventured within sight of the cabin during his father's absence.

The family had hardly been two years in their new home when it was desolated by the death of Abraham's mother. This heavy loss was afterward partially repaired by the marriage of his father to Mrs. Sally Johnston, of Elizabethtown, Kentucky. She was the parent of three children by a former husband, and was always a good and affectionate mother to Thomas Lincoln's motherless son.*

The Lincolns continued to live in Spencer county, until 1830, nothing interrupting the even tenor of Abraham's life, except in his nineteeth year, a flat-boat trip to New Orleans. He and a son of the owner composed the crew, and without other assistance, voyaged

> "Down the beautiful river,
> Past the Ohio shore, and past the mouth of the Wabash,
> Into the golden stream of the broad and swift Mississippi,"

Trafficking here and there, in their course, with the

* Mrs. Lincoln is still living, in Coles county, Illinois.

inhabitants, and catching glimpses of the great world so long shut out by the woods. One night, having tied up their "cumbrous boat," near a solitary plantation on the sugar coast, they were attacked and boarded by seven stalwart negroes; but Lincoln and his comrade, after a severe contest in which both were hurt, succeeded in beating their assailants and driving them from the boat. After which they weighed what anchor they had, as speedily as possible, and gave themselves to the middle current again. With this sole adventure, Lincoln resumed his quiet backwoods life in Indiana.

Four years afterward, on the first of March, 1830, his father determined to emigrate once more, and the family abandoned the cabin which had been their home so long, and set out for Illinois. The emigrant company was made up of Thomas Lincoln's family, and the families of Mrs. Lincoln's two sons-in-law. Their means of progress and conveyance were ox-wagons, one of which Abraham Lincoln drove. Before the month was elapsed they had arrived at Macon county, Illinois, where they remained a short time, and Lincoln's family "located" on some new land, about ten miles northwest of Decatur, on the north bank of the Sangamon river, at a junction of forest and prairie land. Here the father and son built a log-cabin, and split rails enough to fence in their land. It is supposed that these are the rails which have since become historic; though they were by no means the only ones which the robust young backwoodsman made. Indeed, there are other particular rails* which dispute a celebrity somewhat indifferent to the sincere admirer of Mr. Lincoln. The work done was in the course of farm labor, and went to the development of Mr. Lincoln's muscle. Otherwise it is difficult to perceive how it has affected his career.

---

*Mr. George Close, the partner of Lincoln in the rail-splitting business, says that Lincoln was, at this time, a farm laborer, working from day to day, for different people, chopping wood, mauling rails, or doing whatever was to be done. The country was poor, and hard work was the common lot; the heaviest share falling to young unmarried men, with whom it was a continual struggle to earn a livelihood. Lincoln and Mr. Close made about one thousand rails together, for James Hawks and William Miller, receiving their pay in homespun clothing. Lincoln's bargain with Miller's wife, was, that he should have one yard of brown jeans, (richly dyed with walnut bark,) for every four hundred rails made, until he should have enough for a pair of trowsers. As Lincoln was already of great altitude, the number of rails that went to the acquirement of his pantaloons was necessarily immense.

CHAPTER II.

In his time, Denton Offutt was a man of substance; an enterprising and adventurous merchant, trading between the up-river settlements and the city of New Orleans, and fitting out frequent flat-boat expeditions to that cosmopolitan port, where the French voyageur and the rude hunter that trapped the beaver on the Osage and Missouri, met the polished old-world exile, and the tongues of France, Spain, and England made babel in the streets. In view of his experience, it is not too extravagant to picture Denton Offutt as a backwoods Ulysses, wise beyond the home-keeping pioneers about him—

> "Forever roaming with a hungry heart,"

bargaining with the Indians, and spoiling them, doubtless, as was the universal custom in those times; learning the life of the wild Mississippi towns, with their lawless frolics, deep potations, and reckless gambling; meeting under his own roof-tree the many-negroed planter of the sugar-coast, and the patriarchal creole of Louisiana; ruling the boatman who managed his craft, and defying the steamboat captain that swept by the slow broad-horn with his stately palace of paint and gilding; with his body inured to toil and privation, and with all his wits sharpened by traffic; such, no doubt, was Denton Offutt, who had seen

> ——"Cities of men,
> And manners, climates, councils, governments,"

and such was one of Lincoln's earliest friends. He quickly discovered the sterling qualities of honesty and fidelity, and the higher qualities of intellect which lay hid under the young Kentuckian's awkward exterior, and he at once took Lincoln into his employment. He was now about sending another flat-boat to New Orleans, and he engaged Lincoln, and the husband of one of Lincoln's step-sisters, together with their comrade, John Hanks,* to take charge of his craft for the voyage from Beardstown, in Illinois, to the Crescent City.

In this winter of 1830–31, a deep snow, long remembered in Illinois, covered the whole land for many weeks, and did not disappear until the first of March, when the waters of the thaw inundated the country. Overland travel from Macon county to Beardstown was rendered impossible; Lincoln, and his relative, therefore, took a canoe and descended the Sangamon river to Springfield, where they found Offutt. He had not succeeded in getting a flat-boat at Beardstown, as he expected; but with innumerable flat-boats growing up in their primal element of timber about him, he was not the man to be baffled by the trifling consideration that he had no flat-boat built. He offered to Lincoln and each of his

* Now a well known railroad man in Illinois.

friends, twelve dollars a month for the time they should be occupied in getting out lumber, and making the boat. The offer was accepted. The ax did its work; the planks were sawed with a whip-saw; Denton's ark was put together, and the trip to New Orleans triumphantly and profitably made.

On his return to Illinois, Lincoln found that his father had (in pursuance of a previous intention) removed from Macon, and was now living in Coles county. His relative rejoined his family there; but New Salem, on the Sangamon river, became the home of Lincoln, whose "location" there was accidental rather than otherwise. He was descending the river with another flat-boat for Offutt, and near New Salem grounded on a dam. An old friend and ardent admirer, who made his acquaintance on this occasion, says that Lincoln was standing in the water on the dam, when he first caught sight of him, devoting all his energies to the release of the boat. His dress at this time consisted of a pair of blue jeans trowsers indefinitely rolled up, a cotton shirt, striped white and blue, (of the sort known in song and tradition as *hickory*,) and a buckeye-chip hat for which a demand of twelve and a half cents would have been exorbitant.

The future president failed to dislodge his boat; though he did adopt the ingenious expedient of lightening it by boring a hole in the end that hung over the dam and letting out the water—an incident which Mr. Douglas humorously turned to account in one of his speeches. The boat stuck there stubborn, immovable.

Offutt, as has been seen, was a man of resource and decision. He came ashore from his flat-boat and resolutely rented the very mill of which the dam had caused his disaster, together with an old store-room, which he filled with a stock of goods, and gave in the clerkly charge of Abraham Lincoln, with the munificent salary of fifteen dollars a month.

Lincoln had already made his first speech. General W. L. D. Ewing, and a politician named Posey, who afterward achieved notoriety in the Black Hawk war, had addressed the freemen of Macon the year previous, "on the issues of the day." Mr. Posey had, however, in violation of venerable precedent and sacred etiquette, failed to invite the sovereigns to drink something. They were justly indignant, and persuaded Lincoln to reply, in the expectation that he would possibly make himself offensive to Posey. Lincoln, however, took the stump with characteristic modesty, and begging his friends not to laugh if he broke down, treated very courteously the two speakers who had preceded him, discussed questions of politics, and in his peroration eloquently pictured the future of Illinois. There was sense and reason in his arguments, and his imaginative flight tickled the State pride of the Illinoians. It was declared that Lincoln had made the best speech of the day; and he, to his great astonishment, found himself a prophet among those of his own household, while his titled fellow-orator cordially complimented his performance.

At New Salem, he now found the leisure and the

opportunity to initiate a system of self-education. At last, he had struggled to a point, where he could not only take breath, but could stoop and drink from those springs of knowledge, which a hopeless poverty, incessant toil, and his roving, uncertain life, had, till then, forbidden to his lips.

There seems never to have been any doubt of his ability among Lincoln's acquaintances, any more than there was a doubt of his honesty, his generosity, and gentle-heartedness. When, therefore, he began to make rapid progress in his intellectual pursuits, it surprised none of them—least of all, Lincoln's shrewd patron, Offutt, who had been known to declare, with pardonable enthusiasm, that Lincoln was the smartest man in the United States.

The first branch of learning which he took up, was English grammar, acquiring that science from the dry and meager treatise of Kirkham. The book was not to be had in the immediate vicinity, and Lincoln walked seven or eight miles to borrow a copy. He then devoted himself to the study with the whole strength of his resolute nature; and in three weeks he had gained a fair practical knowledge of the grammar. No doubt the thing was hard to the uncultivated mind, though that mind *was* of great depth and fertility. One of his friends* relates that Lincoln used to take him aside, and require explanations of the sententious Kirkham, whenever he visited New Salem.

---

*L. M. Green, Esq., of Petersburgh, Illinois.

This young backwoodsman had the stubborn notion that because the Lincolns had always been people of excellent sense, he, a Lincoln, might become a person of distinction. He had talked, he said, with men who were regarded as great, and he did not see where they differed so much from others. He reasoned, probably, that the secret of their success lay in the fact of original capacity, and untiring industry. He was conscious of his own powers; he was a logician, and could not resist logical conclusions. If he studied, why might not he achieve?

And Kirkham fell before him. One incident of his study, was a dispute with the learned man of the place, —a very *savant* among the unlettered pioneers—in regard to a grammatical nicety, and the question being referred to competent authority, it was decided in Lincoln's favor, to his pride and exultation.

Concluding his grammatical studies with Kirkham, he next turned his attention to mathematics, and took up a work on surveying, with which he made himself thoroughly acquainted.

So great was his ardor in study, at this time, that shrewd suspicions with regard to Offutt's clerk got abroad; the honest neighbors began to question whether one who would voluntarily spend all his leisure in

———"poring over miserable books,"

could be altogether right in his mind.

The peculiar manner in which he afterward pursued

his law studies, was not calculated to allay popular feeling. He bought an old copy of Blackstone, one day, at auction, in Springfield, and on his return to New Salem, attacked the work with characteristic energy.

His favorite place of study was a wooded knoll near New Salem, where he threw himself under a wide-spreading oak, and expansively made a reading desk of the hillside. Here he would pore over Blackstone day after day, shifting his position as the sun rose and sank, so as to keep in the shade, and utterly unconscious of everything but the principles of common law. People went by, and he took no account of them; the salutations of acquaintances were returned with silence, or a vacant stare; and altogether the manner of the absorbed student was not unlike that of one distraught.

Since that day, his habits of study have changed somewhat, but his ardor remains unabated, and he is now regarded as one of the best informed, as he is certainly the ablest, man in Illinois.

When practicing law, before his election to Congress, a copy of Burns was his inseparable companion on the circuit; and this he perused so constantly, that it is said he has now by heart every line of his favorite poet. He is also a diligent student of Shakspeare, "to know whom is a liberal education."

The bent of his mind, however, is mathematical and metaphysical, and he is therefore pleased with the absolute and logical method of Poe's tales and sketches, in which the problem of mystery is given, and wrought out into every-day facts by processes of cunning analysis. It is said that he suffers no year to pass without the perusal of this author.

Books, of all sorts, the eager student devoured with an insatiable appetite; and newspapers were no less precious to him. The first publication for which he ever subscribed, was the *Louisville Journal*, which he paid for when he could secure the intellectual luxury only at the expense of physical comfort.

It was a day of great rejoicing with Lincoln, when President Jackson appointed him postmaster at New Salem. He was a Whig, but the office was of so little pecuniary significance, that it was bestowed irrespective of politics. Lincoln, indeed, was the only person in the community whose accomplishments were equal to the task of making out the mail returns for the Department.

An acquaintance says that the Presidency can never make our candidate happier than the post-office did then. He foresaw unlimited opportunities for reading newspapers, and of satisfying his appetite for knowledge.

But it was not through reading alone that Lincoln cultivated his intellect. The grave and practical American mind has always found entertainment and profit in disputation, and the debating clubs are what every American youth is subject to. They are useful in many ways. They safely vent the mental exuberance of youth; those whom destiny intended for the bar and the Senate, they assist; those who have a mistaken vocation to oratory, they mercifully extinguish.

Even in that day, and that rude country, where learning was a marvelous and fearful exception, the debating school flourished, in part as a literary institution, and in part as a rustic frolic.

Lincoln delighted in practicing polemics, as it was called, and used to walk six and seven miles through the woods to attend the disputations in his neighborhood. Of course, many of the debates were infinitely funny, for the disputants were, frequently, men without education. Here, no doubt, Lincoln stored his mind with anecdote and comic illustration, while he delighted his auditors with his own wit and reason, and added to his growing popularity.

This popularity had been early founded by a stroke of firmness and bravery on Lincoln's part, when he first came into Sangamon county.

He had returned from that famous voyage made with Offutt's impromptu flat-boat to New Orleans, and descending the Sangamon river, had, as has been already related, fixed upon the little village of New Salem,* by fortuity rather than intention, as his future home. Nevertheless, he had first to undergo an ordeal to which every new comer was subjected, before his residence could be generally acknowledged. Then, when it was much more necessary to be equal parts of horse and

* Now Petersburgh.

alligator, and to be able to vanquish one's weight in wild cats, than now, there flourished, in the region of New Salem, a band of jolly, roystering blades, calling themselves "Clary's Grove Boys," who not only gave the law to the neighborhood, as Regulators, but united judicial to legislative functions, by establishing themselves a tribunal to try the stuff of every one who came into that region. They were, at once, the protectors and the scourge of the whole country-side, and must have been some such company as that of Brom Bones, in Sleepy Hollow, upon whom the "neighbors all looked with a mixture of awe, admiration, and good-will." Their mode of receiving a stranger was to appoint some one of their number to wrestle with him, fight with him, or run a foot-race with him, according to their pleasure, and his appearance.

As soon as young Lincoln appeared, the "Clary's Grove Boys" determined to signalize their prowess anew by a triumph over a stalwart fellow, who stood six feet three inches without stockings. The leader and champion of their band, (one Jack Armstrong, who seems himself to have been another Brom Bones,) challenged Lincoln to a wrestling-match. When the encounter took place, the "Clary's Grove Boy" found that he had decidedly the worst half of the affair, and the bout would have ended in his ignominious defeat, had not all his fellow-boys come to his assistance. Lincoln then refused to continue the unequal struggle. He would wrestle with them fairly, or he would run a foot-race, or if any of them desired to fight, he generously offered to thrash that particular individual. He looked every word he said, and none of the Boys saw fit to accept his offer. Jack Armstrong was willing to call the match drawn; and Lincoln's fearless conduct had already won the hearts of his enemies. He was invited to become one of their company. His popularity was assured. The Boys idolized him, and when the Black Hawk war broke out, he was chosen their captain, and remained at their head throughout the campaign. Their favor still pursued him, and, at the close of the war, he was elected to the Legislature, through the influence created by his famous wrestling-match.

Many of the Boys are now distinguished citizens of Illinois, and are among Lincoln's warmest friends; though they acknowledge that if he had shown signs of cowardice when they came to the rescue of their champion, it would have fared grievously with him.

Indeed, this seems to have been one of the most significant incidents of his early life. It gave him reputation for courage necessary in a new country, and opened a career to him which his great qualities have enabled him to pursue with brilliance and success.*

---

*Jack Armstrong, in particular, became a fast friend of Lincoln. It is related that he bestowed a terrible pummeling on a person who once ventured to speak slightingly of Lincoln in his presence. Afterward, Lincoln had an opportunity to make a full return to Armstrong for his friendship. A man had been killed in a riot at camp-meeting, in Menard county, and suspicion fell upon a son of Jack Armstrong—a wild young scapegrace, who was known to have taken part in the affair. He was arrested, and brought to trial for murder. Lincoln, who seems to have believed firmly in the young man's innocence, volun-

CHAPTER III.

In 1832, Black Hawk's war broke out. In the light of history, this war seems to have been a struggle involuntarily commenced by the Indians against the white settlers. A treaty had been made by the Sacs and Foxes, ceding to the United States all the land east of the Mississippi—a treaty which the Sac chief, Black Hawk, declared to be illegal. A war with the Sacs ensued, which was terminated by treaty in 1825. Meanwhile Illinois had been admitted to the Union, and the country had filled up with whites, who extended the lines of their settlements around the country of the Indians, and pressed closer and closer upon them. Outrages, on one part and on the other, were of constant occurrence; and in revenge for some wrong, a party of Chippeway Indians fired upon a keel-boat conveying stores to Fort Snelling. Through mistake or injustice, Black Hawk was arrested for this, and lay imprisoned a whole year before he could be brought to trial and acquitted. After his release, it

---

teered in his defense, and throwing aside the well-connected links of circumstantial evidence against him, made a most touching and eloquent appeal to the sympathies of the jury. There was that confidence in Lincoln, that absolute faith, that he would never say anything but the truth, to achieve any end, that the jury listened and were convinced. Young Armstrong was acquitted; and Lincoln refused to accept any reward for his defense.

was believed that he engaged in negotiations to unite all the Indians, from Rock River to the Gulf of Mexico, in a general war upon the whites. The alarm, of course, was very great, and active preparations for hostilities were made. Regular forces were marched against the Indians at Rock Island, and large bodies of militia were called into the field. It appears that Black Hawk never succeeded in rallying about him more than two or three hundred warriors of his tribe; the Indians being desirous of peace, and willing to abide by the treaty of the chief Keokuk, who favored the cession of land. Indeed, Black Hawk himself attempted to treat with the whites several times when he met them, and only fought after his flags of truce had been fired upon. The war was brought to a close by the battle of Bad-Ax, in which glorious action a great number of squaws and papooses, not to mention several warriors, were killed. The Indians then retreated beyond the Mississippi, and Black Hawk was brought a prisoner into the camp of the whites. He made the grand tour of the Atlantic cities, where he received the usual attentions bestowed upon lions of every tribe, and returning to the West a sadder and a wiser Indian, passed into oblivion.

There can not be any doubt that the war was a very serious matter to the people who were engaged in it; and there is as little doubt that their panic exaggerated their danger, and rendered them merciless in their determination to expel the Indians.

Offutt's business had long been failing, and at the

time the war broke out, Lincoln had the leisure, as well as the patriotism, to join one of the volunteer companies which was formed in the neighborhood of New Salem. To his unbounded surprise and satisfaction, he was chosen captain by his fellow-soldiers. The place of rendezvous was at Richland, and as soon as the members of the company met, the election took place. It was expected that the captaincy would be conferred on a man of much wealth and consequence among the people, for whom Lincoln had once worked. He was a harsh and exacting employer, and had treated the young man, whom everybody else loved and esteemed, with the greatest rigor; a course which had not increased his popularity. The method of election was for the candidates to step out of the ranks, when the electors advanced and joined the man whom they chose to lead them. Three-fourths of the company at once went to Lincoln; and when it was seen how strongly the tide was set in his favor, the friends of the rival candidate deserted him, one after another, until he was left standing almost alone. He was unspeakably mortified and disappointed, while Lincoln's joy was proportionably great.

The latter served three months in the Black Hawk war, and made acquaintance with the usual campaigning experiences, but was in no battle. He still owns the lands in Iowa that he located with warrants for service performed in the war.

An incident of the campaign, in which Lincoln is

concerned,* illustrates a trait of his character no less prominent than his qualities of integrity and truth. One day an old Indian wandered into Lincoln's camp, and was instantly seized by his men. The general opinion was that he ought to be put to death. They were in the field for the purpose of killing Indians, and to spare the slaughter of one that Providence had delivered into their hands was something of which these honest pioneers could not abide the thought. It was to little purpose that the wretched aborigine showed a letter signed by General Cass, and certifying him to be not only a model of all the savage virtues, but a sincere friend of the whites. He was about to be sacrificed, when Lincoln boldly declared that the sacrifice should not take place. He was at once accused of cowardice, and of a desire to conciliate the Indians. Nevertheless, he stood firm, proclaiming that even barbarians would not kill a helpless prisoner. If any one thought him a coward, let him step out and be satisfied of his mistake, in any way he chose. As to this poor old Indian, he had no doubt he was all that the letter of General Cass affirmed; he declared that they should kill *him* before they touched the prisoner. His argument, in fine, was so convincing, and his manner so determined, that the copper-colored ally of the whites was suffered to go his ways, and departed out of the hostile camp of his friends unhurt.

---

*The authority for this anecdote is Mr. William G. Green, a tried and intimate friend of Lincoln during early manhood.

After his return from the wars, Lincoln determined to test the strength of his popularity, by offering himself as a candidate for the Legislature. Added to the good-will which had carried him into the captaincy, he had achieved a warmer place in the hearts of those who had followed his fortunes during the war, by his bravery, social qualities, and uprightness. He was warm-hearted and good-natured, and told his stories, of which he had numbers, in better style than any other man in the camp. No one was so fleet of foot; and in those wrestlings which daily enlivened the tedium of camp life, he was never thrown but once, and then by a man of superior science who was not his equal in strength. These were qualities which commended him to the people, and made him the favorite officer of the battalion.

Parties, at this time, were distinguished as Adams parties and Jackson parties, and in Lincoln's county the Jackson men were vastly in the ascendant. He was a stanch Adams man, and, being comparatively unknown in the remoter parts of the county, was defeated. In his own neighborhood the vote was almost unanimous in his favor; though he had only arrived from the war and announced himself as a candidate ten days before the election. Indeed, he received, at this election, one more vote in his precinct than both of the rival candidates for Congress together.*

* The following is the vote taken from the poll-book in Springfield: For Congress—Jonathan H. Pugh, 179, and Joseph Duncan, 97. For Legislature—Lincoln, 277.

Defeated, but far from dismayed, Lincoln once more turned his attention to business. He was still poor, for though thrifty enough, he never could withstand the appeals of distress, nor sometimes refuse to become security for those who asked the use of his name. His first surveying had been done with a grape-vine instead of a chain, and having indorsed a note which was not paid, his compass was seized and sold. One James Short bought it and returned it to Lincoln. The surveyor of Sangamon county, John Calhoun, (since notorious for his candle-box concealment of the election returns in Kansas,) deputed to Lincoln that part of the county in which he resided, and he now assumed the active practice of surveying, and continued to live upon the slender fees of his office until 1834, when he was elected to the Legislature by the largest vote cast for any candidate.

Before this election Lincoln had engaged and failed in merchandising on his own account.

It is supposed that it was at New Salem that Lincoln, while a "clerk" in Offutt's store, first saw Stephen A. Douglas, and, probably, the acquaintance was renewed during Lincoln's proprietorship of the store which he afterward bought in the same place.*

* Lincoln expressly stated, in reply to some badinage of Douglas, during the debates of 1858, that he never kept a grocery anywhere. Out West, a grocery is understood to be a place where the chief article of commerce is whisky. Lincoln's establishment was, in the Western sense, a store; that is, he sold tea, coffee, sugar, powder, lead, and other luxuries and necessaries of pioneer existence. Very possibly his store was not without the "elixir of life," with which nearly everybody renewed the flower of youth in those days; though this is not a matter of absolute history, nor perhaps of vital consequence.

One Reuben Radford was Lincoln's predecessor. He had fallen, by some means, into disfavor with Clary's Grove Boys, who, one evening, took occasion to break in the windows of his establishment. Reuben was discouraged. Perhaps it would not be going too far to allude to his situation as discouraging. At any rate, he told a young farmer,* who came to trade with him the next day, that he was going to close out his business. What would Mr. Green give him for his stock? Mr. Green looked about him and replied, only half in earnest, Four hundred dollars. The offer was instantly accepted, and the business transferred to Mr. Green. On the following day Lincoln chanced to come in, and being informed of the transaction, proposed that he and Green should invoice the stock, and see how much he had made. They found that it was worth about six hundred dollars, and Lincoln gave Mr. Green a hundred and twenty-five dollars for his bargain, while Green indorsed the notes of Lincoln and one Berry, to Radford for the remaining four hundred. Berry was a thriftless soul, it seems, and after a while the store fell into a chronic decay, and, in the idiom of the region, finally *winked out.*

Lincoln was moneyless, having previously invested his whole fortune in a surveyor's compass and books, and Berry was uncertain. Young Green was compelled to pay the notes given to Radford. He afterward removed to Tennessee, where he married, and was living

* Mr. W. T. Green, now one of the most influential and wealthy men of his part of Illinois.

in forgetfulness of his transaction with Lincoln, when he one day received a letter from that person, stating he was now able to pay back to Green the amount for which he had indorsed. Lincoln was by this time in the practice of the law, and it was with the first earnings of his profession, that he discharged this debt, principal and interest.

The moral need not be insisted on, and this instance is not out of the order of Abraham Lincoln's whole life. That the old neighbors and friends of such a man should regard him with an affection and faith little short of man-worship, is the logical result of a life singularly pure, and an integrity without flaw.

CHAPTER IV.

It is seen that Abraham Lincoln was first elected to a seat in the Legislature, in 1834, in the face of the unpopularity of his political principles, by a larger vote than that given to any other candidate. As a legislator he served his constituents so well that he was three times afterward returned to his place; in 1836, in 1838, and in 1840. He then terminated his legislative career by a positive refusal to be again a candidate.

The period embraced by the eight years in which Lincoln represented Sangamon county, was one of the greatest material activity in Illinois. So early as 1820, the young State was seized with the "generous rage" for public internal improvements, then prevalent in New York, Pennsylvania, and Ohio, and in its sessions for a score of succeeding years, the Legislature was occupied by the discussion of various schemes for enhancing the prosperity of the State. The large canal uniting the waters of Lake Michigan and the Illinois river was completed at a cost of more than eight millions. By a Board of Commissioners of Public Works, specially created, provisions were made for expensive improvements of the rivers Wabash, Illinois, Rock, Kaskaskia, and Little Wabash, and the great Western mail route from

Vincennes to St. Louis. Under the charge of the same Board, six railroads connecting principal points were projected, and appropriations made for their completion at an immense outlay.

One effect of a policy so wild and extravagant was to sink the State in debt. Another was to attract vast emigration, and fill up her broad prairies with settlers. Individuals were ruined; the corporate State became embarrassed; but benefits have resulted in a far greater degree than could have been hoped when the crash first came. It is not yet time to estimate the ultimate good to be derived from these improvements, though the immediate evil has been tangible enough.

The name of Abraham Lincoln is not found recorded in favor of the more visionary of these schemes; but he has always favored public improvements, and his voice was for whatever project seemed feasible and practical. During his first term of service, he was a member of the Committee on Public Accounts and Expenditures. He voted for a bill to incorporate agricultural societies; for the improvement of public roads; for the incorporation of various institutions of learning; for the construction of the Illinois and Michigan Canal; he always fostered the interests of public education, and favored low salaries for public officials. In whatever pertained to the local benefit of his own county, he was active and careful; but his record on this subject is of little interest to the general reader.

Lincoln's voice was ever for measures that relieved

the struggling poor man from pecuniary or political difficulties; he had himself experienced these difficulties. He therefore supported resolutions for the removal of the property qualification in franchise, and for the granting of pre-emption rights to settlers on the public lands. He was the author of a measure permitting Revolutionary pensioners to loan their pension money without taxation. He advocated a bill exempting from execution Bibles, school-books, and mechanics' tools.

His first recorded vote against Stephen A. Douglas, was on the election of that politician to the Attorney-Generalship by the Legislature.

He twice voted for the Whig candidates for the United States Senate. Otherwise than in the election of Senators, State Legislatures were not then occupied with national affairs, and it is difficult to find anything in Mr. Lincoln's legislative history which is of great national interest. There were no exciting questions, and Mr. Lincoln's speeches were few and brief.* He was twice the candidate (in 1838 and 1840) of the Whig minority for Speaker of the House.

In 1836, when Lincoln was first re-elected to the Legislature, Sangamon county, then of greater geographical importance than now, was represented by nine members,

---

* A protest from Mr. Lincoln appears on the journal of the House, in regard to some resolutions which had passed. In this protest he pronounces distinctly against slavery, and takes the first public step toward what is now Republican doctrine.

no one of whom was less than six feet in height—several of them considerably exceeding that altitude. This immensity of stature attracted attention, and the Sangamon members were at once nicknamed *The Long-Nine.* They were genial, hearty-humored fellows, famous whittlers, and distinguished spinners of yarns. They all boarded at the same place, and being of gregarious habits, spent their evenings together. Lincoln was the favorite of the circle; admired for his gift of story-telling, and highly esteemed for his excellent qualities of head and heart, his intellectual shrewdness, his reliability, his good-nature, and generosity. The Illinois Legislature then held its sessions at Vandalia, and Lincoln used to perform his journeys between New Salem and the seat of government on foot, though the remaining eight of the Long-Nine traveled on horseback.

A pleasant story connected with this part of his political career is related by Hon. John D. Stuart. Lincoln and Stuart were both candidates for the Legislature in 1834. Stuart's election was conceded, while that of Lincoln was thought to be comparatively uncertain. The two candidates happened to be present together at a backwoods frolic, when some disaffected of Stuart's party took Lincoln aside, and offered to withdraw votes enough from Stuart to elect him. He rejected the proposal, and at once disclosed the scheme to Stuart, declaring that he would not make such a bargain for any office.

It is by such manly and generous acts that Lincoln has endeared himself to all his old neighbors. It may be said of him without extravagance that he is beloved of all—even by those against whose interests he has conscientiously acted. When in the practice of the law he was never known to undertake a cause which he believed founded in wrong and injustice. "You are not strictly in the right," he said to a person who once wished him to bring a certain suit, and who now tells the story with profound admiration. "I might give the other parties considerable trouble, and perhaps beat them at law, but there would be no justice in it. I am sorry—I can not undertake your case." "I never knew Lincoln to do a mean act in his life," said Stuart, the veteran lawyer, who first encouraged Lincoln to adopt his profession. "God never made a finer man," exclaimed the old backwoods-man, Close, when applied to for reminiscences of Lincoln. So by the testimony of all, and in the memory of every one who has known him, Lincoln is a pure, candid, and upright man, unblemished by those vices which so often disfigure greatness, utterly incapable of falsehood, and without one base or sordid trait.

During the Legislative canvass of 1834, John D. Stuart advised Lincoln to study law, and after the election he borrowed some of Stuart's books, and began to read. Other warm and influential friends, (Wm. Butler, the present Treasurer of State in Illinois, was one of these,) came to Lincoln's material aid and encouragement, and assisted him to retrieve his early errors of generosity. With the support of these friends—for

Lincoln is a man who could receive benefits as nobly as he conferred them—and the slender revenues of his surveyorship, he struggled through the term of his law studies, and was admitted to the bar in 1836. Business flowed in upon him, and quitting New Salem, he took up his residence at Springfield, where he united his professional fortunes with those of Major Stuart. The two old friends remained in partnership until Stuart's election to Congress, by which time Lincoln had elevated himself to a position among the first lawyers of the place. In the midst of affairs, however, he never relaxed his habits of study; taking up, one by one, the natural sciences, and thoroughly acquainting himself with the abstrusest metaphysics. He remains to this day a severe and indefatigable student—never suffering any subject to which he directs his attention, to pass without profound investigation.

5

CHAPTER V.

We now find Abraham Lincoln beginning to assume an active part in the political affairs of Illinois.

He is known to the Whigs throughout the State, and his general popularity is as great as the esteem and regard in which he is held by those personally acquainted with him.

The talented young Whig has founded his reputation upon qualities that make every man proud to say he is the friend of Lincoln.

No admirer, who speaks in his praise, must pause to conceal a stain upon his good name. No true man falters in his affection at the remembrance of any mean action or littleness in the life of Lincoln.

The purity of his reputation, the greatness and dignity of his ambition, ennoble every incident of his career, and give significance to all the events of his past.

It is true that simply to have mauled rails, and commanded a flat-boat, is not to have performed splendid actions. But the fact that Lincoln has done these things, and has risen above them by his own force, confers a dignity upon them; and the rustic boy, who is to be President in 1900, may well be consoled and encouraged in his labors when he recalls these incidents in the history of one whose future once wore no brighter aspect than his own wears now.

The emigrant, at the head of the slow oxen that drag his household gods toward the setting sun—toward some Illinois yet further west—will take heart and hope when he remembers that Lincoln made no prouder entrance into the State of which he is now the first citizen.

The young student, climbing unaided up the steep ascent—he who has begun the journey after the best hours of the morning are lost forever—shall not be without encouragement when he finds the footprints of another in the most toilsome windings of his path.

Lincoln's future success or unsuccess can affect nothing in the past. The grandeur of his triumph over all the obstacles of fortune, will remain the same. Office can not confer honors brighter than those he has already achieved; it is the Presidency, not a great man, that is elevated, if such be chosen chief magistrate.

We have seen that, in 1842, he declines re-election to the State Legislature, after eight years' service in that body. He has already been on the Harrison electoral ticket, and has distinguished himself in the famous canvass of 1840.

But it is not as a politician alone, that Lincoln is heard of at this time. After Stuart's election to Congress has dissolved their connection, Lincoln forms a partnership with Judge Logan, one of the first in his profession at Springfield, and continues the practice of the law, with rising repute.

His characteristics as an advocate, are an earnestness and sincerity of manner, and a directness, conciseness, and strength of style; he appeals, at other times, to the weapons of good-humored ridicule as ably as to the heavier arms of forensic combat. He is strongest in civil cases, but in a criminal cause that enlists his sympathy he is also great. It is then that the advocate's convictions, presented to the jury in terse and forcible, yet eloquent language, sometimes outweigh the charge of the judge. Juries listen to him, and concur in his arguments; for his known truth has preceded his arguments, and he triumphs. There may be law and evidence against him, but the belief that Lincoln is *right*, nothing can shake in the minds of those who know the man.

He prepares his cases with infinite care, when he has nothing but technical work before him. The smallest detail of the affair does not escape him. All the parts are perfectly fitted together, and the peculiar powers of his keen, analytic mind are brought into full play. He has not the quickness which characterizes Douglas, and which is so useful to the man who adventures in law or politics. But he is sufficiently alert, and recovers himself in time to achieve success.

Lincoln does not grow rich at the law, and has not grown rich to this day, though possessing a decent competence, and owing no man anything. Poor men, who have the misfortune to do with courts, come to Lincoln, who has never been known to exact an exorbitant fee, and whose demands are always proportioned to their poverty. There is record of a case which he gained for a young mechanic, after carrying it through three courts, and of his refusal to receive more than a comparative trifle in return.

Meantime, in the year 1842, Lincoln married a woman worthy to be the companion of his progress toward honor and distinction. Miss Mary Todd, who became his wife, is the daughter of Robert Todd, of Lexington, Kentucky, a man well known in that State, and formerly the clerk of the lower House of Congress. At the time of her marriage, Miss Todd was the belle of Springfield society—accomplished and intellectual, and possessing all the social graces native in the women of Kentucky.*

If, at this point of his career, Lincoln looked back over his past life with proud satisfaction, his feeling was one in which every reader, who has traced his history, must sympathize.

It was hardly more than a half-score of years since he had entered Illinois, driving an ox-wagon, laden with the "plunder" of a backwoods emigrant. He was utterly unknown, and without friends who could advance him in any way. He was uneducated, and almost unlettered.

In ten years he had reversed all the relations of his

* Three living sons are the children of this marriage; the first of whom was born in 1843, the second in 1850, and the third in 1853. Another son, who was born in 1846, is now dead.

life. No man had now more friends among all classes of people. No man among his neighbors had a wider intelligence, or more eager and comprehensive mind. No man of his age stood better in his profession, or in politics. No one was in a fairer road to happiness and success. And all this had been accomplished through his own exertion, and the favor which his many noble traits awakened in those around him.

He might well exult in view of all that had been, and all that was.

But, however this may have been, Lincoln did not pause to exult. He exulted in full career; for already the great battle of 1844 was approaching, and he was to take a prominent part in the contest. Many of the people of Illinois have distinct recollection of the brilliant debates which he conducted with Calhoun and Thomas, and these are loth to concede that they have ever been surpassed. The debaters met in all the principal cities and towns of that State, and afterward carried the war into Indiana.

It may be supposed that the fortunes of the war varied, but there are popular stories related of these encounters that give rather amusing results of one of Lincoln's frequent successes.

The contest turned upon the annexation of Texas, to which measure Lincoln was opposed, in proportion as he loved and honored Henry Clay. It has been said that no man ever had such friends as Clay possessed. It may be said that he never possessed a friend more ardent, attached, and faithful than Abraham Lincoln. Throughout that disastrous campaign of 1844, Lincoln was a zealous and indefatigable soldier in the Whig cause. His name was on the electoral ticket of Illinois, and he shared the defeat of his gallant leader—a defeat which precipitated the Mexican war, with its attendant evils, and the long train of dissensions, discords, and pro-slavery aggressions which have followed.

In the lull which comes after a Presidential battle, Lincoln, while mingling in State politics, devoted himself more particularly to professional affairs, though he continued an enemy to the Mexican war, and his election to Congress in 1846, took place in full view of this enmity. It is worthy of note, in this connection, that he was the only Whig elected in Illinois at that time.

CHAPTER VI.

THE period over which Lincoln's Congressional career extends, is one of the most interesting of our history.

Mr. Polk's favorite scheme of a war of glory and aggrandizement, had been in full course of unsatisfactory experiment. Our little army in Mexico had conquered a peace as rapidly as possible. The battles of Palo Alto, Reseca de la Palma, Monterey, Buena Vista, Cerro Gordo, and the rest, had been fought to the triumph and honor of the American arms. Everywhere, the people had regarded these successes with patriotic pride. They had felt a yet deeper interest in them because the volunteer system had taken the war out of the hands of mercenaries, and made it, in some sort, the crusade of Anglo-Saxon civilization and vigor against the semi-barbarism and effeteness of the Mexican and Spanish races.

Yet, notwithstanding the popular character thus given to the army, the war itself had not increased in popularity. People, in their sober second thought, rejected the specious creed, "Our country, right or wrong," and many looked forward earnestly and anxiously to a conclusion of hostilities.

The elections of Congressmen had taken place, and in

the Thirtieth Congress, which assembled on the 6th of December, 1847, the people, by a majority of seven Whigs in the House, pronounced against the war, though hardly more than a year had elapsed since their Representatives, by a vote of one hundred and twenty-two to fourteen, had declared war to exist through the act of Mexico.

In those days, great men shaped the destinies of the nation. In the Senate sat Clay, Calhoun, Benton, Webster, Corwin. In the House were Palfrey, Winthrop, Wilmot, Giddings, Adams.

The new member from Illinois, who had distinguished himself in 1844 as the friend of Clay and the enemy of Texan annexation, took his seat among these great men as a representative of the purest Whig principles; he was opposed to the war, as Corwin was; he was anti-slavery, as Clay was; he favored internal improvements, as all the great Whigs did.

And as Abraham Lincoln never sat astride of any fence, unless in his rail-splitting days; as water was never carried on both of his square shoulders; as his prayers to Heaven have never been made with reference to a compromise with other powers; so, throughout his Congressional career, you find him the bold advocate of the principles which he believed to be right. He never dodged a vote. He never minced matters with his opponents. He had not been fifteen days in the House when he made known what manner of man he was.

On the 22d of December he offered a series of resolutions,* making the most damaging inquiries of the President, as to the verity of certain statements in his messages of May and December. Mr. Polk had represented that the Mexicans were the first aggressors in the

---

* The following are the resolutions, which it is judged best to print here in full:

"*Whereas*, the President of the United States, in his Message of May 11, 1846, has declared that 'the Mexican government refused to receive him, [the envoy of the United States,] or listen to his propositions, but, after a long-continued series of menaces, have at last invaded *our territory*, and shed the blood of our fellow-citizens on *our own soil*.'

"And again, in his Message of December 8, 1846, that 'we had ample cause of war against Mexico long before the breaking out of hostilities; but even then we forbore to take redress into our own hands, until Mexico basely became the aggressor, by invading *our soil* in hostile array, and shedding the blood of our citizens.'

"And yet again, in his Message of December 7, 1847, 'The Mexican government refused even to hear the terms of adjustment which he (our minister of peace) was authorized to propose, and finally, under wholly unjustifiable pretexts, involved the two countries in war, by invading the territory of the State of Texas, striking the first blow, and shedding the blood of our citizens on *our own soil*.'

"And whereas this House is desirous to obtain a full knowledge of all the facts which go to establish whether the particular spot on which the blood of our citizens was so shed, was, or was not, at that time, *our own soil*. Therefore,

"*Resolved, by the House of Representatives*, That the President of the United States be respectfully requested to inform this House—

"1st. Whether the spot on which the blood of our citizens was shed, as in his memorial declared, was, or was not within the territory of Spain, at least, after the treaty of 1819, until the Mexican revolution.

"2d. Whether that spot is, or is not within the territory which was wrested from Spain by the revolutionary government of Mexico.

"3d. Whether that spot is, or is not within a settlement of people, which settlement has existed ever since long before the Texas Revolution, and until its inhabitants fled before the approach of the United States army.

"4th. Whether that settlement is, or is not isolated from any and all other settlements of the Gulf and the Rio Grande on the south and west, and of wide uninhabited regions on the north and east.

"5th. Whether the people of that settlement, or a majority of them, have ever submitted themselves to the government or laws of Texas, or of the United States, of consent or of compulsion, either of accepting office or voting at elections, or paying taxes, or serving on juries, or having process served on them or in any other way.

"6th. Whether the people of that settlement did or did not flee at the ap-

existing hostilities, by an invasion of American soil, and an effusion of American blood, after rejecting the friendly overtures made by this country.

Mr. Lincoln's resolutions demanded to know whether the spot on which American blood had been shed, was not Mexican, or at least, disputed territory; whether the Mexicans who shed this blood had not been driven from their homes by the approach of our arms; whether the Americans killed were not armed soldiers sent into Mexican territory, by order of the President of the United States.

Parliamentary strategy defeated the proposed inquiry, the resolutions going over under the rules.

On the 12th of January, Mr. Lincoln made a speech* on the reference of different parts of the President's message. In this speech he justified a previous vote of sentiment, declaring that the war had been "unnecessarily and unconstitutionally commenced by the President of the United States." That vote had been pressed upon the opposition of the House, by the President's

---

proaching of the United States army, leaving unprotected their homes and their growing crops *before* the blood was shed, as in the message stated; and whether the first blood so shed was, or was not shed within the inclosure of one of the people who had thus fled from it.

"7th. Whether our *citizens* whose blood was shed, as in his message declared, were, or were not, at that time, armed officers and soldiers sent into that settlement by the military order of the President, through the Secretary of War.

"8th. Whether the military force of the United States was, or was not so sent into that settlement after General Taylor had more than once intimated to the War Department that, in his opinion, no such movement was necessary to the defense or protection of Texas."—*Congressional Globe*, vol. xviii, 1st session, 30th Congress, page 64.

* *Globe* Appendix, vol, xix, page 93.

friends, in order to force an expression of opinion which should seem unjust to that functionary. Discussing this point, Mr. Lincoln coolly argued to conclusions the most injurious to the administration; showing that even though the President had attempted to construe a vote of supplies for the army into a vote applauding his official course, the opposition had remained silent, until Mr. Polk's friends forced this matter upon them. Mr. Lincoln then took up the arguments of the President's message, one by one, and exposed their fallacy; and following the line of inquiry marked out by his resolutions of December, proved that the first American blood shed by Mexicans, was in retaliation for injuries received from us, and that hostilities had commenced on Mexican soil. The speech was characterized by all the excellences of Lincoln's later style—boldness, trenchant logic, and dry humor.

He next appears in the debates,* as briefly advocating a measure to give bounty lands to the surviving volunteer soldiers of the war of 1812, and arguing the propriety of permitting all soldiers holding land warrants, to locate their lands in different parcels, instead of requiring the location to be made in one body.

As Lincoln is a man who never talks unless he has something particular to say, (rare and inestimable virtue!) a period of some three months elapsed before he made another speech in Congress. On the 20th of June,

---

Globe, vol. xviii, page 550.

1848, the Civil and Diplomatic Appropriation bill being under consideration, he addressed to the House and the country, a clear and solid argument in favor of the improvement of rivers and harbors.* As a Western man, and as a man whom his own boating experiences had furnished with actual knowledge of the perils of snags and sawyers, he had always been in favor of a measure which commended itself at once to the heart and the pocket of the West. As the representative of a State with many hundred miles of Mississippi river, and vast river interests, he argued to show that an enlightened system of internal improvements, must be of national as well as local benefit.† The prevailing Democratic errors on this subject, as Mr. Lincoln succinctly stated them, were as follows:

"That internal improvements ought not to be made by the General Government:

"1. Because they would overwhelm the Treasury.

"2. Because, while their *burdens* would be general, their *benefits* would be *local* and *partial*, involving an obnoxious inequality; and,

"3. Because they would be unconstitutional.

"4. Because the States may do enough by the levy and collection of tonnage duties; or, if not,

"5. That the Constitution may be amended.

Globe Appendix, vol. xix, page 709.

† This speech will be found printed at length in the appendix to the present biography.

'The sum," said Lincoln, "of these positions is, Do nothing at all, lest you do something wrong."

He then proceeded to assail each of the positions, demolishing them one after another. That admirable simplicity of diction which dashes straight at the heart of a subject, and that singular good sense which teaches a man to stop when he is done, are no less the characteristics of this effort than of all the other speeches of Mr. Lincoln.

Of a different manner, but illustrating a phase of his mind equally marked, is the speech he made in the House on the 27th of July,* when he discussed the political questions of the day with reference to the Presidential contest between General Taylor and Mr. Cass. It abounds in broad ridicule and broad drollery—the most effective and the most good-natured. Severe and sarcastic enough, when treating a false principle, it seems never to have been one of Lincoln's traits to indulge in bitter personalities. His only enemies, therefore, are those who hate his principles.

On the 21st of December, 1848, Mr. Gott, of New York, offered a resolution in the House, instructing the Committee on the District of Columbia to report a bill for the abolition of the slave-trade in that District. There were men in Congress then who had not forgotten the traditions of the Republican fathers, and who were indignant that slaves should be bought and sold

---

* *Globe Appendix*, vol. xix, page 1041.

in the shadow of the capital—that the slave-trader should make the political metropolis of the Republic a depot on the line of his abominable traffic.

As soon as the resolution of Mr. Gott was read, a motion was made to lay it on the table, which was lost by a vote of eighty-one to eighty-five. A hot struggle ensued; but the resolution was adopted. An immediate attempt to reconsider proved ineffectual. The action upon reconsideration was postponed from day to day, until the 10th of January following, when Mr. Lincoln proposed that the committee should be instructed to report a bill forbidding the sale, beyond the District of Columbia, of any slave born within its limits, or the removal of slaves from the District, except such servants as were in attendance upon their masters temporarily residing at Washington; establishing an apprenticeship of twenty-one years for all slaves born within the District subsequent to the year 1850; providing for their emancipation at the expiration of the apprenticeship; authorizing the United States to buy and emancipate all slaves within the District, whose owners should desire to set them free in that manner; finally submitting the bill to a vote of the citizens of the District for approval.

It is well known that the efforts to abolish the slave-trade in the District of Columbia have resulted in nothing.* The wise, humane, and temperate measure of Mr. Lincoln shared the fate of all the rest.

---

* Mr. Lincoln's proposition had received the approval of Mayor Seaton, of Washington, who informed him that it would meet the approbation of the

Another great measure of the Congress in which Mr. Lincoln figured, was the Wilmot Proviso—now a favorite Republican measure—and so pervading, with its distinctive principle (opposition to slavery extension) the whole Republican soul, that, whether in or out of platforms, it remains the life and strength of the party. To this measure Mr. Lincoln was fully committed. Indeed, it is a peculiarity of this man, that he has *always* acted decidedly one way or the other. He thought the Mexican war wrong. He opposed it with his whole heart and strength. He thought the Wilmot Proviso right, and he says he "had the pleasure of voting for it, in one way or another, *about forty times*."

Mr. Lincoln was one of those who advocated the nomination of General Taylor, in the National Whig Convention of 1848. Returning to Illinois after the adjournment of Congress, he took the stump for his favorite candidate, and was active throughout that famous canvass. In 1849, he retired from Congress, firmly declining re-nomination, and resumed the practice of his profession.

The position which he maintained in the House of Representatives was eminently respectable. His name appears oftener in the ayes and noes, than in the debates; he spoke therefore with the more force and effect when he felt called upon to express his opinion.

---

leading citizens. Afterward, Southern Congressmen visited the Mayor and persuaded him to withdraw the moral support given to the measure. When this had been done, the chief hope of success was destroyed, and the bill, of which Mr. Lincoln gave notice, was never introduced.

The impression that his Congressional speeches give you, is the same left by all others that he has made. You feel that he has not argued to gain a point, but to show the truth; that it is not Lincoln he wishes to sustain, but Lincoln's principles.

6

CHAPTER VII.

Peace to the old Whig party, which is dead! When a man has ceased to live, we are cheaply magnanimous in the exaltation of his virtues, and we repair whatever wrong we did him when alive by remorselessly abusing every one who hints that he may have been an imperceptible trifle lower than the angels.

It is with such post-mortem greatness of soul that the leaders of the Democracy have cherished the memory of the Whig party, and gone about the stump, clad in moral sackcloth and craped hats.

If you will believe these stricken mourners, virtue went out with that lamented organization; and there is but one true man unhanged in America, and he is a stoutish giant, somewhat under the middle size.

In speaking, therefore, of the Whig party, you have first to avoid offense to the gentlemen who reviled its great men in their lifetime, and who have a fondness for throwing the honored dust of the past into the eyes of the present. Then, respect is due to the feelings of those Republicans who abandoned the Whig party only after the last consolations of religion had been administered, and who still remember it with sincere regret.

The prejudices of another class of our friends must

be treated with decent regard. Very many old Democrats in the Republican ranks are earnestly persuaded that in former times they were right in their opposition to the Whigs.

Yet one more variety of opinion must be consulted—the opinion that the Whig party had survived its usefulness, and that all which was good in it has now entered upon a higher and purer state of existence in the Republican organization.

Doubtless it would be better not to mention the Whig party at all. Unfortunately for the ends of strict prudence, the story of Abraham Lincoln's life involves allusion to it, since he was once a Whig, and became a Republican, and not a Democrat. But as every Republican is a code of by-laws unto himself—subject only to the Chicago platform—perhaps we may venture to reverently speak of the shade which still, it is said, revisits the glimpses of Boston; and to recount the events which preceded its becoming a shade.

So early as 1848 the dismemberment of the Whig party commenced. It had been distinguished by many of the characteristics of the Republican party, among which is the reserved right of each member of the organization to think and act for himself, on his own responsibility, as already intimated. Whenever its leaders deflected from the straight line of principle, their followers called them to account; and a persistence in the advocacy of measures repugnant to the individual sense of right, caused disaffection.

Many sincere and earnest men, who supported Henry Clay with ardor, ceased to be Whigs when General Taylor was nominated, because they conceived that his nomination was a departure from the Clay Whig principles of opposition to the Mexican war and the acquisition of slave territory.

This is not the place to pronounce upon the wisdom or justice of their course. Others, as sincere and earnest as they, supported General Taylor, and continued to act with the Whig party throughout the Fillmore administration.

The assimilation of the two great parties on the slavery question in 1852, widened the distance between the Whigs and the Free Soilers, and the former were, in the opinion of the latter, demoralized before the election in which they suffered so total an overthrow, though they continued steadfast in their devotion to the Whig name until 1854, when the first organization of the Republicans took place, under the name of the Anti-Nebraska party.

The Whig Free Soilers were eager and glad to fraternize with their old friends; and all greeted with enthusiasm the vast accessions which the new party received from the men who had given spiritual vitality to the Democracy.

Those members of both the old parties, who were particularly sensible to the attractions of office, those whom no pro-slavery aggression could render superior to the luxury of a feeble or selfish acquiescence, also coalesced, and now constitute, with a few sincere political reminiscences, the Democracy of the North.

Up to the time of the repeal of the Missouri Compromise, Abraham Lincoln remained a Whig, both from conviction and affection.

In 1848, he had made speeches in favor of the election of General Taylor, in Maryland, in Massachusetts, and in Illinois. In his own Congressional district, where his word has always been platform enough, the success of his canvass was declared by a majority of fifteen hundred for Taylor.

After his retirement from Congress, he devoted himself, with greater earnestness than ever before, to the duties of his profession, and extended his business and repute. He did not reappear in the political arena until 1852, when his name was placed on the Scott electoral ticket.

In the canvass of that year, so disastrous to the Whig party throughout the country, Lincoln appeared several times before the people of his State as the advocate of Scott's claims for the Presidency. But the prospect was everywhere so disheartening, and in Illinois the cause was so utterly desperate, that the energies of the Whigs were paralyzed, and Lincoln did less in this Presidential struggle than any in which he had ever engaged.

During that lethargy which preceded the dissolution of his party, he had almost relinquished political aspirations. Successful in his profession, happy in his home, secure in the affection of his neighbors, with books, competence, and leisure—ambition could not tempt him. It required the more thrilling voice of danger to freedom, to call the veteran of so many good fights into the field. The call was made.

It would be useless to recount here the history of the Missouri Compromise, and the circumstances attending the violation of that compact, though that history is properly a part of the biography of every public man in the country. Throughout the fierce contest which preceded the repeal of the Compromise, and the storm of indignation which followed that repeal, the whole story was brought vividly before the people, and can not now have faded from their recollection. Those to whom it is yet strange, will find it briefly and faithfully related in the speech of Abraham Lincoln, made in reply to Douglas, at Peoria, in October, 1854.*

---

* Printed in full in this volume. Douglas and Lincoln had previously met at Springfield, where the latter played David to the abbreviated Goliah of the former. The following spirited sketch of the scene is by the editor of the Chicago *Press and Tribune*, who was present:

"The affair came off on the fourth day of October, 1854. The State Fair had been in progress two days, and the capital was full of all manner of men. The Nebraska bill had been passed on the previous twenty-second of May. Mr. Douglas had returned to Illinois to meet an outraged constituency. He had made a fragmentary speech in Chicago, the people filling up each hiatus in a peculiar and good-humored way. He called the people a mob—they called him a rowdy. The 'mob' had the best of it, both then and at the election which succeeded. The notoriety of all these events had stirred up the politics of the State from bottom to top. Hundreds of politicians had met at Springfield, expecting a tournament of an unusual character—Douglas, Breese, Koerner, Lincoln, Trumbull, Matteson, Yates, Codding, John Calhoun, (of the order of the candle-box,) John M. Palmer, the whole house of the McConnells, Singleton, (known to fame in the Mormon war,) Thomas L. Harris, and a host of others. Several speeches were made before, and several after, the passage between Lincoln and Douglas, but that was justly held to be *the* event of the season.

"We do not remember whether a challenge to debate passed between the

The people were glad to hear the voice of their favorite once more, and Lincoln's canvass of Illinois was most triumphant. The legislative elections were held, and those who denounced the repeal of the Missouri Compromise, were found to be in the majority.

---

friends of the speakers or not, but there was a perfectly amicable understanding between Lincoln and Douglas, that the former should speak two or three hours, and the latter reply in just as little or as much time as he chose. Mr. Lincoln took the stand at two o'clock—a large crowd in attendance, and Mr. Douglas seated on a small platform in front of the desk. The first half hour of Mr. Lincoln's speech was taken up with compliments to his distinguished friend Judge Douglas, and dry allusions to the political events of the past few years. His distinguished friend, Judge Douglas, had taken his seat, as solemn as the Cock-Lane ghost, evidently with the design of not moving a muscle till it came his turn to speak. The laughter provoked by Lincoln's exordinm, however, soon began to make him uneasy; and when Mr. L. arrived at his (Douglas's) speech, pronouncing the Missouri Compromise 'a sacred thing, which no ruthless hand would ever be reckless enough to disturb,' he opened his lips far enough to remark, 'A first-rate speech!' This was the beginning of an amusing colloquy.

"'Yes,' continued Mr. Lincoln, 'so affectionate was my friend's regard for this Compromise line, that when Texas was admitted into the Union, and it was found that a strip extended north of 36° 30′, he actually introduced a bill extending the line and prohibiting slavery in the northern edge of the new State.'

"'And you voted against the bill,' said Douglas.

"'Precisely so,' replied Lincoln; 'I was in favor of running the line *a great deal deal further south.*'

"'About this time,' the speaker continued, 'my distinguished friend introduced me to a particular friend of his, one David Wilmot, of Pennsylvania.' [Laughter.]

"'I thought,' said Douglas, 'you would find him congenial company.'

"'So I did,' replied Lincoln. 'I had the pleasure of voting for his proviso, in one way and another, about forty times. It was a *Democratic* measure then, I believe. At any rate, General Cass scolded honest John Davis, of Massachusetts, soundly, for talking away the last hours of the session, so that he (Cass) could n't crowd it through. *A propos* of General Cass: if I am not greatly mistaken, he has a prior claim to my distinguished friend, to the authorship of Popular Sovereignty. The old general has an infirmity for writing letters. Shortly after the scolding he gave John Davis, he wrote his Nicholson letter'—

"Douglas (solemnly)—'God Almighty placed man on the earth, and told him to choose between good and evil. That was the origin of the Nebraska bill!'

"Lincoln—'Well, the priority of invention being settled, let us award all credit to Judge Douglas for being the first to discover it.'

"It would be impossible, in these limits, to give an idea of the strength of

The election of a United States Senator took place the following winter, and General Shields was superseded. This gentleman, who, listening to the seductive persuasions of his voiceful colleague, was said to have voted for the repeal of the Compromise against his own convictions, was a candidate for re-election. On the part of the opposition majority there were two candidates, Lincoln and Trumbull. The great body of the opposition voted steadily for the former on several ballots; but some Democrats who had been elected on the anti-Nebraska issue, continued to cast their votes for Trumbull.

Lincoln feared that this dissension might result in the election of a less positive man than Trumbull, and with

---

Mr. Lincoln's argument. We deemed it by far the ablest effort of the campaign, from whatever source. The occasion was a great one, and the speaker was every way equal to it. The effect produced on the listeners was magnetic. No one who was present will ever forget the power and vehemence of the following passage:

"My distinguished friend says it is an insult to the emigrants to Kansas and Nebraska to suppose they are not able to govern themselves. We must not slur over an argument of this kind because it happens to tickle the ear. It must be met and answered. I admit that the emigrant to Kansas and Nebraska is competent to govern *himself*, but,' the speaker rising to his full hight, '*I deny his right to govern any other person* WITHOUT THAT PERSON'S CONSENT.' The applause which followed this triumphant refutation of a cunning falsehood, was but an earnest of the victory at the polls which followed just one month from that day.

"When Mr. Lincoln had concluded, Mr. Douglas strode hastily to the stand. As usual, he employed ten minutes in telling how grossly he had been abused. Recollecting himself, he added, 'though in a perfectly courteous manner'—abused in a perfectly courteous manner! He then devoted half an hour to showing that it was indispensably necessary to California emigrants, Santa Fè traders and others, to have organic acts provided for the Territories of Kansas and Nebraska—that being precisely the point which nobody disputed. Having established this premise to his satisfaction, Mr. Douglas launched forth into an argument wholly apart from the positions taken by Mr. Lincoln. He had about half finished at six o'clock, when an adjournment to tea was effected. The speaker insisted strenuously upon his right to resume in the evening, but we believe the second part of that speech has not been delivered to this day.

his usual unselfishness, appealed to his friends to vote for Trumbull, adjuring them by their friendship to him to make this concession of individual preference. His appeal was not in vain, and Trumbull was elected Senator.

This, however, was not the first sacrifice which he made to conciliation and union. The anti-Nebraska party of the same year offered him the nomination for Governor; but in the existing state of organizations, he declined for the sake of the cause which all had espoused. It occurs in politics that a force which suddenly rallies about a principle, may be disheartened by the choice of a leader whom recent animosities have rendered obnoxious. Lincoln, as a Whig, had been one of the most decided and powerful opponents of Democracy in Illinois. The period since his opposition to many Democratic members of the anti-Nebraska party had ceased was very brief, and old feelings of antagonism had not died away. He perceived that the advancement of himself might impede the advancement of his principles. Doubtless, he could be elected Governor of Illinois, but the victory which bore him into office might be less brilliant and useful than that which could be achieved under another. He therefore withdrew his name, and threw his influence in favor of Governor Bissell, who had been a Democrat, and who was triumphantly elected.

It must be remembered that the Republican party had, as yet, no definite existence in Illinois. The anti-Nebraska party was the temporary name of the Whigs, Democrats, and Free Soilers, who opposed the repeal of the Missouri Compromise. It is true that a Mass State Convention, with a view to forming a permanent organization, had been held at Springfield, in October; but many anti-Nebraska men, who still adhered to old names, had not taken part in it. The following resolutions were adopted at this Convention:

"1. *Resolved*, That we believe this truth to be self-evident, that when parties become subversive of the ends for which they are established, or incapable of restoring the Government to the true principles of the Constitution, it is the right and duty of the people to dissolve the political bands by which they may have been connected therewith, and to organize new parties upon such principles and with such views as the circumstances and exigencies of the nation may demand.

"2. *Resolved*, That the times imperatively demand the reorganization of parties, and, repudiating all previous party attachments, names, and predilections, we unite ourselves together in defense of the liberty and Constitution of the country, and will hereafter co-operate as the Republican party, pledged to the accomplishment of the following purposes: To bring the administration of the Government back to the control of first principles; to restore Nebraska and Kansas to the position of free territories; that, as the Constitution of the United States vests in the States, and not in Congress, the power to legislate for the extradition of fugitives from labor, to repeal and entirely abrogate the Fugitive Slave law; to restrict slavery to those states in which it exists; to prohibit the admission of any more slave states into the Union; to abolish slavery in the District of Columbia; to exclude slavery from all the territories over which the General Government has exclusive jurisdiction; and to resist the acquirement of any more territories unless the practice of slavery therein forever shall have been prohibited.

"3. *Resolved*, That in furtherance of these principles we will use such Constitutional and lawful means as shall seem best adapted to their accomplishment, and that we will support no man for office, under the General or State Government, who is not positively and fully committed to the support of these principles, and whose personal character and conduct is not a guarantee that he is reliable, and who shall not have abjured old party allegiance and ties."

In the course of the first debate between Douglas and Lincoln, which was held at Ottawa, in August, 1858, Douglas read these resolutions, declaring that Lincoln had participated in the Convention, and assisted in their adoption. Lincoln met this earliest of a series of misrepresentations with prompt denial, and proved that he was not a member of the Convention.

The actual Republican party of Illinois, dates its formation from a period somewhat later; and Lincoln was one of the first members of the present organization. Not so ultra, probably, as the indignant men who framed the resolutions quoted, he was quite as firmly opposed to slavery. In the speech from which he read, in reply to the charge of Douglas, he gives with Wesleyan point, the reason why indifference to slavery should be abhorred:

"This *declared* indifference, but, as I must think, covert *real* zeal for the spread of slavery, I can not but hate. I hate it because of the monstrous injustice of slavery itself. I hate it because it deprives our republican example of its just influence in the world—enables the enemies of free institutions, with plausibility, to taunt us as hypocrites—causes the real friends of freedom to doubt our sincerity, and especially because it forces so many really good men among ourselves into an open war with the very fundamental principles of civil liberty—criticising the Declaration of Independence, and insisting that there is no right principle of action but *self-interest.*"

CHAPTER VIII.

In the Republican National Convention of 1856, Abraham Lincoln received one hundred and two votes for the Vice-Presidential nomination. When the standard-bearers of the party had been selected, he took his rank in the army of freedom, and engaged in the great conflict which followed. The Republicans showed their appreciation of his strength and ability by placing him at the head of their electoral ticket in Illinois; and when in 1858 it was determined to give the Senatorial question the form of a popular contest, by the election of a Legislature pledged to the people, for or against Douglas, Abraham Lincoln was chosen without dissent as the champion of his party.

Much might here be said with regard to his eminent fitness for the conduct of such a canvass; but the result of the election, and his published debates with Douglas, are the best commentary upon his qualifications.

The Republican State ticket of that year was carried by a decisive majority, and the Legislature was lost only through the unfair manner in which the State was districted, and which threw that body into the hands of the Democrats in spite of the popular will.

It may not be improper to allude particularly to circumstances connected with the debates between Lincoln and Douglas, which have been so significant in their result, and which have practically made United States Senators in Illinois elective by the people instead of the Legislature.

Lincoln's first great speech of that year was made at Springfield, on the 17th of June, before the State Convention which named him as the Republican candidate for Senator. In this speech he preached the moral conflict, which has always existed and always must exist between the principle of freedom and the principle of slavery; noticed the repeal of the Missouri Compromise, the Dred Scott decision, and the revival of the slave-trade; and with masterly effect exhibited the secret concert with which all the enemies of freedom had acted in their assaults upon our liberties. The speaker concluded with these memorable words, which every Republican should keep in mind, for they have gathered significance in the two years elapsed since their utterance:

"Our cause, then, must be intrusted to, and conducted by, its own undoubted friends—those whose hands are free, whose hearts are in the work—who *do care* for the result. Two years ago the Republicans of the nation mustered over thirteen hundred thousand strong. We did this under the single impulse of resistance to a common danger, with every external circumstance against us. Of strange, discordant, and even hostile elements, we gathered from the four winds, and formed and fought the battle through, under the constant hot fire of a disciplined, proud, and pampered enemy. Did we brave all then, to falter now?—now, when that same enemy is wavering, dissevered, and belligerent? The result is not doubtful. We shall not fail—if we stand firm, we *shall not fail.* Wise counsels may accelerate, or mistakes delay it, but, sooner or later, the victory is sure to come."

The reply made by Douglas to this speech was on the occasion of his reception at Chicago in the July following. Lincoln was present, and spoke in the same city on the next day. Two more great speeches by Douglas, and one more speech by Lincoln were made before they entered the lists in debate.

In one of those speeches, Douglas found occasion—for he was then addressing Lincoln's old friends at Springfield—to pay his tribute to the worth and greatness of his opponent:

"You all know that I am an amiable, good-natured man, and I take great pleasure in bearing testimony to the fact that Mr. Lincoln is a kind-hearted, amiable, good-natured gentleman, with whom no man has a right to pick a quarrel, even if he wanted one. He is a worthy gentleman. I have known him for twenty-five years, and there is no better citizen, and no kinder-hearted man. He is a fine lawyer, possesses high ability, and there is no objection to him, except the monstrous revolutionary doctrines with which he is identified."

On the 24th of July, Lincoln wrote to Douglas proposing the debates which have since become so famous.

Douglas made answer that "recent events had interposed difficulties in the way of such an arrangement," that the Democratic Central Committee had already made appointments for him at different places; but in order to accommodate Mr. Lincoln, he would meet him in seven of the nine Congressional Districts where they had not yet spoken. He expressed surprise, that if it was Lincoln's original intention to propose these debates, he should have waited until after the plan of the campaign had been arranged by the Democratic Central Committee, before he made known his proposition.

This letter was also written on the 24th of July. On the 29th Lincoln replied, from Springfield:

"Protesting that your insinuations of attempted unfairness on my part are unjust, and with the hope that you did not very considerately make them, I proceed to reply. To your statement that 'It has been suggested, recently, that an arrangement had been made to bring out a third candidate for the United States Senate, who, with yourself, should canvass the State in opposition to me,' etc.,* I can only say, that such suggestion must

---

* The following is the statement, in Douglas's letter, alluded to by Lincoln:

"Besides, there is another consideration which should be kept in mind. It has been suggested, recently, that an arrangement had been made to bring out a third candidate for the United States Senate, who, with yourself, should canvass the State in opposition to me, with no other purpose than to insure my defeat, by dividing the Democratic party for your benefit. If I should make this arrangement with you, it is more than probable that this other candidate, who has a common object with you, would desire to become a party to it, and claim the right to speak from the same stand; so that he and you, in concert, might be able to take the opening and closing speech in every case."

have been made by yourself, for certainly none such has been made by or to me, or otherwise, to my knowledge. Surely, you did not *deliberately* conclude, as you insinuate, that I was expecting to draw you into an arrangement of terms, to be agreed on by yourself, by which a third candidate and myself, 'in concert, might be able to take the opening and closing speech in every case.'

"As to your surprise that I did not sooner make the proposal to divide time with you, I can only say, I made it as soon as I resolved to make it. I did not know but that such proposal would come from you; I waited, respectfully, to see. It may have been well known to you that you went to Springfield for the purpose of agreeing on the plan of campaign; but it was not so known to me. When your appointments were announced in the papers, extending only to the 21st of August, I, for the first time, considered it certain that you would make no proposal to me, and then resolved that, if my friends concurred, I would make one to you. As soon thereafter as I could see and consult with friends satisfactorily, I did make the proposal. It did not occur to me that the proposed arrangement could derange your plans after the latest of your appointments already made. After that, there was, before the election, largely over two months of clear time.

"For you to say that we have already spoken at Chicago and Springfield, and that on both occasions I had the concluding speech, is hardly a fair statement. The truth rather is this: At Chicago, July 9th, you made a carefully-prepared conclusion on my speech of June 16th. Twenty-four hours after, I made a hasty conclusion on yours of the 9th. You had six days to prepare, and concluded on me again at Bloomington on the 16th. Twenty-four hours after, I concluded again on you at Springfield. In the mean time, you had made another conclusion on me at Springfield, which I did not hear, and of the contents of which I knew nothing when I spoke; so that your speech made in daylight, and mine at night, of the 17th, at Springfield, were both made in perfect independence of each other. The dates of making all these speeches will show, I think, that in the matter of time for preparation, the advantage has all been on your side; and that none of the external circumstances have stood to my advantage."

Lincoln having left all the arrangements of time, place, and manner of debate to Douglas, the latter made the following proposition, which, (although it allowed Douglas four openings and closes to Lincoln's three, and so gave considerable advantage to him,) Lincoln promptly accepted:

"BEMENT, PIATT CO., ILL., July 30, 1858.

"DEAR SIR:

"Your letter, dated yesterday, accepting my proposition for a joint discussion at one prominent point in each Congressional District, as stated in my previous letter, was received this morning.

"The times and places designated are as follows:

Ottawa, La Salle county	August	21st,	1858.
Freeport, Stephenson county	"	27th,	"
Jonesboro, Union county	September	15th,	"
Charleston, Coles county	"	18th,	"
Galesburgh, Knox county	October	7th,	"
Quincy, Adams county	"	13th,	"
Alton, Madison county	"	15th,	"

"I agree to your suggestion that we shall alternately open and close the discussion. I will speak at Ottawa one hour, you can reply, occupying an hour and a half, and I will then follow for half an hour. At Freeport, you shall open the discussion and speak one hour; I will follow for an hour and a half, and you can then reply for half an hour. We will alternate in like manner in each successive place.

"Very respectfully, your obedient servant,

"S. A. DOUGLAS.

"HON. A. LINCOLN, Springfield, Ill."

In the intervals between the debates, which took place as arranged, both speakers addressed audiences separately, and the work on both sides was carried on with unflagging energy.

No one, it seems to me, can read these debates without admiration of Lincoln's ability, courage, and truth, while the impression left by Douglas is that of a great mind bending all its energies to a purpose beneath it; of an acute logician resorting to sophistry when meeting his opponent's arguments, and to adroit misrepresentation of language and position, when assailing his opinions.

The questions discussed were substantially the same that are at issue now. The spirit of pro-slavery aggression takes many forms, but in nature remains unchanged. Lincoln pursued it through all its disguises, and exposed it at every turn. The subtlest and most audacious champion of slavery that had ever proved false to freedom, was not equal to the conflict. As the pretended advocate of the right of every man to govern himself and regulate his own affairs, Douglas was full of words. When a flash of truth showed him the real advocate of one man's right to enslave another, he was dumb. The banner of popular sovereignty smote pleasantly upon the sight. When Lincoln reversed it, and men read the true inscription, they saw that it was the signal of discord, oppression, and violence. There were old stains upon that gay piece of bunting; stains of blood from the cabin hearths of Kansas, and from the marble floor of the Senate hall; and a marvelous ill-odor of cruelty hung about it, as if it were, in fact, no better than the flag of a slave-ship. Where its shadow fell across the future of a State, civilization and humanity seemed to shrink back, and a race of bondmen and their masters thinly peopled a barren land that would have "laughed in harvests" in the light of freedom.

The Douglas dogma never has been so thoroughly refuted, as by Lincoln's speeches in those debates; and Douglas himself never suffered such entire defeat, in the eyes of the country. The truth gave the victory to Lincoln; a trick bestowed the Senatorship upon Douglas.

In May, 1859, when the amendment to the Constitution of Massachusetts, extending the term of naturalization, aroused the apprehensions of many German Republicans, Dr. Theodor Canisius, a German citizen of Illinois, addressed a letter to Lincoln, asking his opinion of the amendment, and inquiring whether he favored a fusion of the Republicans with the other elements of opposition in 1860. Writing from Springfield, Lincoln replies:

"Massachusetts is a sovereign and independent State, and I have no right to advise her in her policy. Yet, if any one is desirous to draw a conclusion as to what I would do from what she has done, I may speak without impropriety. I say, then, that so far as I understand the Massachusetts provision, I am against its adoption, not only in Illinois, but in every other place in which I have the right to oppose it. As I understand the spirit of our institutions, it is designed to promote the *elevation* of men. I am, therefore, hostile to anything that tends to their debasement. It is well known that I deplore the oppressed condition of the blacks, and it would, therefore, be very inconsistent for me to look with approval upon any measure that infringes upon the inalienable rights of white men, whether or not they are born in another land or speak a different language from our own.

"In respect to a fusion, I am in favor of it whenever it can be effected on Republican principles, but upon *no other condition.* A fusion upon any other platform would be as insane as unprincipled. It would thereby lose the whole North, while the common enemy would still have the support of the entire South. The question in relation to men is different. There are good and patriotic men and able statesmen in the South whom I would willingly support if they would place themselves on Republican ground; but I shall oppose the lowering of the Republican standard even by a *hair's-breadth.*"

During the gubernatorial canvass of 1859, in Ohio, Lincoln was invited to address the people of that State, and appeared before them, at Columbus and Cincinnati, in September. The impression made was one of universal favor; and it was through the interest awakened by these speeches, that the Republican Central Committee and State officers of Ohio, were led to request copies of his debates with Douglas, for publication in book-form. The Ohioans went to hear him with full allowances for the exaggerations of Illinois enthusiasm; when they had heard him, their own admiration equaled that of the Illinoians.

It was, doubtless, with still greater surprise that New England and New York listened to him. His speech at the Cooper Institute, in the commercial and intellectual metropolis, was the most brilliant success in everything that makes such an effort successful. His audience was vast in numbers, and profoundly attentive. They found him, indeed, lank and angular in form, but of fine oratorial presence; lucid and simple in his style, vigorous in argument, speaking with a full, clear voice. He addressed appeals of reason to the sense and conscience of his hearers, and skillfully hit the humor of a critical and unfamiliar people.

CHAPTER IX.

THE Republican National Convention, which assembled at Chicago on the 16th of May, was no less marked by a diversity of preferences than a unity of interests. In three days it accomplished its work—the conciliation of men and the assimilation of sections on minor points of difference. In three days Abraham Lincoln was nominated, and the armies of the irrepressible conflict were united under the banner of the man who was the first to utter that great truth, which all men felt.*

I need hardly recount the incidents of that Convention, of which the great event has proven so satisfactory. They are all fresh in the minds of the people, who watched, hour by hour, and day by day, the proceedings of one of the most distinguished bodies which ever assembled in this country.

The Convention met in Chicago without factitious advantages. The failure of the Democracy to nominate at Charleston left the Republicans in the dark as to the champion whom they were to combat, and there was nothing to be gained by the choice of a man with reference to a Democratic probability.

---

* See Lincoln's speech at Springfield, June 17, 1858.

What lay before the Convention, then, was the task of choosing a positive man embodying decided Republican principles, whose strength and decision of opinions should attract one side of the party, while nothing in his history should repel the other.

Up to the time of the third ballot, which resulted in the nomination of Abraham Lincoln, all the indications were favorable to the success of William H. Seward. That great man, whom no fortuity can lessen in the proud regard of the party, had rallied to his cause a host of friends—attached, powerful, vigilant. These came to Chicago, and into the Convention, with a solid strength that swept everything before it.

Mr. Lincoln was the only candidate upon whom a considerable number of those who opposed Mr. Seward from policy, were united; but it was not until after two votes of sentiment that a sufficient force was diverted from other favorites to swell Mr. Lincoln's vote into a majority.

The leader of the New York delegation, who had worked so faithfully for Mr. Seward, was the first to move the unanimous nomination of Lincoln, which was done amid demonstrations of the wildest enthusiasm, in the wigwam of the Convention and throughout the city of Chicago. At the same instant the lightning flashed the tidings throughout the land, and in a thousand towns and cities the cannon thundered back the jubilant responses of the people.

The fact of his nomination was at once telegraphed

to Lincoln, at Springfield. He received it with characteristic quiet. Seated in the *Illinois State Journal* office, talking over the Convention with a number of friends, he was approached by the telegraphic operator. "Mr. Lincoln, you are nominated for the Presidency." Lincoln took the proffered dispatch in silence, and read it. At length he folded it carefully, and saying to the exuberant bystanders, "There is a little woman down street who would like to know something about this," went home to communicate the news to his wife.

The little city of Springfield was in a phrensy of excitement; and that night all the streets were ablaze with bonfires, and thronged by the rejoicing Republicans. The fact of the nomination of the man whom every one of his fellow-townsmen regarded with pride, was excuse enough for all sorts of vocal and pyrotechnic extravagances.

The next day, the excursion train arrived from Chicago with a large number of delegates, and the Committee appointed by the Convention to make Lincoln officially acquainted with his nomination.

The deputation was received at Mr. Lincoln's house, and when the guests had assembled in the parlor, Mr. Ashmun, the President of the Convention, said:

"I have, sir, the honor, in behalf of the gentlemen who are present, a Committee appointed by the Republican Convention, recently assembled at Chicago, to discharge a most pleasant duty. We have come, sir, under a vote of instructions to that Committee, to notify you that you have been selected by the Convention of the Republicans at Chicago, for President of the United States. They instruct us, sir, to notify you of that selection, and that Committee deem it not only respectful to yourself, but appropriate to the important matter which they have in hand, that they should come in person, and present to you the authentic evidence of the action of that Convention; and, sir, without any phrase which shall either be considered personally plauditory to yourself, or which shall have any reference to the principles involved in the questions which are connected with your nomination, I desire to present to you the letter which has been prepared, and which informs you of the nomination, and with it the platform, resolutions, and sentiments which the Convention adopted. Sir, at your convenience we shall be glad to receive from you such a response as it may be your pleasure to give us."

To this address Mr. Lincoln listened with grave attention, and replied:

"MR. CHAIRMAN AND GENTLEMEN OF THE COMMITTEE:

"I tender to you and through you to the Republican National Convention, and all the people represented in it, my profoundest thanks for the high honor done me, which you now formally announce. Deeply, and even painfully sensible of the great responsibility which is inseparable from this high honor—a responsibility which

I could almost wish had fallen upon some one of the far more eminent men and experienced statesmen whose distinguished names were before the Convention, I shall, by your leave, consider more fully the resolutions of the Convention denominated the platform, and without unnecessary or unreasonable delay, respond to you, Mr. Chairman, in writing, not doubting that the platform will be found satisfactory, and the nomination gratefully accepted.

"And now I will not longer defer the pleasure of taking you, and each of you, by the hand."

After this response, it is proper to immediately add the letter in which Mr. Lincoln has since formally accepted the nomination:

"SPRINGFIELD, ILLINOIS, May 23, 1860.

"HON. GEORGE ASHMUN,

'*President of the Republican National Convention:*

"SIR: I accept the nomination tendered me by the Convention over which you presided, of which I am formally apprised in the letter of yourself and others acting as a Committee of the Convention for that purpose. The declaration of principles and sentiments which accompanies your letter meets my approval, and it shall be my care not to violate it, or disregard it in any part.

"Imploring the assistance of Divine Providence, and with due regard to the views and feelings of all who were represented in the Convention, to the rights of all the states and territories and people of the nation, to the inviolability of the Constitution, and the perpetual union, harmony, and prosperity of all, I am most happy to co-operate for the practical success of the principles declared by the Convention.

"Your obliged friend and fellow-citizen,

"ABRAHAM LINCOLN."

People who visit Mr. Lincoln are pleased no less at the simple and quiet style in which he lives, than at the perfect ease and cordiality with which they are received. The host puts off half his angularity at home, or hides it beneath the mantle of hospitality; and the hostess is found "a pattern of lady-like courtesy and polish," who "converses with freedom and grace, and is thoroughly *au fait* in all the little amenities of society," and who will "do the honors of the White House with appropriate grace." Intellectually, she is said to be little her husband's inferior.

Lincoln's residence is a comfortable two-story frame house, not now new in appearance, and situated in the northeast part of Springfield. The grounds about it, which are not spacious, are neatly and tastefully kept.

Mr. Lincoln's political room is an apartment in the State House, at the door of which you knock unceremoniously. A sturdy voice calls out, "Come in!" and you find yourself in the presence of a man who rises to the hight of six feet three inches, as you enter. He shakes you with earnest cordiality by the hand—

receiving you as in the old days he would have received a friend who called upon him at his farm-work; for those who have always known him, say that, though Lincoln is now more distinguished, he has always been a great man, and his simple and hearty manners have undergone no change. You find him, in physique, thin and wiry, and he has an appearance of standing infirmly upon his feet, which often deceived those who contended with him in the wrestle, in his younger days.

The great feature of the man's face is his brilliant and piercing eye, which has never been dimmed by any vice, great or small. His rude and vigorous early life contributed to strengthen the robust constitution which he inherited, and he is now, at fifty, in the prime of life, with rugged health, though bearing, in the lines of his face, the trace of severe and earnest thought.

The biographer's task ends here, and he does not feel that any speculations with regard to the future would be of great worth or pertinence, though conjecture is easy and a prophetic reputation possible. He prefers to leave the future of Lincoln to Providence and to the people, who often make history without the slightest respect to the arrangements of sagacious writers.

THE REPUBLICAN WIGWAM AT CHICAGO.

MEMORABILIA

OF THE

CHICAGO CONVENTION.

MEMORABILIA

OF THE

CHICAGO CONVENTION.

THE Convention was called to order, on the morning of the 16th, by Governor Morgan, of New York.

Mr. David Wilmot, of Pennsylvania, took the chair as temporary President.

In the afternoon, Mr. George Ashmun, of Massachusetts, was chosen permanent President.

CHICAGO REPUBLICAN PLATFORM,

ADOPTED MAY 17, 1860, BY THE REPUBLICAN NATIONAL CONVENTION.

Resolved, That we, the delegated representatives of the Republican electors of the United States, in Convention assembled, in the discharge of the duty we owe to our constituents and our country, unite in the following declarations:

First. That the history of the nation during the last four years has fully established the propriety and necessity of the organization and perpetuation of the Republican party, and that the causes which called it into existence are permanent in their nature, and now, more than ever before, demand its peaceful and constitutional triumph.

Second. That the maintenance of the principles promulgated in the Declaration of Independence, and embodied in the Federal Constitution, is essential to the preservation of our Republican institutions, and that the Federal Constitution, the rights of the states, and the Union of the states, must and shall be preserved.

Third. That to the Union of the states this nation owes its unprecedented increase in population; its surprising development of material resources; its rapid augmentation of wealth; its happiness at home and its honor abroad, and we hold in abhorrence all schemes for disunion, come from whatever source they may; and we congratulate the country that no Republican member of Congress has uttered or countenanced a threat of disunion, so often made by Democratic members of Congress, without rebuke and with applause from their political associates; and we denounce those threats of disunion, in case of a popular overthrow of their ascendency, as denying the vital principles of a free government, and as an avowal of contemplated treason, which it is the imperative duty of an indignant people strongly to rebuke and forever silence.

Fourth. That the maintenance inviolate of the rights of the states, and especially the right of each state to order and control its own domestic institutions, according to its own judgment exclusively, is essential to that balance of power on which the perfection and endurance of our political faith depends, and we denounce the lawless invasion by an armed force of any state or territory, no matter under what pretext, as among the gravest of crimes.

Fifth. That the present Democratic administration has far exceeded our worst apprehensions in its measureless subserviency to the exactions of a sectional interest, as is especially evident in its desperate exertions to force the infamous Lecompton Constitution upon the protesting people of Kansas; in construing the personal relation between master and servant to involve an unqualified property in persons; in its attempted enforcement everywhere, on land and sea, through the intervention of Congress and the Federal courts, of the extreme pretensions of a purely local interest, and in its general and unvarying abuse of the power intrusted to it by a confiding people.

Sixth. That the people justly view with alarm the reckless extravagance which pervades every department of the Federal Government; that a return to rigid economy and accountability is indispensable to arrest the system of plunder of the public treasury by favored partisans; while the recent startling developments of fraud and corruption at the Federal Metropolis show that an entire change of administration is imperatively demanded.

Seventh. That the new dogma that the Constitution of its own force carries slavery into any or all the territories of the United States, is a dangerous political heresy, at variance with the explicit provisions of that instrument itself, with cotemporaneous exposition, and with legislative and judicial precedent; is revolutionary in its tendency, and subversive of the peace and harmony of the country.

Eighth. That the normal condition of all the territory of the United States is that of freedom; that as our republican fathers, when they had abolished slavery in all our national territory, ordained that no person should be deprived of life, liberty, or property, without due process of law, it becomes our duty, by legislation, whenever such legislation is necessary, to maintain this provision of the Constitution against all attempt to violate it; and we deny the authority of Congress, or a Territorial Legislature, or of any individuals, to give legal existence to slavery in any territory of the United States.

Ninth. That we brand the recent reopening of the African slave-trade, under the cover of our national flag, aided by perversions of judicial power, as a crime against humanity, a burning shame to our country and age; and we call upon Congress to take prompt and efficient measures for the total and final suppression of that execrable traffic.

Tenth. That in the recent vetoes by their Federal Governors of the acts of the Legislatures of Kansas and Nebraska, prohibiting slavery in those territories, we find a practical illustration of the boasted Democratic principle of non-intervention and popular sovereignty, embodied in the Kansas and Nebraska bill, and a denunciation of the deception and fraud involved therein.

Eleventh. That Kansas should, of right, be immediately admitted as a state under the Constitution recently formed and adopted by her people, and accepted by the House of Representatives.

Twelfth. That while providing revenue for the support of the General Government by duties upon imposts, sound policy requires such an adjustment of these imposts as to encourage the development of the industrial interest of the whole country; and we commend that policy of national exchanges which secures to the workingmen liberal wages, to agriculture remunerating prices, to mechanics and manufacturers an adequate reward for their skill, labor, and enterprise, and to the nation commercial prosperity and independence.

Thirteenth. That we protest against any sale or alienation to others of the public lands held by actual settlers, and against any view of the Free Homestead policy which regards the settlers as paupers or supplicants for public bounty, and we demand the passage by Congress of the complete and satisfactory Homestead measure which has already passed the House.

Fourteenth. That the National Republican party is opposed to any change in our naturalization laws, or any state legislation by which the rights of citizenship hitherto accorded to emigrants from foreign lands shall be abridged or impaired, and in favor of giving a full and efficient protection to the rights of all classes of citizens, whether native or naturalized, both at home and abroad.

Fifteenth. That appropriations by Congress for River and Harbor improvements of a national character, required for the accommodation and security of our existing commerce, are authorized by the Constitution and justified by an obligation of the Government to protect the lives and property of its citizens.

Sixteenth. That a railroad to the Pacific Ocean is imperatively demanded by the interests of the whole country; that the Federal Government ought to render immediate and efficient aid in its construction, and that as preliminary thereto, a daily overland mail should be promptly established.

Seventeenth. Finally, having thus set forth our distinctive principles and views, we invite the co-operation of all citizens, however differing on other questions, who substantially agree with us in their affirmance and support.

On motion of GEORGE WILLIAM CURTIS, of New York, the following was added to the second resolution:

"That we solemnly reassert the self-evident truths that all are endowed by the Creator with certain inalienable rights, among which are those of life, liberty, and the pursuit of happiness; that governments are instituted among men to secure the enjoyment of these rights."

BALLOTS FOR PRESIDENT IN THE CHICAGO CONVENTION.

FIRST BALLOT.

STATES.	Seward....	Lincoln...	Wade......	Cameron...	Bates......	McLean ...	Reed......	Chase	Dayton....	Sumner ...	Fremont...	Collamer ..
Maine	10	6	...	...	...	...	...	...	...	...	...	...
New Hampshire	1	7	...	...	...	...	...	1	...	...	1	...
Vermont	...	...	...	...	...	...	...	...	...	...	..	10
Massachusetts	21	4	...	...	...	...	...	...	...	...	...	...
Rhode Island	...	...	...	...	1	5	1	1	...	...	...	...
Connecticut	...	2	1	...	7	...	...	2	...	...	...	...
New York	70	...	...	...	...	...	...	...	...	...	...	...
New Jersey	...	...	...	...	...	...	...	...	14	...	...	...
Pennsylvania	1½	4	...	47½	...	1	...	...	...	...	...	...
Maryland	3	...	...	...	8	...	...	...	...	...	...	...
Delaware	...	...	...	...	6	...	...	...	...	...	...	...
Virginia	8	14	...	1	...	...	...	...	...	...	...	...
Kentucky	5	6	2	...	...	1	...	8	...	1	...	...
Ohio	...	8	...	...	...	4	...	34	...	...	...	...
Indiana	...	26	...	...	...	...	...	...	...	...	...	...
Missouri	...	...	...	...	18	...	...	...	...	...	...	...
Michigan	12	...	...	...	...	...	...	...	...	...	...	...
Illinois	...	22	...	...	...	...	...	...	...	...	...	...
Texas	4	...	...	...	2	...	...	...	...	...	...	...
Wisconsin	10	...	...	...	...	...	...	...	...	...	...	...
Iowa	2	2	...	1	1	1	...	1	...	...	...	...
California	8	...	...	...	...	...	...	...	...	...	...	...
Minnesota	8	...	...	...	...	...	...	...	...	...	...	...
Oregon	...	...	...	...	5	...	...	...	...	...	...	...
TERRITORIES.												
Kansas	6	...	...	...	...	...	...	...	...	...	...	...
Nebraska	2	1	...	1	...	...	...	2	...	...	...	...
District of Columbia	2	...	...	...	...	...	...	...	...	...	...	...

SECOND BALLOT.

STATES.	Seward....	Lincoln....	Bates	Cameron..	McLean ...	Chase.......	Dayton....	C. M. Clay.
Maine	10	6	...	...	...	...	...	...
New Hampshire......	1	9	...	...	...	...	...	...
Vermont.................	...	10	...	...	...	...	...	...
Massachusetts.........	22	4	...	...	...	...	...	...
Rhode Island..........	...	3	...	...	2	3	...	...
Connecticut	...	4	4	...	...	2	...	2
New York...............	70	...	...	...	...	...	...	...
New Jersey............	4	...	...	...	...	...	10	...
Pennsylvania..........	2½	48	...	1	2½	...	...	...
Maryland	3	...	8	...	...	...	...	...
Delaware	...	6	...	...	...	...	...	...
Virginia	8	14	...	1	...	...	...	...
Kentucky	7	9	...	...	...	6	...	...
Ohio.......................	...	14	...	...	3	29	...	...
Indiana..................	...	26	...	...	...	...	...	...
Missouri	...	...	18	...	...	...	...	...
Michigan	12	...	...	...	...	...	...	...
Illinois...................	...	22	...	...	...	...	...	...
Texas	6	...	...	...	...	...	...	...
Wisconsin...............	10	...	...	...	...	...	...	...
Iowa	2	5	...	...	½	½	...	...
California	8	...	...	...	...	...	...	...
Minnesota..............	8	...	...	...	...	...	...	...
Oregon.	...	...	5	...	...	...	...	...
TERRITORIES.								
Kansas....................	6	...	...	...	...	...	...	...
Nebraska................	3	1	...	...	...	2	...	...
District of Columbia.	2	...	...	...	...	...	...	...

THIRD BALLOT.

STATES.	Seward.....	Bates.......	Chase.......	Lincoln ...	McLean ...	Dayton	C. M. Clay.
Maine	10	...	...	6	...	...	...
New Hampshire......	1	...	...	9	...	...	...
Vermont.................	...	...	...	10	...	...	...
Massachusetts.........	18	...	...	8	...	...	...
Rhode Island..........	1	...	1	5	1	...	...
Connecticut.............	1	4	2	4	...	...	1
New York...............	70	...	...	...	...	...	...

THIRD BALLOT.—CONTINUED.

STATES.	Seward....	Bates......	Chase......	Lincoln....	McLean....	Dayton....	C. M. Clay.
New Jersey............	5	...	...	8	...	1	...
Pennsylvania..........	...	...	...	52	2	...	...
Maryland..............	2	...	...	9	...	...	...
Delaware...............	...	...	...	6	...	...	...
Virginia................	8	...	...	14	...	...	...
Kentucky..............	6	...	4	13	...	...	...
Ohio......................	...	...	15	29	2	...	...
Indiana..................	...	...	...	26	...	...	...
Missouri................	...	18	...	...	...	...	...
Michigan..............	12	...	...	...	...	...	...
Illinois..................	...	...	...	22	...	...	...
Texas.....................	6	...	...	...	...	...	...
Wisconsin..............	10	...	...	...	...	...	...
Iowa......................	2	...	½	5½	...	...	...
California..............	8	...	...	...	...	...	...
Minnesota..............	8	...	...	...	...	...	...
Oregon..................	1	...	...	4	...	...	...
TERRITORIES.							
Kansas..................	6	...	...	...	...	...	...
Nebraska..............	3	...	2	1	...	...	...
District of Columbia.	2	...	...	...	...	...	...
Total,..............	180	22	24½	231½	5	1	1

MR. EVARTS, OF NEW YORK, ON HIS MOTION TO MAKE THE NOMINATION OF MR. LINCOLN UNANIMOUS.

MR. LINCOLN being announced as nominated on the third ballot, MR. EVARTS, Chairman of the New York delegation, took the stand and said:

MR. PRESIDENT AND GENTLEMEN OF THE NATIONAL REPUBLICAN CONVENTION: The State of New York, by a full delegation, with complete unanimity of purpose at home, came to this Convention and presented to its choice one of its citizens, who had served the State from boyhood up, who had labored for and loved it.

We came from a great state, with, as we thought, a great statesman, (prolonged cheers;) and our love of the great Republic for which we are all delegates--the great American Union—and our love of the great Republican party of the Union, and our love of our statesman and candidate, made us think that we did our duty to the country, and the whole country, in expressing our preference and love for him. (Loud cheers.) For, gentlemen, it was from Governor Seward that most of us learned to love Republican principles and the Republican party. (Renewed cheers.) His fidelity to the country, the Constitution, and the laws, his fidelity to the party and the principle that the majority govern, his interest in the advancement of our party to its victory, that our country may rise to its true glory, induces me to assume to speak his sentiments as I do indeed the opinions of our delegation, when I move you, as I do now, that the nomination of Abraham Lincoln, of Illinois, as the Republican candidate for the suffrages of the whole country for the office of Chief Magistrate of the American Union, be made unanimous. (Enthusiastic cheers.)

MR. BROWNING, OF ILLINOIS, RESPONDS.

Mr. President and Gentlemen of the Convention: On behalf of the Illinois delegation I have been requested to make some proper response to the speeches that we have heard from our friends of the other states. Illinois ought hardly on this occasion to be expected to make a speech, or called upon to do so. We are so much elated at present that we are scarcely in a condition to collect our own thoughts, or to express them intelligently to those who may listen to us.

I desire to say, gentlemen of the Convention, that in the contest through which we have just passed, we have been actuated by no feeling of hostility to the illustrious statesman from New York, who was in competition with our own loved and gallant son. We were actuated solely by a desire for the certain advancement of Republicanism. The Republicans of Illinois, believing the principles of the Republican party are the same principles which embalmed the hearts and nerved the arms of our patriot sires of the Revolution; that they are the same principles which were vindicated upon every battle-field of American freedom, were actuated solely by the conviction that the triumph of these principles was necessary not only to the salvation of our party, but to the perpetuation of the free institutions whose blessings we now enjoy; and we have struggled against the nomination of the illustrious statesman of New York, solely because we believed here that we could go into battle on the prairies of Illinois with more hope and more prospect of success under the leadership of our own noble son. No Republican who has a love of freedom in his heart, and who has marked the course of Governor Seward of New York, in the councils of our nation, who has witnessed the many occasions upon which he has risen to the very hight of moral sublimity in his conflicts with the enemies of free institutions; no heart that has the love of freedom in it and has witnessed these great conflicts of his, can do otherwise than venerate his name on this occasion. I desire to say only, that the hearts of Illinois are to-day filled with emotions of gratification, for which they have no utterance. We are not more overcome by the triumph of our noble Lincoln, loving him as we do, knowing the purity of his past life, the integrity of his character, and devotion to the principles of our party, and the gallantry with which we will be conducted through this contest, than we are by the magnanimity of our friends of the great and glorious State of New York in moving to make this nomination unanimous. On behalf of the delegation from Illinois, for the Republican party of this great and growing prairie State, I return to all our friends, New York included, our heartfelt thanks and gratitude for the nomination of this Convention.

PRESIDENT ASHMUN'S VALEDICTORY.

Gentlemen of the Convention: It becomes now my duty to put to you the last motion which, in the order of parliamentary law, the President has the power to propose. It will probably be the last proposition which he can ever make to most of you in any Convention. But before doing it, and before making a single other remark, I beg to tender you each and all my cordial thanks for the kind manner in which you have sustained me in the performance of the duties of this station. I confess to you, when I assumed it, I did it with some apprehension that I might not be able to come up to the expectations which had been formed. It was a bold undertaking, in every respect, and I know that I could not have accomplished it half so well as I have done, but for the extreme generosity manifested on all sides of the house. There was a solemn purpose here in the minds and in the hearts of not merely the Convention, but of the vast assemblage which has surrounded us, that before we separated we would accomplish the high duty. That duty, gentlemen, we have accomplished. Your sober judgments, your calm deliberations, after a comparison and discussion, free, frank, brotherly, and patriotic, have arrived at a conclusion at which the American people will arrive. Every symptom, every sign, every indication accompanying the Convention, in all its stages, are a high assurance of success, and I will not doubt, and none of us do doubt, that it will be a glorious success.

Allow me to say of the nominee that, although it may be of no consequence to the American people or to you, they are both personally known to me. It was my good fortune to have served with Mr. Lincoln in the Congress of the United States, and I rejoice in the opportunity to say that there was never elected to the House of Representatives a purer, nor a more intelligent and loyal representative than Abraham Lincoln. (Great applause.) The contest through which he passed during the last two years has tried him as by fire; and in that contest in which we are about to go for him now, I am sure that there is not one man in this country that will be compelled to hang his head for anything in the life of Abraham Lincoln. You have a candidate worthy of the cause; you are pledged to his success; humanity is pledged to his success; the cause of free government is pledged to his success. The decree has gone forth that he shall succeed. (Tremendous applause.)

I have served also in public life with Hannibal Hamlin. In the House of Representatives we were ranged on different sides. He was a firm Democrat of the old school, while I was as firmly, and perhaps too much so, a copy of the Webster school. (Applause.) But, as is known to many of the gentlemen who sit here before me to-day, there was always a sympathetic chord between him and me upon the question that has brought us here to-day. (Great applause.) And while the old divisions of party have crumbled away, and the force of circumstances have given rise to new issues, it is not strange that we are found battling together in the common cause. I say then, gentlemen, that you have got a ticket worthy of the cause, and worthy of the country.

Now, gentlemen, that we have completed so well, so thoroughly, the great work which the people sent us here to do, let us adjourn to our several constituencies; and, thanks be to God who giveth the victory, we will triumph. (Applause.)

SPEECHES.

SPEECH

DELIVERED AT CINCINNATI, OHIO, SEPTEMBER, 1859.

[THE following speech is here republished, with the insertion of Mr. Lincoln's views upon labor, and the ability of the laborer to become an employer. These were omitted in the first report, and the passages are supplied by the reporter for the present work.]

MY FELLOW-CITIZENS OF THE STATE OF OHIO: This is the first time in my life that I have appeared before an audience in so great a city as this. I therefore—though I am no longer a young man—make this appearance under some degree of embarrassment. But I have found that when one is embarrassed, usually the shortest way to get through with it is to quit talking or thinking about it, and go at something else.

I understand that you have had recently with you my very distinguished friend, Judge Douglas, of Illinois, and I understand, without having had an opportunity (not greatly sought to be sure) of seeing a report of the speech that he made here, that he did me the honor to mention my humble name. I suppose that he did so for the purpose of making some objection to some sentiment at some time expressed by me. I should expect, it is true, that Judge Douglas had reminded you, or informed you, if you had never before heard it, that I had once in my life declared it as my opinion that this Government can not "endure permanently half slave and half free; that a house divided against itself can not stand," and, as I had expressed it, I did not expect the house to fall; that I did not expect the Union to be dissolved; but that I did expect that it would cease to be divided; that it would become all one thing or all the other; that either the opposition of slavery would arrest the further spread of it, and place it where the public mind would rest in the belief that it was in the course of ultimate extinction; or the friends of slavery will push it forward until it becomes alike lawful in all the states, old or new, free as well as slave. I did, fifteen months ago, express that opinion, and upon many occasions Judge Douglas has denounced it, and has greatly, intentionally or unintentionally, misrepresented my purpose in the expression of that opinion.

I presume, without having seen a report of his speech, that he did so here. I presume that he alluded also to that opinion, in different language, having been expressed at a subsequent time by Governor Seward of New York, and that he took the two in a lump and denounced them; that he tried to point out that there was something couched in this opinion which led to the making of an entire uniformity of the local institutions of the various states of the Union, in utter disregard of the different states, which in their nature would seem to require a variety of institutions, and a variety of laws, conforming to the differences in the nature of the different states.

Not only so; I presume he insisted that this was a declaration of war between the free and slave states—that it was the sounding to the onset of continual war between the different states, the slave and free states.

This charge, in this form, was made by Judge Douglas on, I believe, the 9th of July, 1858, in Chicago, in my hearing. On the next evening, I made some reply to it. I informed him that many of the inferences he drew from that expression of mine were altogether foreign to any purpose entertained by me, and in so far as he should ascribe these inferences to me, as my purpose, he was entirely mistaken; and in so far as he might argue that whatever might be my purpose, actions conforming to my views would lead to these results, he might argue and establish if he could; but, so far as purposes were concerned, he was totally mistaken as to me.

When I made that reply to him—when I told him, on the question of declaring war between the different states of the Union, that I had not said that I did not expect any peace upon this question until slavery was exterminated; that I had only said I expected peace when that institution was put where the public mind should rest in the belief that it was in course of ultimate extinction; that I believed from the organization of our Government, until a very recent period of time, the institution had been placed and continued upon such a basis; that we had had comparative peace upon that question through a portion of that period of time, only because the public mind rested in that belief in regard to it, and that when we returned to that position in relation to that matter, I supposed we should again have peace as we previously had. I assured him, as I now assure you, that I neither then had, nor have, or ever had, any purpose in any way of interfering with the institution of slavery, where it exists. I believe we have no power, under the Constitution of the United States; or rather under the form of Government under which we live, to interfere with the institution of slavery, or any other of the institutions of our sister states, be they free or slave states. I declared then, and I now redeclare, that I have as little inclination to interfere with the institution of slavery, where it now exists, through the instrumentality of the General Government, or any other instrumentality, as I believe we have no power to do so.

I accidentally used this expression : I had no purpose of entering into the slave states to disturb the institution of slavery! So, upon the first occasion that Judge Douglas got an opportunity to reply to me, he passed by the whole body of what I had said upon that subject, and seized upon the particular expression of mine, that I had no purpose of entering into the slave states to disturb the institution of slavery. "O, no," said he, "he (Lincoln) won't enter into the slave states to disturb the institution of slavery; he is too prudent a man to do such a thing as that; he only means that he will go on to the line between the free and slave states, and shoot over at them. This is all he means to do. He means to do them all the harm he can, to disturb them all he can, in such a way as to keep his own hide in perfect safety."

Well, now, I did not think, at that time, that that was either a very dignified or very logical argument; but so it was, I had to get along with it as well as I could.

It has occurred to me here to-night, that if I ever do shoot over the line at the people on the other side of the line into a slave state, and purpose to do so, keeping my skin safe, that I have now about the best chance I shall ever have. I should not wonder that there are some Kentuckians about this audience; we are close to Kentucky; and whether that be so or not, we are on elevated ground, and by speaking distinctly, I should not wonder if some of the Kentuckians would hear me on the other side of the river. For that reason, I propose to address a portion of what I have to say to the Kentuckians.

I say, then, in the first place, to the Kentuckians, that I am what they call, as I understand it, a "Black Republican." I think slavery is wrong, morally and politically. I desire that it should be no further spread in these United States, and I should not object if it should gradually terminate in the whole Union. While I say this for myself, I say to you, Kentuckians, that I understand you differ radically with me upon this proposition; that you believe slavery is a good thing; that slavery is right; that it ought to be extended and perpetuated in this Union. Now, there being this broad difference between us, I do not pretend in addressing myself to you, Kentuckians, to attempt proselyting you; that would be a vain effort. I do not enter upon it. I only propose to try to show you that you ought to nominate for the next Presidency, at Charleston, my distinguished friend, Judge Douglas. In all that there is a difference between you and him, I understand he is sincerely for you, and more wisely for you than you are for yourself. I will try to demonstrate that proposition. Understand now, I say that I believe he is as sincerely for you, and more wisely for you, than you are for yourselves.

What do you want more than anything else to make successful your views of slavery—to advance the outspread of it, and to secure and perpetuate the nationality of it? What do you want more than anything else? What is needed absolutely? What is indispensable to you? Why! if I may be allowed to answer the question, it is to retain a hold upon the North—it is to retain support and strength from the free states. If you can get this support and strength from the free states you can succeed. If you do not get this support and this strength from the free states, you are in the minority, and you are beaten at once.

If that proposition be admitted—and it is undeniable—then the next thing I say to you is, that Douglas, of all the men in this nation, is the only man that affords you any hold upon the free states; that no other man can give you any strength in the free states. This being so, if you doubt the other branch of the proposition, whether he is for you—whether he is really for you, as I have expressed it, I propose asking your attention for a while to a few facts.

The issue between you and me, understand, is, that I think slavery is wrong, and ought not to be outspread, and you think it is right and ought to be extended and perpetuated. (A voice, "O Lord.") That is my Kentuckian I am talking to now.

I now proceed to try to show you that Douglas is sincerely for you, and more wisely for you, than you are for yourselves.

In the first place, we know that in a Government like this, in a Government of the people, where the voice of all the men of that country, substantially, enters into the execution—or administration rather—of the Government—in such a Government, what lies at the bottom of all of it, is public opinion. I lay down the proposition, that Judge Douglas is not only the man that promises you in advance a hold upon the North, and support in the North, but that he constantly molds public opinion to your ends; that in every possible way he can, he constantly molds the public opinion of the North to your ends; and if there are a few things in which he seems to be against you—a few things which he says that appear to be against you, and a few that he forbears to say which you would like to have him say—you ought to remember that the saying of the one, or the forbearing to say the other, would lose his hold upon the North, and, by consequence, would lose his capacity to serve you.

Upon this subject of molding public opinion, I call your attention to the fact—for a well-established fact it is—that the judge never says your institution of slavery is wrong; he never says it is right, to be sure, but he never says it is wrong. There is not a public man in the United States, I believe, with the exception of Senator Douglas, who has not, at some time in his life, declared his opinion whether the thing is right or wrong; but Senator Douglas never declares it is wrong. He leaves himself at perfect liberty to do all in your favor which he would be hindered from doing if he were to declare the thing to be wrong. On the contrary, he takes all the chances that he has for inveigling the sentiment of the North, opposed to slavery, into your support, by never saying it is right. This you ought to set down to his credit. You ought to give him full credit for this much, little though it be, in comparison to the whole which he does for you.

Some other things I will ask your attention to. He said upon the floor of the United States Senate, and he has repeated it, as I understand, a great many times, that he does not care whether slavery is "voted up or voted down." This again shows you, or ought to show you, if you would reason upon it, that he does not believe it to be wrong; for a man may say, when he sees nothing wrong in a thing, that he does not care whether it be voted up or voted down; but no man can logically say that he cares not whether a thing goes up or goes down, which to him appears to be wrong. You therefore have a demonstration in this, that to Judge Douglas's mind, your favorite institution, which you would have spread out, and made perpetual, is no wrong.

Another thing he tells you, in a speech made at Memphis, in Tennessee, shortly after the canvass in Illinois, last year. He there distinctly told the people that there was a "line drawn by the Almighty across this continent, on the one side of which the soil must always be cultivated by slaves;" that he did not pretend to know exactly where that line was, but that there was such a line. I want to ask your attention to that proposition again: that there is one portion of this continent where the Almighty has designed the soil shall always be cultivated by slaves; that its being cultivated by slaves at that place is right; that it has the direct sympathy and authority of the Almighty. Whenever you can get these Northern audiences to adopt the opinion that slavery is right on the other side of the Ohio; whenever you can get them, in pursuance of Douglas's views, to adopt that sentiment, they will very readily make the other argument, which is perfectly logical, that that which is right on that side of the Ohio, can not be wrong on this; and that if you have that property on that side of the Ohio, under the seal and stamp of the Almighty, when by any means it escapes over here, it is wrong to have Constitutions and laws "to devil" you about it. So Douglas is molding the public opinion of the North, first to say that the thing is right in your state over the Ohio river, and hence to say that that which is right there is not wrong here, and that all laws and Constitutions here, recognizing it as being wrong, are themselves wrong, and ought to be repealed and abrogated. He will tell you, men of Ohio, that if you choose here to have laws against slavery, it is in conformity to the idea that your climate is not suited to it; that your climate is not suited to slave labor, and therefore you have Constitutions and laws against it.

Let us attend to that argument for a little while, and see if it be sound. You do not raise sugar-cane, (except the new-fashioned sugar-cane, and you won't raise that long,) but they do raise it in Louisiana. You don't raise it in Ohio because you can't raise it profitably, because the climate don't suit it. They do raise it in Louisiana because there it is profitable. Now, Douglas will tell you that is precisely the slavery question. That they do have slaves there because they are profitable, and you don't have them here because they are not profitable. If that is so, then it leads to dealing with the one precisely as with the other. Is there anything in the Constitution or laws of Ohio against raising sugar-cane? Have you found it necessary to put any such provision in your law? Surely not! No man desires to raise sugar-cane in Ohio; but, if any man did desire to do so, you would say it was a tyrannical law that forbids his doing so; and whenever you shall agree with Douglas, whenever your minds are brought to adopt his argument, as surely you will have reached the conclusion, that although slavery is not profitable in Ohio, if any man wants it, it is wrong to him not to let him have it.

In this matter Judge Douglas is preparing the public mind for you of Kentucky, to make perpetual that good thing in your estimation, about which you and I differ.

In this connection let me ask your attention to another thing. I believe it is safe to assert that, five years ago, no living man had expressed the opinion that the negro had no share in the Declaration of Independence. Let me state that again: five years ago no living man had expressed the opinion that the negro had no share in the Declaration of Independence. If there is in this large audience any man who ever knew of that opinion being put upon paper as much as five years ago, I will be obliged to him now or at a subsequent time to show it.

If that be true I wish you then to note the next fact; that within the space of five years Senator Douglas, in the argument of this question, has got his entire party, so far as I know, without exception, to join in saying that the negro has no share in the Declaration of Independence. If there be now, in all these United States, one Douglas man that does not say this, I have been unable upon any occasion to scare him up. Now, if none of you said this five years ago, and all of you say it now, that is a matter that you Kentuckians ought to note. That is a vast change in the Northern public sentiment upon that question.

Of what tendency is that change? The tendency of that change is to bring the public mind to the conclusion that when men are spoken of, the negro is not meant; that when negroes are spoken of, brutes alone are contemplated. That change in public sentiment has already degraded the black man in the estimation of Douglas and his followers from the condition of a man of some sort, and assigned him to the condition of a brute. Now, you Kentuckians ought to give Douglas credit for this. That is the largest possible stride that can be made in regard to the perpetuation of your thing of slavery.

A voice—"Speak to Ohio men, and not to Kentuckians!"

Mr. Lincoln—I beg permission to speak as I please.

In Kentucky perhaps, in many of the slave states certainly, you are trying to establish the rightfulness of slavery by reference to the Bible. You are trying to show that slavery existed in the Bible times by Divine ordinance. Now, Douglas is wiser than you, for your own benefit, upon that subject. Douglas knows that whenever you establish that slavery was right by the Bible, it will occur that that slavery was the slavery of the *white* man—of men without reference to color—and he knows very well that you may entertain that idea in Kentucky as much as you please, but you will never win any Northern support upon it. He makes a wiser argument for you; he makes the argument that the slavery of the *black* man, the slavery of the man who has a skin of a different color from your own, is right. He thereby brings to your support Northern voters who could not for a moment be brought by your own argument of the Bible-right of slavery. Will you not give him credit for that? Will you not say that in this matter he is more wisely for you than you are for yourselves?

Now, having established with his entire party this doctrine, having been entirely successful in that branch of his efforts in your behalf, he is ready for another.

At this same meeting at Memphis, he declared that, while in all contests between the negro and the white man, he was for the white man, but that in all questions between the negro and the crocodile he was for the negro. He did not make that declaration accidentally at Memphis. He made it a great many times in the canvass in Illinois last year, (though I don't know that it was reported in any of his speeches there,) but he frequently made it. I believe he repeated it at Columbus, and I should not wonder if he repeated it here. It is, then, a deliberate way of expressing himself upon that subject. It is a matter of mature deliberation with him thus to express himself upon that point of his case. It therefore requires some deliberate attention.

The first inference seems to be that if you do not enslave the negro you are wronging the white man in some way or other; and that whoever is opposed to the negro being enslaved, is, in some way or other, against the white man. Is not that a falsehood? If there was a necessary conflict between the white man and the negro, I should be for the white man as much as Judge Douglas; but I say there is no such necessary conflict. I say that there is room enough for us all to be free, and that it not only does not wrong the white man that the negro should be free, but it positively wrongs the mass of the white men that the negro should be enslaved; that the mass of white men are really injured by the effects of slave labor in the vicinity of the fields of their own labor.

But I do not desire to dwell upon this branch of the question more than to say that this assumption of his is false, and I do hope that the fallacy will not long prevail in the minds of intelligent white men. At all events, you ought to thank Judge Douglas for it. It is for your benefit it is made.

The other branch of it is, that in a struggle between the negro and the crocodile, he is for the negro. Well, I don't know that there is any struggle between the negro and the crocodile either. I suppose that if a crocodile (or, as we old Ohio river boatmen used to call them, alligators) should come across a white man, he would kill him if he could, and so he would a negro. But what, at last, is this proposition? I believe that it is a sort of proposition in proportion, which may be stated thus: "As the negro is to the white man, so is the crocodile to the negro; and as the negro may rightfully treat the crocodile as a beast or reptile, so the white man may rightfully treat the negro as a beast or reptile." That is really the "knip" of all that argument of his.

Now, my brother Kentuckians, who believe in this,

you ought to thank Judge Douglas for having put that in a much more taking way than any of yourselves have done.

Again, Douglas's *great principle*, "Popular Sovereignty," as he calls it, gives you, by natural consequence, the revival of the slave-trade whenever you want it. If you question this, listen a while, consider a while, what I shall advance in support of that proposition.

He says that it is the sacred right of the man who goes into the territories, to have slavery if he wants it. Grant that for argument's sake. Is it not the sacred right of the man who don't go there equally to buy slaves in Africa, if he wants them? Can you point out the difference? The man who goes into the Territories of Kansas and Nebraska, or any other new territory, with the sacred right of taking a slave there which belongs to him, would certainly have no more right to take one there than I would, who own no slave, but who would desire to buy one and take him there. You will not say—you, the friends of Judge Douglas—but that the man who does not own a slave, has an equal right to buy one and take him to the territory, as the other does?

A VOICE—"I want to ask a question. Don't foreign nations interfere with the slave-trade?"

MR. LINCOLN—Well! I understand it to be a principle of Democracy to whip foreign nations whenever they interfere with us.

VOICE—"I only ask for information. I am a Republican myself."

MR. LINCOLN—You and I will be on the best terms in the world, but I do not wish to be diverted from the point I was trying to press.

I say that Douglas's Popular Sovereignty, establishing

his sacred right in the people, if you please, if carried to its logical conclusion, gives equally the sacred right to the people of the states or the territories themselves to buy slaves, wherever they can buy them cheapest; and if any man can show a distinction, I should like to hear him try it. If any man can show how the people of Kansas have a better right to slaves because they want them, than the people of Georgia have to buy them in Africa, I want him to do it. I think it can not be done. If it is "Popular Sovereignty" for the people to have slaves because they want them, it is "Popular Sovereignty" for them to buy them in Africa, because they desire to do so.

I know that Douglas has recently made a little effort—not seeming to notice that he had a different theory—has made an effort to get rid of that. He has written a letter, addressed to somebody, I believe, who resides in Iowa, declaring his opposition to the repeal of the laws that prohibit the African slave-trade. He bases his opposition to such repeal, upon the ground that these laws are themselves one of the compromises of the Constitution of the United States. Now it would be very interesting to see Judge Douglas, or any of his friends, turn to the Constitution of the United States and point out that compromise, to show where there is any compromise in the Constitution, or provision in the Constitution, express or implied, by which the administrators of that Constitution are under any obligation to repeal the African slave-trade. I know, or at least I think I know, that the framers of that Constitution did expect that the African slave-trade would be abolished at the end of twenty years, to which time their prohibition against its being abolished extended. I think there is abundant cotemporaneous history to show that the framers of the

Constitution expected it to be abolished. But while they so expected, they gave nothing for that expectation, and they put no provision in the Constitution requiring it should be so abolished. The migration or importation of such persons as the states shall see fit to admit, shall not be prohibited, but a certain tax might be levied upon such importation. But what was to be done after that time? The Constitution is as silent about that, as it is silent, personally, about myself. There is absolutely nothing in it about that subject; there is only the expectation of the framers of the Constitution that the slave-trade would be abolished at the end of that time, and they expected it would be abolished, owing to public sentiment, before that time, and they put that provision in, in order that it should not be abolished before that time, for reasons which I suppose they thought to be sound ones, but which I will not now try to enumerate before you.

But while they expected the slave-trade would be abolished at that time, they expected that the spread of slavery into the new territories should also be restricted. It is as easy to prove that the framers of the Constitution of the United States expected that slavery should be prohibited from extending into the new territories, as it is to prove that it was expected that the slave-trade should be abolished. Both these things were expected. One was no more expected than the other, and one was no more a compromise of the Constitution than the other. There was nothing said in the Constitution in regard to the spread of slavery into the territory. I grant that, but there was something very important said about it by the same generation of men in the adoption of the old ordinance of '87, through the influence of which, you here in Ohio, our neighbors in Indiana, we in Illinois, our neighbors in Michigan and Wisconsin are happy, prosperous, teeming millions of free men. That generation of men, though not to the full extent members of the Convention that framed the Constitution, were to some extent members of that Convention, holding seats at the same time in one body and the other, so that if there was any compromise on either of these subjects, the strong evidence is, that that compromise was in favor of the restriction of slavery from the new territories.

But Douglas says that he is unalterably opposed to the repeal of those laws; because, in his view, it is a compromise of the Constitution. You Kentuckians, no doubt, are somewhat offended with that! You ought not to be! You ought to be patient! You ought to know that if he said less than that, he would lose the power of "lugging" the Northern States to your support. Really, what you would push him to do would take from him his entire power to serve you. And you ought to remember how long, by precedent, Judge Douglas holds himself obliged to stick by compromises. You ought to remember that by the time you yourselves think you are ready to inaugurate measures for the revival of the African slave-trade, that sufficient time will have arrived, by precedent, for Judge Douglas to break through that compromise. He says now nothing more strong than he said in 1849, when he declared in favor of the Missouri Compromise—that precisely four years and a quarter after he declared that compromise to be a sacred thing, which "no ruthless hand would ever dare to touch," he, himself, brought forward the measure, ruthlessly to destroy it. By a mere calculation of time, it will only be four years more until he is ready to take back his profession about the sacredness of the Compromise abolishing the slave-trade. Precisely as soon as you are ready to have his services in that direction, by fair calculation, you may be sure of having them.

But you remember and set down to Judge Douglas's debt, or discredit, that he, last year, said the people of territories can, in spite of the Dred Scott decision, exclude your slaves from those territories; that he declared by "unfriendly legislation," the extension of your property into the new territories may be cut off in the teeth of the decision of the Supreme Court of the United States.

He assumed that position at Freeport, on the 27th of August, 1858. He said that the people of the territories can exclude slavery, in so many words. You ought, however, to bear in mind that he has never said it since. You may hunt in every speech that he has since made, and he has never used that expression once. He has never seemed to notice that he is stating his views differently from what he did then; but, by some sort of accident, he has always really stated it differently. He has always, since then, declared that "the Constitution does not carry slavery into the territories of the United States, beyond the power of the people legally to control it, as other property." Now, there is a difference in the language used upon that former occasion and in this latter day. There may or may not be a difference in the meaning, but it is worth while considering whether there is not also a difference in meaning.

What is it to exclude? Why, it is to drive it out; it is in some way to put it out of the territory; it is to force it across the line, or change its character, so that as property it is out of existence. But what is the controlling of it "as other property?" Is controlling it as other property the same thing as destroying it, or driving it away? I should think not. I should think the controlling of it as other property would be just about what you in Kentucky should want. I understand the controlling of property means the controlling of it for the benefit of the owner of it. While I have no doubt the Supreme Court of the United States would say "God speed" to any of the territorial Legislatures that should thus control slave property, they would sing quite a different tune, if by the pretense of controlling it they were to undertake to pass laws which virtually excluded it, and that upon a very well known principle to all lawyers, that what a Legislature can not directly do, it can not do by indirection; that as the Legislature has not the power to drive slaves out, they have no power by indirection, by tax, or by imposing burdens in any way on that property, to effect the same end, and that any attempt to do so would be held by the Dred Scott court unconstitutional.

Douglas is not willing to stand by his first proposition that they can exclude it, because we have seen that that proposition amounts to nothing more nor less than the naked absurdity, that you may lawfully drive out that which has a lawful right to remain. He admitted at first that the slave might be lawfully taken into the territories under the Constitution of the United States, and yet asserted that he might be lawfully driven out. That being the proposition, it is the absurdity I have stated. He is not willing to stand in the face of that direct, naked, and impudent absurdity; he has, therefore, modified his language into that of being "*controlled as other property.*"

The Kentuckians do n't like this in Douglas! I will tell you where it will go. He now swears by the court. He was once a leading man in Illinois to break down a court, because it had made a decision he did not like. But he now not only swears by the court, the courts having got to working for you, but he denounces all men that do not swear by the courts, as unpatriotic, as bad citizens.

When one of these acts of unfriendly legislation shall impose such heavy burdens as to, in effect, destroy property in slaves in a territory, and show plainly enough that there can be no mistake in the purpose of the Legislature to make them so burdensome, this same Supreme Court will decide that law to be unconstitutional, and he will be ready to say for your benefit, "I swear by the court; I give it up;" and while that is going on, he has been getting all his men to swear by the courts, and to give it up with him. In this again he serves you faithfully, and, as I say, more wisely than you serve yourselves.

Again: I have alluded in the beginning of these remarks to the fact, that Judge Douglas has made great complaint of my having expressed the opinion that this Government "can not endure permanently half slave and half free." He has complained of Seward for using different language, and declaring that there is an "irrepressible conflict" between the principles of free and slave labor. [A VOICE—"He says it is not original with Seward. That is original with Lincoln."] I will attend to that immediately, sir. Since that time, Hickman, of Pennsylvania, expressed the same sentiment. He has never denounced Mr. Hickman. Why? There is a little chance, notwithstanding that opinion in the mouth of Hickman, that he may yet be a Douglas man. That is the difference! It is not unpatriotic to hold that opinion if a man is a Douglas man.

But neither I, nor Seward, nor Hickman, is entitled to the enviable or unenviable distinction of having first expressed that idea. That same idea was expressed by the *Richmond Enquirer*, in Virginia, in 1856; quite two years before it was expressed by the first of us. And while Douglas was pluming himself, that in his conflict with my humble self, last year, he had "squelched out" that fatal heresy, as he delighted to call it, and had suggested that if he only had had a chance to be in New York and meet Seward, he would have "squelched" it there also, it never occurred to him to breathe a word against Pryor. I do n't think that you can discover that Douglas ever talked of going to Virginia to "squelch" out that idea there. No. More than that: that same Roger A. Pryor was brought to Washington City and made the editor of the *par excellence* Douglas paper, after making use of that expression, which, in us, is so unpatriotic and heretical. From all this, my Kentucky friends may see that this opinion is heretical in his view only when it is expressed by men suspected of a desire that the country shall all become free, and not when expressed by those fairly known to entertain the desire that the whole country shall become slave. When expressed by that class of men, it is in nowise offensive to him. In this again, my friends of Kentucky, you have Judge Douglas with you.

There is another reason why you Southern people ought to nominate Douglas at your Convention at Charleston. That reason is the wonderful capacity of the man; the power he has of doing what would seem to be impossible. Let me call your attention to one of these apparently impossible things.

Douglas had three or four very distinguished men of the most extreme antislavery views of any men in the Republican party, expressing their desire for his re-election to the Senate last year. That would, of itself, have seemed to be a little wonderful, but that wonder is hightened when we see that Wise, of Virginia, a man exactly opposed to them, a man who believes in the Divine right of slavery, was also expressing his desire that Douglas should be re-elected; that another man that may be said to be kindred to Wise, Mr. Breckinridge, the Vice-President, and of your own state, was also agreeing with the antislavery men in the North, that Douglas ought to be re-elected. Still to heighten the wonder, a Senator from Kentucky, whom I have always loved with an affection as tender and endearing as I have ever loved any man; who was opposed to the antislavery men for reasons which seemed sufficient to him, and equally opposed to Wise and Breckinridge, was writing letters into Illinois to secure the re-election of Douglas.

Now that all these conflicting elements should be brought, while at dagger's points, with one another, to support him, is a feat that is worthy for you to note and consider. It is quite probable that each of these classes of men thought, by the re-election of Douglas, their peculiar views would gain something; it is probable that the antislavery men thought their views would gain something; that Wise and Breckinridge thought so too, as regards their opinions; that Mr. Crittenden thought that his views would gain something, although he was opposed to both these other men. It is probable that each and all of them thought that they were using Douglas, and it is yet an unsolved problem whether he was not using them all. If he was, then it is for you to consider whether that power to perform wonders, is one for you lightly to throw away.

There is one other thing that I will say to you in this relation. It is but my opinion, I give it to you without a fee. It is my opinion that it is for you to take him or be defeated; and that if you do take him you may be beaten. You will surely be beaten if you do not take him. We, the Republicans and others forming the opposition of the country, intend to "stand by our guns," to be patient and firm, and in the long run to beat you whether you take him or not. We know that before we fairly beat you, we have to beat you both together. We know that you are "all of a feather," and that we have to beat you altogether, and we expect to do it. We do n't intend to be very impatient about it. We mean to be as deliberate and calm about it as it is possible to be, but as firm and resolved as it is possible for men to be. When we do as we say, beat you, you perhaps want to know what we will do with you.

I will tell you, so far as I am authorized to speak for the opposition, what we mean to do with you. We mean to treat you, as near as we possibly can, as Washington, Jefferson, and Madison treated you. We mean to leave you alone, and in no way to interfere with your institution; to abide by all and every compromise of the Constitution, and, in a word, coming back to the original proposition, to treat you, so far as degenerated men (if we have degenerated) may, according to the examples of those noble fathers—Washington, Jefferson, and Madison.

We mean to remember that you are as good as we; that there is no difference between us other than the difference of circumstances. We mean to recognize and bear in mind always that you have as good hearts in your bosoms as other people, or as we claim to have, and treat you accordingly. We mean to marry your girls when we have a chance—the white ones I mean; and I have the honor to inform you that I once did have a chance in that way.

I have told you what we mean to do. I want to know now, when that thing takes place, what do you mean to do? I often hear it intimated that you mean to divide the Union whenever a Republican, or anything like it, is elected President of the United States.

A VOICE—That is so.

MR. LINCOLN—"That is so," one of them says; I wonder if he is a Kentuckian?

A VOICE—He is a Douglas man.

MR. LINCOLN—Well, then, I want to know what you are going to do with your half of it? Are you going to split the Ohio down through, and push your half off a piece? Or are you going to keep it right alongside of us outrageous fellows? Or are you going to build up a wall some way between your country and ours, by which that movable property of yours can't come over here any more, to the danger of your losing it? Do you think you can better yourselves on that subject, by leaving us here under no obligation whatever to return those specimens of your movable property that come hither? You have divided the Union because we would not do right with you, as you think, upon that subject; when we cease to be under obligations to do anything for you, how much better off do you think you will be? Will you make war upon us, and kill us all? Why, gentlemen, I think you are as gallant and as brave men as live; that you can fight as bravely in a good cause, man for man, as any other people living; that you have shown yourselves capable of this upon various occasions; but man for man, you are not better than we are, and there are not so many of you as there are of us. You will never make much of a hand at whipping us. If we were fewer in numbers than you, I think that you could whip us; if we were equal, it would likely be a drawn battle; but being inferior in numbers, you will make nothing by attempting to master us.

But perhaps I have addressed myself as long, or longer, to the Kentuckians than I ought to have done, inasmuch as I have said that whatever course you take we intend in the end to beat you.

I propose to address a few remarks to our friends, by way of discussing with them the best means of keeping that promise that I have in good faith made.

It may appear a little episodical for me to mention the topic of which I shall speak now. It is a favorite proposition of Douglas's that the interference of the General Government, through the ordinance of '87, or through any other act of the General Government, never has made or ever can make a free state; that the ordinance of '87 did not make free states of Ohio, Indiana, or Illinois. That these states are free upon his "great principle" of popular sovereignty, because the people of those several states have chosen to make them so. At Columbus, and probably here, he undertook to compliment the people that they themselves have made the State of Ohio free, and that the ordinance of '87 was not entitled, in any degree, to divide the honor with them. I have no doubt that the people of the State of Ohio did make her free according to their own will and judgment, but let the facts be remembered.

In 1802, I believe, it was you made your first Constitution, with the clause prohibiting slavery, and you did it, I suppose, very nearly unanimously; but you should bear in mind that you—speaking of you as one people—that you did so unembarrassed by the actual presence of the institution among you; that you made it a free state, not with the embarrassment upon you of already having among you many slaves, which, if they had been here, and you had sought to make a free state, you would not know what to do with. If they had been among you, embarrassing difficulties, most probably, would have induced you to tolerate a slave Constitution instead of a free one, as indeed these very difficulties have constrained every people on this continent who have adopted slavery.

Pray what was it that made you free? What kept you free? Did you not find your country free when you came to decide that Ohio should be a free state? It is important to inquire by what reason you found it so? Let us take an illustration between the States of Ohio and Kentucky. Kentucky is separated by this river Ohio, not a mile wide. A portion of Kentucky, by reason of the course of the Ohio, is further north than this portion of Ohio, in which we now stand. Kentucky is entirely covered with slavery—Ohio is entirely free from it. What made that difference? Was it climate? No! A portion of Kentucky was further north than this portion of Ohio. Was it soil? No! There is nothing in the soil of the one more favorable to slave labor than the other. It was not climate or soil that caused one side of the line to be entirely covered with slavery, and the other side free of it. What was it? Study over it. Tell us, if you can, in all the range of conjecture, if there be anything you can conceive of that made that difference, other than that there was no law of any sort keeping it out of Kentucky, while the ordinance of '87 kept it out of Ohio? If there is any other reason than this, I confess that it is wholly beyond my power to conceive of it. This, then, I offer to combat the idea that that ordinance has never made any state free.

I do n't stop at this illustration. I come to the State of Indiana; and what I have said as between Kentucky and Ohio, I repeat as between Indiana and Kentucky; it is equally applicable. One additional argument is applicable also to Indiana. In her territorial condition she more than once petitioned Congress to abrogate the ordinance entirely, or at least so far as to suspend its operation for a time, in order that they should exercise the "popular sovereignty" of having slaves if they wanted them. The men then controlling the General Government, imitating the men of the Revolution, refused Indiana that privilege. And so we have the evidence that Indiana supposed she could have slaves if it were not for that ordinance; that she besought Congress to put that barrier out of the way; that Congress refused to do so, and it all ended at last in Indiana being a free state. Tell me not, then, that the ordinance of '87 had nothing to do with making Indiana a free state, when we find some men chafing against and only restrained by that barrier.

Come down again to our State of Illinois. The great Northwest Territory, including Ohio, Indiana, Illinois, Michigan, and Wisconsin, was acquired first, I believe, by the British Government, in part, at least, from the French. Before the establishment of our independence, it became a part of Virginia; enabling Virginia afterward to transfer it to the General Government. There were French settlements in what is now Illinois, and at the same time there were French settlements in what is now Missouri—in the tract of country that was not purchased till about 1803. In these French settlements negro slavery had existed for many years—perhaps more than a hundred, if not as much as two hundred years—at Kaskaskia, in Illinois, and at St. Genevieve, or Cape Girardeau, perhaps, in Missouri. The number of slaves was not very great, but there was about the same number in each place. They were there when we acquired the territory. There was no effort made to break up the relation of master and slave, and even the ordinance of 1787 was not so enforced as to destroy that slavery in Illinois; nor did the ordinance apply to Missouri at all.

What I want to ask your attention to, at this point, is that Illinois and Missouri came into the Union about the same time, Illinois in the latter part of 1818, and Missouri, after a struggle, I believe some time in 1820. They had been filling up with American people about the same period of time; their progress enabling them to come into the Union about the same. At the end of that ten years, in which they had been so preparing, (for it was about that period of time,) the number of slaves in Illinois had actually decreased; while in Missouri, beginning with very few, at the end of that ten years, there were about ten thousand. This being so, and it being remembered that Missouri and Illinois are, to a certain extent, in the same parallel of latitude—that the northern half of Missouri and the southern half of Illinois are in the same parallel of latitude—so that climate would have the same effect upon one as upon the other, and that in the soil there is no material difference so far as bears upon the question of slavery being settled upon one or the other—there being none of those natural causes to produce a difference in filling them, and yet there being a broad difference in their filling up, we are led again to inquire what was the cause of that difference.

It is most natural to say that in Missouri there was no law to keep that country from filling up with slaves, while in Illinois there was the ordinance of '87. The ordinance being there slavery decreased during that ten years—the ordinance not being in the other, it increased from a few to ten thousand. Can anybody doubt the reason of the difference?

I think all these facts most abundantly prove that my friend Judge Douglas's proposition, that the ordinance of '87, or the national restriction of slavery, never had a tendency to make a free state, is a fallacy—a proposition without the shadow or substance of truth about it.

Douglas sometimes says that all the states (and it is part of this same proposition I have been discussing) that have become free, have become so upon his "great principle;" that the State of Illinois itself came into the Union as a slave state, and that the people, upon the "great principle" of Popular Sovereignty, have since made it a free state. Allow me but a little while to state to you what facts there are to justify him in saying that Illinois came into the Union as a slave state.

I have mentioned to you that there were a few old French slaves there. They numbered, I think, one or two hundred. Besides that, there had been a territorial law for indenturing black persons. Under that law, in violation of the ordinance of '87, but without any enforcement of the ordinance to overthrow the system, there had been a small number of slaves introduced as indentured persons. Owing to this the clause for the prohibition of slavery was slightly modified. Instead of running like yours, that neither slavery nor involuntary servitude, except for crime of which the party shall have been duly convicted, should exist in the state, they said that neither slavery nor involuntary servitude should thereafter be introduced, and that the children of indentured servants should be born free; and nothing was said about the few old French slaves. Out of this fact, that the clause for prohibiting slavery was modified because of the actual presence of it, Douglas asserts again and again that Illinois came into the Union as a slave state. How far the facts sustain the conclusion that he draws, it is for intelligent and impartial men to decide. I leave it with you with these remarks, worthy of being remembered, that that little thing, those few indentured servants being there, was of itself sufficient to modify a Constitution made by a people ardently desiring to have a free Constitution; showing the power of the actual presence of the institution of slavery to prevent any people, however anxious to make a free state, from making it perfectly so.

I have been detaining you longer, perhaps, than I ought to do.

I am in some doubt whether to introduce another topic upon which I could talk a while. [Cries of "Go on," and "Give us it."] It is this then: Douglas's popular sovereignty, as a principle, is simply this: If one man chooses to make a slave of another man, neither that man nor anybody else has a right to object. Apply it to government, as he seeks to apply it, and it is this: if, in a new territory, into which a few people are beginning to enter for the purpose of making their homes, they choose to either exclude slavery from their limits, or to establish it there, however one or the other may affect the persons to be enslaved, or the infinitely greater number of persons who are afterward to inhabit that territory, or the other members of the family of communities of which they are but an incipient member, or the general head of the family of states as parent of all—however their action may affect one or the other of these, there is no power or right to interfere. That is Douglas's popular sovereignty applied. Now I think that there is a real popular sovereignty in the world. I think a definition of popular sovereignty, in the abstract, would be about this: that each man shall do precisely as he pleases with himself, and with all those things which exclusively concern him. Applied in government, this principle would be, that a general government shall do all those things which pertain to it, and all the local governments shall do precisely as they please in respect to those matters which exclusively concern them.

[Upon what principle shall it be said the planting of

a new territory by the first thousand people that migrate to it, is a matter concerning them exclusively? What kind of logic is it that argues that it in no wise concerns, if you please, the black men who are to be enslaved? Or if you are afraid to say anything about that; if you have been bedeviled for your sympathy for the negro; if noses have been turned up at you; and if you have been accused of having wanted the negro as your social equal, for a juror, to be a witness against your white brethren, or even to marry with him; if you have been accused of all this, until you are afraid to speak of the colored race;—then, I ask you, what right is there to say that the planting of free soil with slavery has no effect upon the white men that are to go there afterward as emigrants from the older states? By what right do a few of the first settlers fix that first condition beyond the power of succeeding millions to eradicate it? Why shall a few men be allowed, as it were, to sow that virgin soil with Canada thistles, or any other pest of the soil, which the farmer, in subsequent ages, cannot eradicate without endless toil. Is it a matter that exclusively concerns those few people that settle there first?

Douglas argues that it is a matter of exclusive local jurisdiction. What enables him to say that? It is because he looks upon slavery as so insignificant that the people may decide that question for themselves, albeit they are not fit to decide who shall be their governor, judge, or secretary, or who have been any of their officers. These are vast national matters, in his estimation; but the little matter, in his estimation, is the planting of slavery there. That is of purely local interest, which nobody should be allowed to say a word about. It is a great national question that Sammedary shall be appointed by the President as Governor of Kansas, that he may go there for a year or two, and come away without there being left behind him a sign for good or evil of his having been there; but the question of planting slavery on that soil is a little, local, unimportant matter, that nobody ought to be allowed to speak of. Such an expression is absolutely shameful.

Labor is the great source from which nearly all, if not all, human comforts and necessaries are drawn. There is a difference of opinion about the elements of labor in a society. Some men assume that there is a necessary connection between capital and labor, and that connection draws within it all of the labor of the community. They assume that nobody works unless capital excites him to work. They begin next to consider what is the best way for capital to be used to induce people to work. They say that there are but two ways; one is, to hire men and to allure them to labor by their own consent, and the other is, to buy the men, and drive them to labor. This latter is slavery. Having assumed so much, they proceed to discuss the question of whether the laborers themselves are better off in the condition of slavery or of hired laborers; and they usually decide that they are better off in the condition of slaves.

In the first place, I say that that whole theory is a mistake. That there is a certain relation between capital and labor I admit. That it does exist, and rightfully exist, and that it is proper that it should exist, I think is true. I think, in the progress of things, that men who are industrious, and sober, and honest in the pursuit of their own interests, should, after a while, accumulate capital, and then should be allowed to enjoy it in peace, and also, if they choose, when they have accumulated it, use it to save themselves from actual labor, by hiring other people to labor for them. In doing so, they do not wrong the man they employ, for they find young men who have not of their own land to work upon, or shops to labor in, and who are benefited by working for others in the capacity of hired laborers, receiving their capital for it. Thus, a few men that own capital, hire others, and thus establish the relation of capital and labor rightfully; a relation of which I make no complaint. But I insist that the relation, after all, does not embrace more than one-eighth of all the labor of the country. At least seven-eighths of the labor is done without relation to it.

Take the State of Ohio. Out of eight bushels of wheat, seven are raised by those men who labor for themselves, aided by their boys growing to manhood, neither being hired nor hiring, but literally laboring upon their own hook, asking no favor of capital, of hired laborer, or of the slave. That is the true condition of the larger portion of all the labor done in this community, or that should be the condition of labor in well-regulated communities of agriculturists. Thus much for that part of the subject.

Again: the assumption that the slave is in a better condition than the hired laborer, includes the further assumption that he who is once a hired laborer always remains a hired laborer; that there is a certain class of men who remain through life in a dependent condition. Then they endeavor to point out that when they get old they have no kind masters to take care of them, and that they fall dead in the traces, with the harness of actual labor upon their feeble backs. In point of fact that is a false assumption. There is no such thing as a man who is a hired laborer, of a necessity, always remaining in his early condition. The general rule is otherwise. I know it is so, and I will tell you why.

When at an early age, I was myself a hired laborer, at twelve dollars per month; and therefore I do know that there is not always the necessity for actual labor because once there was propriety in being so. My understanding of the hired laborer is this: A young man finds himself of an age to be dismissed from parental control; he has for his capital nothing, save two strong hands that God has given him, a heart willing to labor, and a freedom to choose the mode of his work and the manner of his employer; he has got no soil nor shop, and he avails himself of the opportunity of hiring himself to some man who has capital to pay him a fair day's wages for a fair day's work. He is benefited by availing himself of that privilege. He works industriously, he behaves soberly, and the result of a year or two's labor is a surplus of capital. Now he buys land on his own hook; he settles, marries, begets sons and daughters, and in course of time he too has enough capital to hire some new beginner.

In this same way every member of the whole community benefits and improves his condition. That is the true condition of labor in the world, and it breaks up the saying of these men that there is a class of men chained down throughout life to labor for another. There is no such case unless he be of that confiding and leaning disposition that makes it preferable for him to choose that course, or unless he be a vicious man, who, by reason of his vice, is, in some way prevented from improving his condition, or else he be a singularly unfortunate man. There is no such thing as a man being bound down in a free country through his life as a laborer. This progress by which the poor, honest, industrious, and resolute man raises himself, that he may work on his own account, and hire somebody else, is that progress that human nature is entitled to, is that improvement in condition that is intended to be secured by those institutions under which we live, is the great principle for which this government was really formed. Our government was not established that one man might do with himself as he pleases, and with another man too.

I hold that if there is any one thing that can be proved to be the will of God by external nature around us, without reference to revelation, it is the proposition that whatever any one man earns with his hands and by the sweat of his brow, he shall enjoy in peace. I say that whereas God Almighty has given every man one mouth to be fed, and one pair of hands adapted to furnish food for that mouth, if anything can be proved to be the will of Heaven, it is proved by this fact, that that mouth is to be fed by those hands, without being interfered with by any other man who has also his mouth to feed and his hands to labor with. I hold if the Almighty had ever made a set of men that should do all the eating and none of the work, he would have made them with mouths only and no hands, and if he had ever made another class that he had intended should do all the work and none of the eating, he would have made them without mouths and with all hands. But inasmuch as he has not chosen to make man in that way, if anything is proved, it is that those hands and mouths are to be co-operative through life and not to be interfered with. That they are to go forth and improve their condition as I have been trying to illustrate, is the inherent right given to mankind directly by the Maker.

In the exercise of this right you must have room. In the filling up of countries, it turns out after a while that we get so thick that we have not quite room enough for the exercise of that right, and we desire to go somewhere else. Where shall we go to? Where shall you go to escape from over-population and competition? To those new territories which belong to us, which are God-given for that purpose. If, then, you will go to those territories that you may improve your condition, you have a right to keep them in the best condition for those going into them, and can they make that natural advance in their condition if they find the institution of slavery planted there?

My good friends, let me ask you a question—you who have come from Virginia or Kentucky, to get rid of this thing of slavery—let me ask you what headway would you have made in getting rid of it, if by popular sovereignty you find slavery on that soil which you looked for to be free when you get there? You would not have made much headway if you had found slavery already here, if you had to sit down to your labor by the side of the unpaid workman.

I say, then, that it is due to yourselves as voters, as owners of the new territories, that you shall keep those territories free, in the best condition for all such of your gallant sons as may choose to go there.

I do not desire to elaborate this branch of the general subject of political discussion at this time further. I did not think I would get upon this topic at all, and I have detained you already too long in its discussion.]

I have taken upon myself, in the name of some of you, to say that we expect, upon these principles, to ultimately beat them. In order to do so, I think we want and must have a national policy in regard to the institution of slavery, that acknowledges and deals with that institution as being wrong. Whoever desires the prevention of the spread of slavery and the nationalization of that institution, yields all, when he yields to any policy that either recognizes slavery as being right, or as being an indifferent thing. Nothing will make you successful but setting up a policy which shall treat the thing as being wrong. When I say this, I do not mean to say that this General Government is charged with the duty of redressing or preventing all the wrongs in the world; but I do think that it is charged with preventing and redressing all wrongs which are wrongs to itself. This Government is expressly charged with the duty of providing for the general welfare. We believe that the spreading out and perpetuity of the institution of slavery impairs the general welfare. We believe—nay, we know, that that is the only thing that has ever threatened the perpetuity of the Union itself. The only thing which has ever menaced the destruction of the government under which we live is this very thing. To repress this thing, we think, is providing for the general welfare. Our friends in Kentucky differ from us. We need not make our argument for them; but we, who think it is wrong in all its relations, or in some of them at least, must decide as to our own actions, and our own course, upon our own judgment.

I say that we must not interfere with the institution of slavery in the states where it exists, because the Constitution forbids it, and the general welfare does not require us to do so. We must not withhold an efficient fugitive slave law; because the Constitution requires us, as I understand it, not to withhold such a law. But we must prevent the outspreading of the institution; because neither the Constitution nor general welfare requires us to extend it. We must prevent the revival of the African slave-trade, and the enacting, by Congress, of a territorial slave code. We must prevent each of these things being done by either congresses or courts. The people of these United States are the rightful masters of both congresses and courts, not to overthrow the Constitution, but to overthrow the men who pervert the Constitution.

To do these things we must employ instrumentalities. We must hold conventions; we must adopt platforms, if we conform to ordinary custom; we must nominate candidates, and we must carry elections. In all these things, I think that we ought to keep in view our real purpose, and in none do anything that stands adverse to our purpose. If we shall adopt a platform that fails to recognize or express our purpose, or elect a man that declares himself inimical to our purpose, we not only make nothing by our success, but we tacitly admit that we act upon no other principle than a desire to have "the loaves and fishes," by which, in the end, our apparent success is really an injury to us.

I know that this is very desirable with me, as with everybody else, that all the elements of the Opposition shall unite in the next Presidential election and in all future time. I am anxious that that should be, but there are things seriously to be considered in relation to that matter. If the terms can be arranged, I am in favor of the Union. But, suppose we shall take up some man and put him upon one end or the other of the ticket, who declares himself against us in regard to the prevention of the spread of slavery—who turns up his nose, and says he is tired of hearing anything more about it—who is more against us than against the enemy, what will be the issue? Why, he will get no slave states after all—he has tried that already, until being beat is the rule for him. If we nominate him upon that ground, he will not carry a slave state, and not only so, but that portion of our men who are high-strung upon the principle we really fight for, will not go for him, and he won't get a single electoral vote anywhere, except, perhaps, in the State of Maryland. There is no use in saying to us that we are stubborn and obstinate, because we won't do some such thing as this. We can not do it. We can not get our men to vote it. I speak by the card, that we can not give the State of Illinois, in such case, by fifty thousand. We would be flatter down than the "Negro Democracy" themselves have the heart to wish to see us.

After saying this much, let me say a little on the other side. There are plenty of men in the slave states that are altogether good enough for me, to be either President or Vice-President, provided they will profess their sympathy with our purpose, and will place themselves on the ground that our men, upon principle, can vote for them. There are scores of them, good men in their character for intelligence and talent and integrity. If such a one will place himself upon the right ground, I am for his occupying one place upon the next Republican or Opposition ticket. I will heartily go for him. But, unless he does so place himself, I think it a matter of perfect nonsense to attempt to bring about a union upon any other basis; that if a union be made, the elements will scatter so that there can be no success for such a ticket, nor anything like success. The good old maxims of the Bible are applicable, and truly applicable, to human affairs; and in this, as in other things, we may say here that "He who is not for us is against us;" "He who gathereth not with us scattereth." I should be glad to have some of the many good, and able, and noble men of the South to place themselves where we can confer upon them the high honor of an election, upon one or the other end of our ticket. It would do my soul good to do that thing. It would enable us to teach them that, inasmuch as we select one of their own number to carry out our principles, we are free from the charge that we mean more than we say.

But, my friends, I have detained you much longer than I expected to do. I believe I may do myself the compliment to say, that you have stayed and heard me with great patience, for which I return you my most sincere thanks.

SPEECH

ON

INTERNAL IMPROVEMENTS,

IN THE HOUSE OF REPRESENTATIVES,
JUNE 20, 1848.

IN Committee of the Whole on the state of the Union, on the Civil and Diplomatic Appropriation Bill, Mr. LINCOLN said:

MR. CHAIRMAN: I wish at all times in no way to practice any fraud upon the House or the Committee, and I also desire to do nothing which may be very disagreeable to any of the members. I therefore state, in advance, that my object in taking the floor is to make a speech on the general subject of internal improvements; and if I am out of order in doing so, I give the Chair an opportunity of so deciding, and I will take my seat.

The CHAIR.—I will not undertake to anticipate what the gentleman may say on the subject of internal improvements. He will, therefore, proceed in his remarks, and, if any question of order shall be made, the Chair will then decide it.

Mr. LINCOLN.—At an early day of this session the President sent to us what may properly be called an internal-improvement veto message. The late Democratic

Convention which sat at Baltimore, and which nominated General Cass for the Presidency, adopted a set of resolutions, now called the Democratic platform, among which is one in these words:

> "That the Constitution does not confer upon the General Government the power to commence and carry on a general system of internal improvements."

General Cass, in his letter accepting the nomination, holds this language:

> "I have carefully read the resolutions of the Democratic National Convention, laying down the platform of our political faith, and I adhere to them as firmly as I approve them cordially."

These things, taken together, show that the question of internal improvements is now more distinctly made—has become more intense, than at any former period. It can no longer be avoided. The veto message and the Baltimore resolution I understand to be, in substance, the same thing; the latter being the mere general statement, of which the former is the amplification—the bill of particulars. While I know there are many Democrats, on this floor and elsewhere, who disapprove that message, I understand that all who shall vote for General Cass will thereafter be counted as having approved it, as having indorsed all its doctrines. I suppose all, or nearly all, the Democrats will vote for him. Many of them will do so, not because they like his position on this question, but because they prefer him, being wrong in this, to another whom they consider further wrong on other questions. In this way the internal improvement Democrats are to be, by a sort of forced consent, carried over, and arrayed against themselves on this measure of policy. General Cass, once elected, will not trouble himself to make a constitutional argument, or, perhaps, any argument at all, when he shall veto a river or harbor bill. He will consider it a sufficient answer to all Democratic murmurs, to point to Mr. Polk's message, and to the "Democratic platform." This being the case, the question of improvements is verging to a final crisis; and the friends of the policy must now battle, and battle manfully, or surrender all. In this view, humble as I am, I wish to review, and contest, as well as I may, the general positions of this veto message. When I say *general* positions, I mean to exclude from consideration so much as relates to the present embarrassed state of the treasury, in consequence of the Mexican war.

Those general positions are: That internal improvements ought not to be made by the General Government:

1. Because they would overwhelm the treasury.

2. Because, while their *burdens* would be general, their *benefits* would be *local* and *partial*, involving an obnoxious inequality; and

3. Because they would be unconstitutional.

4. Because the States may do enough by the levy and collection of tonnage duties; or, if not,

5. That the Constitution may be amended.

"Do nothing at all, lest you do something wrong," is the sum of these positions—is the sum of this message; and this, with the exception of what is said about constitutionality, applying as forcibly to making improvements by State authority, as by the national authority. So that we must abandon the improvements of the country altogether, by any and every authority, or we must resist and repudiate the doctrines of this message. Let us attempt the latter.

The first position is, that a system of internal improvement would overwhelm the treasury.

That in such a system there is a *tendency* to undue expansion, is not to be denied. Such tendency is founded in the nature of the subject. A member of Congress will prefer voting for a bill which contains an appropriation for his district, to voting for one which does not; and when a bill shall be expanded till every district shall be provided for, that it will be too greatly expanded is obvious. But is this any more true in Congress than in a State Legislature? If a member of Congress must have an appropriation for his district, so a member of the Legislature must have one for his county; and if one will overwhelm the national treasury, so the other will overwhelm the State treasury. Go where we will, the difficulty is the same. Allow it to drive us from the halls of Congress, and it will just as easily drive us from the State Legislatures. Let us, then, grapple with it, and test its strength. Let us, judging of the future by the past, ascertain whether there may not be, in the discretion of Congress, a sufficient power to limit and restrain this expansive tendency within reasonable and proper bounds. The President himself values the evidence of the past. He tells us, that at a certain point of our history, more than two hundred millions of dollars had been *applied for*, to make improvements; and this he does to prove that the treasury would be overwhelmed by such a system. Why did he not tell us how much was *granted?* Would not that have been better evidence? Let us turn to it, and see what it proves. In the message, the President tells us that "during the four succeeding years, embraced by the administration of President Adams, the power not only to appropriate money, but to apply it, under the direction and authority of the General Government, as well to the construction of roads as to the improvement of harbors and rivers, was fully asserted and exercised."

This, then, was the period of greatest enormity. These, if any, must have been the days of the two hundred millions. And how much do you suppose was really expended for improvements during that four years? Two hundred millions? One hundred? Fifty? Ten? Five? No, sir, less than two millions. As shown by authentic documents, the expenditures on improvements, during 1825, 1826, 1827, and 1828, amounted to $1,879,-627 01. These four years were the period of Mr. Adams's administration, nearly, and substantially. This fact shows, that when the power to make improvements "was fully asserted and exercised," the Congresses *did* keep within reasonable limits; and what *has* been done, it seems to me, *can* be done again.

Now for the second position of the message, namely, that the burdens of improvements would be *general*, while their *benefits* would be *local* and *partial*, involving an obnoxious inequality. That there is some degree of truth in this position I shall not deny. No commercial object of government patronage can be so exclusively *general*, as not to be of some peculiar *local* advantage; but, on the other hand, nothing is so *local* as not to be of some general advantage. The navy, as I understand it, was established, and is maintained, at a great annual expense, partly to be ready for war, when war shall come, but partly also, and perhaps chiefly, for the protection of our commerce on the high seas. This latter object is, for all I can see, in principle, the same as internal improvements. The driving a pirate from the track of commerce on the broad ocean, and the removing a snag from its more narrow path in the Mississippi river, can not, I think, be distinguished in principle. Each is done to save life and property, and for nothing else. The navy, then, is the most general in its benefits of all this class of objects; and yet even the navy is of some peculiar advantage to Charleston, Baltimore, Philadelphia, New York, and Boston, beyond what it is to the interior towns of Illinois. The next most general object I can think of, would be improvements on the Mississippi river and its tributaries. They touch thirteen of our states—Pennsylvania, Virginia, Kentucky, Tennessee, Mississippi, Louisiana, Arkansas, Missouri, Illinois, Indiana, Ohio, Wisconsin, and Iowa. Now, I suppose it will not be denied, that these thirteen states are a little more interested in improvements on that great river than are the remaining seventeen. These instances of the navy and the Mississippi river, show clearly that there is something of local advantage in the most general objects. But the converse is also true. Nothing is so *local* as not to be of some *general* benefit. Take, for instance, the Illinois and Michigan canal. Considered apart from its effects, it is perfectly local. Every inch of it is within the State of Illinois. That canal was first opened for business last April. In a very few days we were all gratified to learn, among other things, that sugar had been carried from New Orleans, through the canal, to Buffalo, in New York. This sugar took this route, doubtless, because it was cheaper than the old route. Supposing the benefit in the reduction of the cost of carriage to be shared between seller and buyer, the result is, that the New Orleans merchant sold his sugar a little *dearer*, and the people of Buffalo sweetened their coffee a little *cheaper* than before; a benefit resulting *from* the canal, not to Illinois where the canal *is*, but to Louisiana and New York, where it is *not*. In other transactions Illinois will, of course, have her share, and perhaps the larger share too, in the benefits of the canal; but the instance of the sugar clearly shows, that the *benefits* of an improvement are by no means confined to the particular locality of the improvement itself.

The just conclusion from all this is, that if the nation refuse to make improvements of the more general kind, because their benefits may be somewhat local, a state may, for the same reason, refuse to make an improvement of a local kind, because its benefits may be somewhat general. A state may well say to the nation: "If you will do nothing for me, I will do nothing for you." Thus it is seen, that if this argument of "inequality" is sufficient anywhere, it is sufficient everywhere, and puts an end to improvements altogether. I hope and believe, that if both the nation and the states would, in good faith, in their respective spheres, do what they could in the way of improvements, what of inequality might be produced in one place might be compensated in another, and that the sum of the whole might not be very unequal. But suppose, after all, there should be some degree of inequality: inequality is certainly never to be embraced for its own sake; but is every good thing to be discarded which may be inseparably connected with some degree of it? If so, we must discard all government. This capitol is built at the public expense, for the public benefit; but does any one doubt that it is of some peculiar local advantage to the property holders and business people of Washington? Shall we remove it for this reason? And if so, where shall we set it down, and be free from the difficulty? To make sure of our object, shall we locate it nowhere? And have Congress hereafter to hold its sessions, as the loafer lodged, "in spots about?" I make no special allusion to the present President when I say, there are few stronger cases in this world of, "burden to the many, and benefit to the few"—of "inequality"—than the Presidency itself is by some thought to be. An honest laborer digs coal at about seventy cents a day, while the President digs abstractions at about seventy dollars a day. The *coal* is clearly worth more than the *abstractions*, and yet what a monstrous inequality in the prices. Does the President, for this reason, propose to abolish the Presidency? He *does* not, and he *ought* not. The true rule, in determining to embrace or reject anything, is not whether it have *any* evil in it, but whether it have more of evil than of good. There are few things *wholly* evil or *wholly* good. Almost everything, especially of governmental policy, is an inseparable compound of the two; so that our best judgment of the preponderance between them is continually demanded. On this principle, the President, his friends, and the world generally, act on most subjects. Why not apply it, then, upon this question? Why, as to improvements, magnify the *evil*, and stoutly refuse to see any *good* in them?

Mr. Chairman, on the third position of the message, (the constitutional question,) I have not much to say. Being the man I am, and speaking when I do, I feel that in any attempt at an original, constitutional argument, I should not be, and ought not to be, listened to patiently. The ablest and the best of men have gone over the whole ground long ago. I shall attempt but little more than a brief notice of what some of them have said. In relation to Mr. Jefferson's views, I read from Mr. Polk's veto message:

"President Jefferson, in his message to Congress in 1806, recommended an amendment of the Constitution, with a view to apply an anticipated surplus in the treasury, 'to the great purposes of the public education, roads, rivers, canals, and such other objects of public improvements as it may be thought proper to add to the constitutional enumeration of the Federal powers.' And he adds: 'I suppose an amendment to the Constitution, by consent of the states, necessary, because the objects now recommended, are not among those enumerated in the Constitution, and to which it permits the public moneys to be applied.' In 1825, he repeated, in his published letters, the opinion that no such power has been conferred upon Congress."

I introduce this, not to controvert, just now, the constitutional opinion, but to show, that on the question of *expediency*, Mr. Jefferson's opinion was against the present President—that this opinion of Mr. Jefferson, in one branch at least, is, in the hands of Mr. Polk, like McFingal's gun:

"Bears wide and kicks the owner over."

But, to the constitutional question. In 1826, Chancellor Kent first published his Commentaries on American Law. He devoted a portion of one of the lectures to the question of the authority of Congress to appropriate public moneys for internal improvements. He mentions that the question had never been brought under judicial consideration, and proceeds to give a brief summary of the discussions it had undergone between the legislative and the executive branches of the government. He shows that the legislative branch had usually been *for*, and the executive *against*, the power, till the period of Mr. J. Q. Adams's administration; at which point he considers the executive influence as withdrawn from opposition, and added to the support of the power. In 1844, the chancellor published a new edition of his Commentaries, in which he adds some notes of what had transpired on the question since 1826.

I have not time to read the original text, or the notes, but the whole may be found on page 267, and the two or three following pages of the first volume of the edition of 1844. As what Chancellor Kent seems to consider the sum of the whole, I read from one of the notes:

"Mr. Justice Story, in his Commentaries on the Constitution of the United States, vol. 2, page 429-440, and again, page 519-538, has stated at large the arguments for and against the proposition that Congress have a constitutional authority to lay taxes, and to apply the power to regulate commerce, as a means directly to encourage and protect domestic manufactures; and, without giving any opinion of his own on the contested doctrine, he has left the reader to draw his own conclusions. I should think, however, from the arguments as stated, that every mind which has taken no part in the discussions, and felt no prejudice or territorial bias on either side of the question, would deem the arguments in favor of the Congressional power vastly superior."

It will be seen, that in this extract, the power to make improvements is not directly mentioned; but by examining the context, both of Kent and of Story, it will appear that the power mentioned in the extract and the power to make improvements, are regarded as identical. It is not to be denied that many great and good men have been *against* the power; but it is insisted that quite as many, as great and as good, have been *for* it; and it is shown that, on a full survey of the whole, Chancellor Kent was of opinion that the arguments of the latter were *vastly* superior. This is but the opinion of a man; but who was that man? He was one of the ablest and most learned lawyers of his age, or of any age. It is no disparagement to Mr. Polk, nor, indeed, to any one who devotes much time to politics, to be placed far behind Chancellor Kent as a lawyer. His attitude was most favorable to correct conclusions. He wrote coolly, and in retirement. He was struggling to rear a durable monument of fame; and he well knew that *truth* and thoroughly sound reasoning were the only sure foundations. Can the party opinion of a party President, on a law question, as this purely is, be at all compared or set in opposition to that of such a man, in such an attitude, as Chancellor Kent?

This constitutional question will probably never be better settled than it is, until it shall pass under judicial consideration; but I do think no man who is clear on this question of expediency need feel his conscience much pricked upon this.

Mr. Chairman, the President seems to think that enough may be done in the way of improvements, by means of tonnage duties, under state authority, with the consent of the General Government. Now, I suppose this manner of tonnage duties is well enough in its own sphere. I suppose it may be efficient, and perhaps *sufficient*, to make slight improvements and repairs in harbors already in use, and not much out of repair. But if I have any correct general idea of it, it must be wholly inefficient for any generally beneficent purposes of improvement. I know very little, or rather nothing at all, of the practical matter of levying and collecting tonnage duties; but I suppose one of its principles must be, to lay a duty, for the improvement of any particular harbor, *upon the tonnage coming into that harbor*. To do otherwise—to collect money in *one* harbor to be expended on improvements in *another*—would be an extremely aggravated form of that inequality which the President so much deprecates. If I be right in this, how could we make any entirely new improvements by means of tonnage duties? How make a road, a canal, or clear a greatly obstructed river? The idea that we could, involves the same absurdity of the Irish bull about the new boots: "I shall niver get 'em on," says Patrick, "till I wear 'em a day or two, and stretch 'em a little." We shall never make a canal by tonnage duties, until it shall already have been made a while, so the tonnage can get into it.

After all, the President concludes that possibly there may be some great objects of improvements which can not be effected by tonnage duties, and which, therefore, may be expedient for the General Government to take in hand. Accordingly, he suggests, in case any such be discovered, the propriety of amending the Constitution. Amend it for what? If, like Mr. Jefferson, the President thought improvements *expedient*, but not constitutional, it would be natural enough for him to recommend such an amendment; but hear what he says in this very message:

> "In view of these portentous consequences, I cannot but think that this course of legislation should be arrested, even were there nothing to forbid it in the fundamental laws of our Union."

For what, then, would *he* have the Constitution amended? With *him* it is a proposition to remove *one* impediment, merely to be met by *others*, which, in his opinion, can not be removed—to enable Congress to do what, in his opinion, they ought not to do if they could.

[Here Mr. MEADE, of Virginia, inquired if Mr. L. understood the President to be opposed, on grounds of expediency, to any and every improvement?]

To which Mr. LINCOLN answered: In the very part of his message of which I am now speaking, I understand him as giving some vague expressions in favor of some possible objects of improvements; but, in doing so, I understand him to be directly in the teeth of his own arguments in other parts of it. Neither the President, nor any one, can possibly specify an improvement which shall not be clearly liable to one or another of the objections he has urged on the score of expediency. I have shown, and might show again, that no work—no object—can be so general as to dispense its benefits with precise equality; and this inequality is chief among the "portentous consequences" for which he declares that improvements should be arrested. No, sir; when the President intimates that something in the way of improvements may properly be done by the General Government, he is shrinking from the conclusions to which his own arguments would force him. He feels that the improvements of this broad and goodly land are a mighty interest; and he is unwilling to confess to the people, or perhaps to himself, that he has built an argument, which, when pressed to its conclusion, entirely annihilates this interest.

I have already said that no one who is satisfied of the expediency of making improvements, need be much uneasy in his conscience about its constitutionality. I wish now to submit a few remarks on the general proposition of amending the Constitution. As a general rule, I think we would do much better to let it alone. No slight occasion should tempt us to touch it. Better not take the first step, which may lead to a habit of altering it. Better rather habituate ourselves to think of it as unalterable. It can scarcely be made better than it is. New provisions would introduce new difficulties, and thus create and increase appetite for still further change. No, sir; let it stand as it is. New hands have never touched it. The men who made it have done their work, and have passed away. Who shall improve on what *they* did?

Mr. Chairman, for the purpose of reviewing this message in the least possible time, as well as for the sake of distinctness, I had analyzed its arguments as well as I could, and reduced them to the propositions I have stated. I have now examined them in detail. I wish to detain the committee only a little while longer with some general remarks upon the subject of improvements.

That the subject is a difficult one, can not be denied. Still, it is no more difficult in Congress than in the State Legislatures, in the counties, or in the smallest municipal districts which anywhere exist. All can recur to instances of this difficulty in the case of county roads, bridges, and the like. One man is offended because a road passes over his land; and another is offended because it does *not* pass over his; one is dissatisfied because the bridge, for which he is taxed, crosses the river on a different road from that which leads from his house to town; another can not bear that the county should get in debt for these same roads and bridges; while not a few struggle hard to have roads located over their lands, and then stoutly refuse to let them be opened, until they are first paid the damages. Even between the different wards and streets of towns and cities, we find this same wrangling and difficulty. Now, these are no other than the very difficulties against which, and out of which, the President constructs his objections of "inequality," "speculation," and "crushing the treasury." There is but a single alternative about them—they are *sufficient*, or they are *not*. If sufficient, they are sufficient *out* of Congress as well as *in* it, and there is the end. We must reject them as insufficient, or lie down and do nothing by any authority. Then, difficulty though there be, let us meet and overcome it.

> "Attempt the end, and never stand to doubt;
> Nothing so hard, but search will find it out.'

Determine that the thing can and shall be done, and then we shall find the way. The tendency to undue expansion is unquestionably the chief difficulty. How to do *something* and still not to do *too much*, is the desideratum. Let each contribute his mite in the way of suggestion. The late Silas Wright, in a letter to the Chicago Convention, contributed his, which was worth something; and I now contribute mine, which may be worth nothing. At all events, it will mislead nobody, and therefore will do no harm. I would not borrow money. I am against an overwhelming, crushing system. Suppose that at each session, Congress shall determine *how much* money can, for that year, be spared for improvements; then apportion that sum to the most *important* objects. So far all is easy; but how shall we determine which *are* the most important? On this question comes the collision of interests. *I* shall be slow to acknowldge that *your* harbor or *your* river is more important than *mine*, and *vice versa*. To clear this difficulty, let us have that same statistical information which the gentleman from Ohio [Mr. VINTON] suggested at the beginning of this session. In that information we shall have a stern, unbending basis of *facts*—a basis in nowise subject to whim, caprice, or local interest. The pre-limited amount of means will save us from doing *too much*, and the statistics will save us from doing what we do, in *wrong places*. Adopt and adhere to this course, and, it seems to me, the difficulty is cleared.

One of the gentlemen from South Carolina, [Mr.

RHETT,] very much deprecates these statistics. He particularly objects, as I understand him, to counting all the pigs and chickens in the land. I do not perceive much force in the objection. It is true, that if everything be enumerated, a portion of such statistics may not be very useful to this object. Such products of the country as are to be *consumed* where they are *produced*, need no roads and rivers, no means of transportation, and have no very proper connection with this subject. The *surplus*, that which is produced in *one* place to be consumed in *another;* the capacity of each locality for producing a *greater* surplus; the natural means of transportation, and their susceptibility of improvement; the hinderances, delays, and losses of life and property during transportation, and the causes of each, would be among the most valuable statistics in this connection. From these it would readily appear where a given amount of expenditure would do the most good. These statistics might be equally accessible, as they would be equally useful, to both the nation and the states. In this way, and by these means, let the nation take hold of the larger works, and the states the smaller ones; and thus, working in a meeting direction, discreetly, but steadily and firmly, what is made unequal in one place may be equalized in another, extravagance avoided, and the whole country put on that career of prosperity which shall correspond with its extent of territory, its natural resources, and the intelligence and enterprise of its people.

SPEECH

IN REPLY TO JUDGE DOUGLAS,

DELIVERED IN REPRESENTATIVES' HALL, SPRINGFIELD, ILL., JUNE 26, 1857.

Fellow-Citizens: I am here to-night, partly by the invitation of some of you, and partly by my own inclination. Two weeks ago, Judge Douglas spoke here on the several subjects of Kansas, the Dred Scott decision, and Utah. I listened to the speech at the time, and have read the report of it since. It was intended to controvert opinions which I think just, and to assail (politically, not personally) those men who, in common with me, entertain those opinions. For this reason I wished then, and still wish, to make some answer to it, which I now take the opportunity of doing.

I begin with Utah. If it prove to be true, as is probable, that the people of Utah are in open rebellion to the United States, then Judge Douglas is in favor of repealing their territorial organization, and attaching them to the adjoining states for judicial purposes. I say, too, if they are in rebellion, they ought to be somehow coerced to obedience; and I am not now prepared to admit or deny that the judge's mode of coercing them is not as good as any. The Republicans can fall in with it, without taking back anything they have ever said. To be sure, it would be a considerable backing down by Judge Douglas from his much-vaunted doctrine of self-government for the territories; but this is only additional proof of what was very plain from the beginning, that that doctrine was a mere deceitful pretense for the benefit of slavery. Those who could not see that much in the Nebraska act itself, which forced Governors, and Secretaries, and Judges, on the people of the territories, without their choice or consent, could not be made to see, though one should rise from the dead.

But in all this, it is very plain the judge evades the only question the Republicans have ever pressed upon the Democracy in regard to Utah. That question the judge well knew to be this: "If the people of Utah shall peacefully form a State Constitution tolerating polygamy, will the Democracy admit them into the Union?" There is nothing in the United States Constitution or law against polygamy; and why is it not a part of the judge's "sacred right of self-government" for the people to have it, or rather to keep it, if they choose? These questions, so far as I know, the judge never answers. It might involve the Democracy to answer them either way, and they go unanswered.

As to Kansas. The substance of the judge's speech on Kansas is an effort to put the Free State men in the wrong for not voting at the election of delegates to the Constitutional Convention. He says:

> "There is every reason to hope and believe that the law will be fairly interpreted and impartially executed, so as to insure to every *bona fide* inhabitant the free and quiet exercise of the elective franchise."

It appears extraordinary that Judge Douglas should

make such a statement. He knows that, by the law, no one can vote who has not been registered; and he knows that the Free State men place their refusal to vote on the ground that but few of them have been registered. It is possible this is not true, but Judge Douglas knows it is asserted to be true in letters, newspapers, and public speeches, and borne by every mail, and blown by every breeze to the eyes and ears of the world. He knows it is boldly declared that the people of many whole counties, and many whole neighborhoods in others, are left unregistered; yet, he does not venture to contradict the declaration, or to point out how they can vote without being registered; but he just slips along, not seeming to know there is any such question of fact, and complacently declares:

"There is every reason to hope and believe that the law will be fairly interpreted and impartially executed, so as to insure to every *bona fide* inhabitant the free and quiet exercise of the elective franchise."

I readily agree that if all had a chance to vote, they ought to have voted. If, on the contrary, as they allege, and Judge Douglas ventures not to particularly contradict, few only of the Free State men had a chance to vote, they were perfectly right in staying from the polls in a body.

By the way, since the judge spoke, the Kansas election has come off. The judge expressed his confidence that all the Democrats in Kansas would do their duty—including "Free State Democrats" of course. The returns received here, as yet, are very incomplete; but so far as they go, they indicate that only about one-sixth of the registered voters, have really voted; and this, too, when not more, perhaps, than one-half of the rightful voters have been registered, thus showing the thing to have been altogether the most exquisite farce ever enacted. I am watching, with considerable interest, to ascertain what figure "the Free State Democrats" cut in the concern. Of course they voted—all Democrats do their duty—and of course they did not vote for Slave State candidates. We soon shall know how many delegates they elected, how many candidates they had pledged to a free state, and how many votes were cast for them.

Allow me to barely whisper my suspicion that there were no such things in Kansas as "Free State Democrats"—that they were altogether mythical, good only to figure in newspapers and speeches in the free states. If there should prove to be one real living Free State Democrat in Kansas, I suggest that it might be well to catch him, and stuff and preserve his skin as an interesting specimen of that soon to be extinct variety of the genus Democrat.

And now as to the Dred Scott decision. That decision declares two propositions—first, that a negro can not sue in the United States Courts; and secondly, that Congress can not prohibit slavery in the territories. It was made by a divided court—dividing differently on the different points. Judge Douglas does not discuss the merits of the decision; and, in that respect, I shall follow his example, believing I could no more improve on McLean and Curtis, than he could on Taney.

He denounces all who question the correctness of that decision, as offering violent resistance to it. But who resists it? Who has, in spite of the decision, declared Dred Scott free, and resisted the authority of his master over him?

Judicial decisions have two uses—first, to absolutely determine the case decided; and secondly, to indicate to the public how other similar cases will be decided when they arise. For the latter use, they are called "precedents" and "authorities."

We believe as much as Judge Douglas (perhaps more) in obedience to, and respect for, the judicial department of governor. We think its decisions on Constitutional questions, when fully settled, should control, not only the particular cases decided, but the general policy of the country, subject to be disturbed only by amendments of the Constitution as provided in that instrument itself. More than this would be revolution. But we think the Dred Scott decision is erroneous. We know the court that made it has often overruled its own decisions, and we shall do what we can to have it overrule this. We offer no resistance to it.

Judicial decisions are of greater or less authority as precedents, according to circumstances. That this should be so, accords both with common sense, and the customary understanding of the legal profession.

If this important decision had been made by the unanimous concurrence of the judges, and without any apparent partisan bias, and in accordance with legal public expectation, and with the steady practice of the departments throughout our history, and had been, in no part, based on assumed historical facts which are not really true ; or, if wanting in some of these, it had been before the court more than once, and had there been affirmed and reaffirmed through a course of years, it then might be, perhaps would be, factious, nay, even revolutionary, not to acquiesce in it as a precedent.

But when, as it is true, we find it wanting in all these claims to the public confidence, it is not resistance, it is not factious, it is not even disrespectful, to treat it as not having yet quite established a settled doctrine for the country. But Judge Douglas considers this view awful. Hear him:

"The courts are the tribunals prescribed by the Constitution and created by the authority of the people to determine, expound, and enforce the law. Hence, whoever resists the final decision of the highest judicial tribunal, aims a deadly blow to our whole Republican system of government—a blow, which, if successful, would place all our rights and liberties at the mercy of passion, anarchy, and violence. I repeat, therefore, that if resistance to the decisions of the Supreme Court of the United States, in a matter like the points decided in the Dred Scott case, clearly within their jurisdiction as defined by the Constitution, shall be forced upon the country as a political issue, it will become a distinct and naked issue between the friends and enemies of the Constitution—the friends and the enemies of the supremacy of the laws."

Why, this same Supreme Court once decided a national bank to be constitutional; but General Jackson, as President of the United States, disregarded the decision, and vetoed a bill for a re-charter, partly on constitutional ground, declaring that each public functionary must support the Constitution, "as he understands it." But hear the general's own words. Here they are, taken from his veto message:

"It is maintained by the advocates of the bank, that its constitutionality, in all its features, ought to be considered as settled by precedent, and by the decision of the Supreme Court. To this conclusion I can not assent. Mere precedent is a dangerous source of authority, and should not be regarded as deciding questions of constitutional power, except where the acquiescence of the people and the States can be considered as well settled. So far from this being the case on this subject, an argument against the bank might be based on precedent. One Congress in 1791, decided in favor of a bank; another in 1811, decided against it. One Congress in 1815 decided against a bank; another, in 1816, decided in its favor. Prior to the present Congress, therefore, the precedents drawn from that source were equal. If we resort to the states, the expressions of legislative, judicial, and executive opinions against the bank have been probably to those in its favor as four to one. There is nothing in precedent, therefore, which, if its authority were admitted, ought to weigh in favor of the act before me."

I drop the quotation merely to remark, that all there ever was, in the way of precedent up to the Dred Scott decision, on the points therein decided, had been against that decision. But hear General Jackson further:

"If the opinion of the Supreme Court covered the whole ground of this act, it ought not to control the co-ordinate authorities of this Government. The Congress, the Executive, and the Court, must each for itself be guided by its own opinion of the Constitution. Each public officer, who takes an oath to support the Constitution, swears that he will support it as he understands it, and not as it is understood by others."

Again and again have I heard Judge Douglas denounce that bank decision, and applaud General Jackson for disregarding it. It would be interesting for him to look over his recent speech, and see how exactly his fierce philippics against us, for resisting Supreme Court decisions, fall upon his own head. It will call to mind a long and fierce political war in this country, upon an issue which, in his own language, and, of course, in his own changeless estimation, was "a distinct issue between the friends and the enemies of the Constitution," and in which war he fought in the ranks of the enemies of the Constitution.

I have said, in substance, that the Dred Scott decision was, in part, based on assumed historical facts which were not really true, and I ought not to leave the subject without giving some reasons for saying this; I therefore give an instance or two, which I think fully sustain me. Chief Justice Taney, in delivering the opinion of the majority of the Court, insists at great length that negroes were no part of the people who made, or for whom was made, the Declaration of Independence, or the Constitution of the United States.

On the contrary, Judge Curtis, in his dissenting opinion, shows that in five of the then thirteen states, to wit: New Hampshire, Massachusetts, New York, New Jersey, and North Carolina, free negroes were voters, and, in proportion to their numbers, had the same part in making the Constitution that the white people had. He shows this with so much particularity as to leave no doubt of its truth; and as a sort of conclusion on that point, holds the following language:

"The Constitution was ordained and established by the people of the United States, through the action, in each state, of those persons who were qualified by its laws to act thereon in behalf of themselves and all other citizens of the state. In some of the states, as we have seen, colored persons were among those qualified by law to act on the subject. These colored persons were not only included in the body of 'the people of the United States,' by whom the Constitution was ordained and established, but in at least five of the states, they had the power to act, and, doubtless, did act, by their suffrages, upon the question of its adoption."

Again, Chief Justice Taney says:

"It is difficult, at this day, to realize the state of public opinion in relation to that unfortunate race, which prevailed in the civilized and enlightened portions of the world at the time of the Declaration of Independence, and when the Constitution of the United States was framed and adopted."

And again, after quoting from the Declaration, he says:

"The general words above quoted would seem to include the whole human family, and if they were used in a similar instrument at this day, would be so understood."

In these the Chief Justice does not directly assert, but plainly assumes, as a fact, that the public estimate of the black man is more favorable now than it was in the days of the Revolution. This assumption is a mistake. In some trifling particulars, the condition of that race has been ameliorated; but, as a whole, in this country, the change between then and now is decidedly the other way; and their ultimate destiny has never appeared so hopeless as in the last three or four years. In two of the five states—New Jersey and North Carolina—that then gave the free negro the right of voting, the right has since been taken away; and in a third—New York—it has been greatly abridged; while it has not been extended, so far as I know, to a single additional state, though the number of the states has more than doubled. In those days, as I understand, masters could, at their own pleasure, emancipate their slaves; but since then, such legal restraints have been made upon emancipation, as to amount almost to prohibition. In those days, Legislatures held the unquestioned power to abolish slavery in their respective states; but now it is becoming quite fashionable for State Constitutions to withhold that power from the Legislatures. In those days, by common consent, the spread of the black man's bondage to the new countries was prohibited, but now, Congress decides that it will not continue the prohibition; and the Supreme Court decides that it could not if it would. In those days, our Declaration of Independence was held sacred by all, and thought to include all; but now, to aid in making the bondage of the negro universal and eternal, it is assailed, and sneered at, and construed, and hawked at, and torn, till, if its framers could rise from their graves, they could not at all recognize it. All the powers of earth seem rapidly combining against him. Mammon is after him, ambition follows, philosophy follows, and the theology of the day is fast joining the cry. They have him in his prison house; they have searched his person, and left no prying instrument with him. One after another they have closed the heavy iron doors upon him; and now they have him, as it were, bolted in with a lock of a hundred keys, which can never be unlocked without the concurrence of every key; the keys in the hands of a hundred different men, and they scattered to a hundred different and distant places; and they stand musing as to what invention, in all the dominions of mind and matter, can be produced to make the impossibility of his escape more complete than it is.

It is grossly incorrect to say or assume that the public estimate of the negro is more favorable now than it was at the origin of the Government.

Three years and a half ago, Judge Douglas brought forward his famous Nebraska bill. The country was at once in a blaze. He scorned all opposition, and carried it through Congress. Since then he has seen himself superseded in a Presidential nomination, by one indorsing the general doctrine of his measure, but at the same time standing clear of the odium of its untimely agitation, and its gross breach of national faith; and he has seen that successful rival constitutionally elected, not by strength of friends, but by the division of adversaries, being in a popular minority of nearly four hundred thousand votes. He has seen his chief aids in his own state, Shields and Richardson, politically speaking, successively tried, convicted, and executed, for an offense not their own, but his. And now he sees his own case, standing next on the docket for trial.

There is a natural disgust in the minds of nearly all white people, to the idea of an indiscriminate amalgamation of the white and black races; and Judge Douglas evidently is basing his chief hope upon the chances of his being able to appropriate the benefit of this disgust to himself. If he can, by much drumming and repeating, fasten the odium of that idea upon his adversaries, he thinks he can struggle through the storm. He therefore clings to this hope, as a drowning man to the last plank. He makes an occasion for lugging it in from the opposition to the Dred Scott decision. He finds the Republicans insisting that the Declaration of Independence includes ALL men, black as well as white, and forthwith he boldly denies that it includes negroes at all, and proceeds to argue gravely that all who contend it does, do so only because they want to vote, and eat, and sleep, and marry with negroes! He will have it that they can not be consistent else. Now I protest against the counterfeit logic which concludes that, because I do not want a black woman for a slave I must necessarily want her for a wife. I need not have her for either. I can just leave her alone. In some respects, she certainly is not my equal; but in her natural right to eat the bread she earns with her own hands without asking leave of any one else, she is my equal, and the equal of all others.

Chief Justice Taney, in his opinion in the Dred Scott case, admits that the language of the Declaration is broad enough to include the whole human family, but he and Judge Douglas argue that the authors of that instrument did not intend to include negroes, by the fact that they did not at once actually place them on an equality with the whites. Now this grave argument comes to just nothing at all, by the other fact, that they did not at once, or ever afterward, actually place all white people on an equality with one another. And this is the staple argument of both the Chief Justice and the Senator, for doing this obvious violence to the plain, unmistakable language of the Declaration.

I think the authors of that notable instrument intended to include *all* men, but they did not intend to declare all men equal *in all respects.* They did not mean to say all were equal in color, size, intellect, moral developments, or social capacity. They defined with tolerable distinctness, in what respects they did consider all men created equal—equal with "certain inalienable rights, among which are life, liberty, and the pursuit of happiness." This they said, and this they meant. They did not mean to assert the obvious untruth, that all were then actually enjoying that equality, nor yet that they were about to confer it immediately upon them. In fact, they had no power to confer such a boon. They meant simply to declare the *right*, so that the *enforcement* of it might follow as fast as circumstances should permit.

They meant to set up a standard maxim for free society, which should be familiar to all, and revered by all; constantly looked to, constantly labored for, and even though never perfectly attained, constantly approximated, and thereby constantly spreading and deepening its influence and augmenting the happiness and value of life to all people of all colors everywhere. The assertion that "all men are created equal," was of no practical use in effecting our separation from Great Britain; and it was placed in the Declaration, not for that, but for future use. Its authors meant it to be as, thank God, it is now proving itself, a stumbling-block to all those who, in after times, might seek to turn a free people back into the hateful paths of despotism. They knew the proneness of prosperity to breed tyrants, and they meant when such should reappear in this fair land and commence their vocation, they should find left for them at least one hard nut to crack.

I have now briefly expressed my view of the *meaning* and *object* of that part of the Declaration of Independence which declares that "all men are created equal."

Now let us hear Judge Douglas's view of the same subject, as I find it in the printed report of his late speech. Here it is:

> "No man can vindicate the character, motives, and conduct of the signers of the Declaration of Independence, except upon the hypothesis that they referred to the white race alone, and not to the African, when they declared all men to have been created equal—that they were speaking of British subjects on this continent being equal to British subjects born and residing in Great Britain—that they were entitled to the same inalienable rights, and among them were enumerated life, liberty, and the pursuit of happiness. The Declaration was adopted for the purpose of justifying the colonists in the eyes of the civilized world in withdrawing their allegiance from the British crown and dissolving their connection with the mother country."

My good friends, read that carefully over some leisure hour, and ponder well upon it—see what a mere wreck—mangled ruin, it makes of our once glorious Declaration.

"They were speaking of British subjects on this continent being equal to British subjects born and residing in Great Britain!" Why, according to this, not only negroes, but white people outside of Great Britain and

America were not spoken of in that instrument. The English, Irish, and Scotch, along with white Americans, were included to be sure, but the French, Germans, and other white people of the world are all gone to pot along with the judge's inferior races.

I had thought the Declaration promised something better than the condition of British subjects; but no, it only meant that we should be *equal* to them in their own oppressed and *unequal* condition. According to that, it gave no promise that, having kicked off the king and lords of Great Britain, we should not at once be saddled with a king and lords of our own.

I had thought the Declaration contemplated the progressive improvement in the condition of all men everywhere; but no, it merely "was adopted for the purpose of justifying the colonists in the eyes of the civilized world in withdrawing their allegiance from the British crown, and dissolving their connection with the mother country." Why, that object having been effected some eighty years ago, the Declaration is of no practical use now—mere rubbish—old wadding left to rot on the battle-field after the victory is won.

I understand you are preparing to celebrate the "Fourth" to-morrow week. What for? The doings of that day had no reference to the present; and quite half of you are not even descendants of those who were referred to at that day. But I suppose you will celebrate; and will even go so far as to read the Declaration. Suppose, after you read it once in the old fashioned way, you read it once more with Judge Douglas's version. It will then run thus: "We hold these truths to be self-evident that all British subjects who were on this continent eighty-one years ago, were created equal to all British subjects born and *then* residing in Great Britain."

And now I appeal to all—to Democrats as well as others—are you really willing that the Declaration shall thus be frittered away?—thus left no more at most than an interesting memorial of the dead past?—thus shorn of its vitality and practical value, and left without the *germ* or even the *suggestion* of the individual rights of man in it?

But Judge Douglas is especially horrified at the thought of the mixing blood by the white and black races. Agreed for once — a thousand times agreed. There are white men enough to marry all the white women, and black men enough to marry all the black women; and so let them be married. On this point, we fully agree with the judge; and when he shall show that his policy is better adapted to prevent amalgamation than ours, we shall drop ours and adopt his. Let us see. In 1850, there were in the United States, 405,751 mulattoes. Very few of these are the offspring of whites and *free* blacks; nearly all have sprung from black *slaves* and white masters. A separation of the races is the only perfect preventive of amalgamation, but as an immediate separation is impossible, the next best thing is to *keep* them apart *where* they are not already together. If white and black people never get together in Kansas, they will never mix blood in Kansas. That is at least one self-evident truth. A few free colored persons may get into the free states, in any event; but their number is too insignificant to amount to much in the way of mixing blood. In 1850, there were in the free states, 56,649 mulattoes; but for the most part they were not born there—they came from the slave states, ready made up. In the same year the slave states had 348,874 mulattoes, all of home production. The proportion of free mulattoes to free blacks—the only colored classes in the free states—is much greater in the slave than in the free states. It is worthy of note, too, that among the free states those which make the colored man the nearest equal to the white, have proportionably the fewest mulattoes, the least of amalgamation. In New Hampshire, the state which goes farthest toward equality between the races, there are just 184 mulattoes, while there are in Virginia—how many do you think?—79,775, being 23,126 more than in all the free states together.

These statistics show that slavery is the greatest source of amalgamation, and next to it, not the elevation, but the degradation of free blacks. Yet Judge Douglas dreads the slightest restraints on the spread of slavery, and the slightest human recognition of the negro, as tending horribly to amalgamation.

The very Dred Scott case affords a strong test as to which party most favors amalgamation, the Republicans or the dear Union-saving Democracy? Dred Scott, his wife, and two daughters were all involved in the suit. We desired the court to have held that they were citizens so far at least as to entitle them to a hearing as to whether they were free or not; and then, also, that they were in fact and in law really free. Could we have had our way, the chances of these black girls ever mixing their blood with that of white people, would have been diminished at least to the extent that it could not have been without their consent. But Judge Douglas is delighted to have them decided to be slaves, and not human enough to have a hearing, even if they were free, and thus left subject to the forced concubinage of their masters, and liable to become the mothers of mulattoes in spite of themselves—the very state of case that produces nine-tenths of all the mulattoes—all the mixing of blood in the nation.

Of course, I state this case as an illustration only, not meaning to say or intimate that the master of Dred Scott and his family, or any more than a per centage of masters generally, are inclined to exercise this particular power which they hold over their female slaves.

I have said that the separation of the races is the only perfect preventive of amalgamation. I have no right to say all the members of the Republican party are in favor of this, nor to say that as a party they are in favor of it. There is nothing in their platform directly on the subject. But I can say, a very large proportion of its members are for it, and that the chief plank in their platform—opposition to the spread of slavery—is most favorable to that separation.

Such separation, if ever effected at all, must be effected by colonization; and no political party, as such, is now doing anything directly for colonization. Party operations, at present, only favor or retard colonization incidentally. The enterprise is a difficult one; but "where there is a will there is a way;" and what colonization needs most is a hearty will. Will springs from the two elements of moral sense and self-interest. Let us be brought to believe it is morally right, and, at the same, time, favorable to, or, at least, not against, our interest, to transfer the African to his native clime, and we shall find a way to do it, however great the task may be. The children of Israel, to such numbers as to include four hundred thousand fighting men, went out of Egyptian bondage in a body.

How differently the respective courses of the Democratic and Republican parties incidentally bear on the question of forming a will—a public sentiment—for colonization, is easy to see. The Republicans inculcate, with whatever of ability they can, that the negro is a man; that his bondage is cruelly wrong, and that the field of his oppression ought not to be enlarged. The Democrats deny his manhood; deny, or dwarf to insignificance, the wrong of his bondage; so far as possible, crush all sympathy for him, and cultivate and excite hatred and disgust against him; compliment themselves as Union-savers for doing so; and call the indefinite outspreading of his bondage "a sacred right of self-government."

The plainest print can not be read through a gold eagle; and it will be ever hard to find many men who will send a slave to Liberia, and pay his passage, while they can send him to a new country—Kansas, for instance—and sell him for fifteen hundred dollars, and the rise.

SPEECH

DELIVERED AT COOPER INSTITUTE, FEBRUARY 27, 1860.

MR. PRESIDENT and FELLOW-CITIZENS of New York: The facts with which I shall deal this evening are mainly old and familiar; nor is there anything new in the general use I shall make of them. If there shall be any novelty, it will be in the mode of presenting the facts, and the references and observations following that presentation.

In his speech last autumn, at Columbus, Ohio, as reported in the New York *Times*, Senator Douglas said:

> "Our fathers, when they framed the government under which we live, understood this question just as well, and even better than we do now."

I fully indorse this, and I adopt it as a text for this discourse. I so adopt it because it furnishes a precise and an agreed starting-point for a discussion between Republicans and that wing of the democracy headed by Senator Douglas. It simply leaves the inquiry: "What was the understanding those fathers had of the question mentioned?"

What is the frame of government under which we live?

The answer must be: "The Constitution of the United

States." That Constitution consists of the original, framed in 1787, (and under which the present government first went into operation,) and twelve subsequently framed amendments, the first ten of which were framed in 1789.

Who were our fathers that framed the Constitution? I suppose the "thirty-nine" who signed the original instrument may be fairly called our fathers who framed that part of our present government. It is almost exactly true to say they framed it, and it is altogether true to say they fairly represented the opinion and sentiment of the whole nation at that time. Their names, being familiar to nearly all, and accessible to quite all, need not now be repeated.

I take these "thirty-nine," for the present, as being "our fathers who framed the government under which we live."

What is the question which, according to the text, those fathers understood just as well and even better than we do now?

It is this: Does the proper division of local from Federal authority, or anything in the Constitution, forbid our Federal Government to control as to slavery in our Federal territories?

Upon this Douglas holds the affirmative, and Republicans the negative. This affirmative and denial form an issue; and this issue—this question—is precisely what the text declares our fathers understood better than we.

Let us now inquire whether the "thirty-nine" or any of them ever acted upon this question; and if they did, how they acted upon it—how they expressed that better understanding.

In 1784—three years before the Constitution—the United States then owning the North-western Territory, and no other—the Congress of the Confederation had before them the question of prohibiting slavery in that territory; and four of the "thirty-nine" who afterward framed the Constitution were in that Congress, and voted on that question. Of these, Roger Sherman, Thomas Mifflin and Hugh Williamson voted for the prohibition—thus showing that, in their understanding, no line dividing local from Federal authority, nor anything else, properly forbade the Federal Government to control as to slavery in Federal territory. The other of the four—James McHenry—voted against the prohibition, showing that, for some cause, he thought it improper to vote for it.

In 1787, still before the Constitution, but while the convention was in session framing it, and while the North-western Territory still was the only territory owned by the United States—the same question of prohibiting slavery in the territory again came before the Congress of the Confederation; and three more of the "thirty-nine" who afterward signed the Constitution were in that Congress and voted on the question. They were William Blount, William Few, and Abraham Baldwin, and they all voted for the prohibition—thus showing that, in their understanding, no line dividing local from Federal authority, nor anything else, properly forbade the Federal Government to control as to slavery in Federal territory. This time the prohibition became a law, being a part of what is now known as the ordinance of '87.

The question of Federal control of slavery in the territories seems not to have been directly before the convention which framed the original Constitution; and hence it is not recorded that the "thirty-nine," or any of them, while engaged on that instrument, expressed any opinion on that precise question.

In 1789, by the first Congress which sat under the Constitution, an act was passed to enforce the ordinance of '87, including the prohibition of slavery in the Northwestern Territory. The bill for this act was reported by one of the "thirty-nine," Thomas Fitzsimmons, then a member of the House of Representatives from Pennsylvania. It went through all its stages without a word of opposition, and finally passed both branches without yeas and nays, which is equivalent to a unanimous passage. In this Congress there were sixteen of the "thirty-nine" fathers who framed the original Constitution. They were:

John Langdon,	George Clymer,	Richard Bassett,
Nicholas Gilman,	William Few,	George Read,
William S. Johnson,	Abraham Baldwin,	Pierce Butler,
Roger Sherman,	Rufus King,	Daniel Carroll,
Robert Morris,	William Patterson,	James Madison,
	Thos. Fitzsimmons.	

This shows that in their understanding no line dividing local from Federal authority, nor anything in the Constitution, properly forbade Congress to prohibit slavery in the Federal territory; else both their fidelity to correct principle, and their oath to support the Constitution, would have constrained them *to oppose* the prohibition.

Again, George Washington, another of the "thirty-nine," was then President of the United States, and, as such, approved and signed the bill, thus completing its validity as a law, and thus showing that, in his understanding, no line dividing local from Federal authority, nor anything in the Constitution, forbade the Federal Government to control as to slavery in Federal territory.

No great while after the adoption of the original Constitution, North Carolina ceded to the Federal Government the country now constituting the State of Tennessee; and a few years later, Georgia ceded that which now constitutes the States of Mississippi and Alabama. In both deeds of cession it was made a condition by the ceding States that the Federal Government should not prohibit slavery in the ceded country. Besides this, slavery was then actually in the ceded country. Under these circumstances, Congress, on taking charge of these countries, did not absolutely prohibit slavery within them. But they did interfere with it—take control of it—even there, to a certain extent. In 1798, Congress organized the territory of Mississippi. In the act of organization, they prohibited the bringing of slaves into the territories, from any place without the United States, by fine, and giving freedom to slaves so brought. This act passed both branches of Congress without yeas and nays. In that Congress were three of the "thirty-nine" who framed the original Constitution. They were John Langdon, George Read, and Abraham Baldwin. They all, probably, voted for it. Certainly they would have placed their opposition to it upon record, if, in their understanding, any line dividing local from Federal authority, or anything in the Constitution, properly forbade the Federal Government to control as to slavery in Federal territory.

In 1803, the Federal Government purchased the Louisiana country. Our former territorial acquisitions came from certain of our own states; but this Louisiana country was acquired from a foreign nation. In 1804, Congress gave a territorial organization to that part of it which now constitutes the State of Louisiana. New Orleans, lying within that part, was an old and comparatively large city. There were other considerable towns and settlements, and slavery was extensively and thoroughly intermingled with the people. Congress did not, in the territorial act, prohibit slavery; but they did interfere with it--take control of it—in a more marked and extensive way than they did in the case of Mississippi. The substance of the provision therein made, in relation to slaves, was:

First: That no slaves should be imported into the territory from foreign parts.

Second: That no slave should be carried into it who had been imported into the United States since the first day of May, 1798.

Third: That no slave should be carried into it, except by the owner, and for his own use as a settler; the penalty in all the cases being a fine upon the violator of the law, and freedom to the slave.

This act, also, was passed without yeas and nays. In the Congress which passed it there were two of the "thirty-nine." They were Abraham Baldwin and Jonathan Dayton. As stated in the case of Mississippi, it is probable they both voted for it; they would not have allowed it to pass without recording their opposition to it, if, in their understanding, it violated either the line properly dividing local from Federal authority or any provision of the Constitution.

In 1819–20 came, and passed, the Missouri question. Many votes were taken by yeas and nays, in both branches of Congress, upon the various phases of the general question. Two of the "thirty-nine"—Rufus King and Charles Pinckney—were members of that Congress. Mr. King steadily voted for slavery prohibition and against all compromises, while Mr. Pinckney as steadily voted against slavery prohibition and against all compromises. By this Mr. King showed that in his understanding, no line dividing local from Federal authority, nor anything in the Constitution, was violated by Congress prohibiting slavery in Federal territory; while Mr. Pinckney, by his votes, showed that in his understanding, there was some sufficient reason for opposing such prohibition in that case.

The cases I have mentioned are the only acts of the "thirty-nine," or any of them, upon the direct issue, which I have been able to discover.

To enumerate the persons who thus acted, as being four in 1784, three in 1787, seventeen in 1789, three in 1798, two in 1804, and two in 1819-20—there would be thirty-one of them. But this would be counting John Langdon, Roger Sherman, William Few, Rufus King, and George Read, each twice, and Abraham Baldwin four times. The true number of those of the "thirty-nine," whom I have shown to have acted upon the question, which, by the text, they understood better than we, is twenty-three, leaving sixteen not shown to have acted upon it in any way.

Here, then, we have twenty-three of our "thirty-nine" fathers who framed the government under which we live, who have, upon their official responsibility and their corporal oaths, acted upon the very question which the text affirms they "understood just as well, and even better than we do now;" and twenty-one of them—a clear majority of the whole "thirty-nine"—so acting upon it as to make them guilty of gross political impropriety and willful perjury, if, in their understanding, any proper division between local and Federal authority, or anything in the Constitution they had made themselves and sworn to support, forbade the Federal Government to control, as to slavery, the Federal territories. Thus the twenty-one acted; and, as actions speak louder than words, so actions under such responsibility speak still louder.

Two of the twenty-three voted against Congressional prohibition of slavery in the Federal territories, in the instances in which they acted upon the question. But for what reasons they so voted is not known. They may have done so because they thought a proper division of local from Federal authority, or some provision or principle of the Constitution, stood in the way; or they may, without any such question, have voted against the prohibition on what appeared to them to be sufficient grounds of expediency. No one who has sworn to support the Constitution can conscientiously vote for what he understands to be an unconstitutional measure, however expedient he may think it; but one may and ought to vote against a measure which he deems constitutional, if, at the same time, he deems it inexpedient. It, therefore, would be unsafe to set down even the two who voted against the prohibition, as having done so because, in their understanding, any proper division of local from Federal authority, or anything in the Constitution, forbade the Federal Government to control, as to slavery, in territory.

The remaining sixteen of the "thirty-nine," so far as I have discovered, have left no record of their understanding upon the direct question of Federal control of slavery in the Federal territories. But there is much reason to believe that their understanding upon that question would not have appeared different from that of their twenty-three compeers, had it been manifested at all.

For the purpose of adhering rigidly to the text, I have purposely omitted whatever understanding may have been manifested, by any person, however distinguished, other than the thirty-nine fathers who framed the original Constitution; and, for the same reason, I have also omitted whatever understanding may have been manifested by any of the "thirty-nine," even, on any other phase of the general question of slavery. If we should look into their acts and declarations on those other phases, as the foreign slave trade, and the morality and policy of slavery generally, it would appear to us that on the direct question of Federal control of slavery in Federal territories, the sixteen, if they had acted at all, would probably have acted just as the twenty-three did. Among that sixteen were several of the most noted anti-slavery men of those times—as Dr. Franklin, Alexander Hamilton, and Gouverneur Morris—while there was not one now known to have been otherwise, unless it may be John Rutledge, of South Carolina.

The sum of the whole is, that of our "thirty-nine" fathers who framed the original Constitution, twenty-one—a clear majority of the whole—certainly understood that no proper division of local from Federal authority, nor any part of the Constitution, forbade the Federal Government to control slavery in the Federal territories; while all the rest probably had the same understanding. Such, unquestionably, was the understanding of our fathers who framed the original Constitution; and the text affirms that they understood the question better than we.

But, so far, I have been considering the understanding of the question manifested by the framers of the original Constitution. In and by the original instrument, a mode was provided for amending it; and, as I have already stated, the present frame of government under which we live consists of that original and twelve amendatory articles framed and adopted since. Those who now insist that Federal control of slavery in Federal territories violates the Constitution, point us to the provisions which they suppose it thus violates; and, as I understand, they all fix upon provisions in these amendatory articles, and not in the original instrument. The Supreme Court, in the Dred Scott case, plant themselves upon the fifth amendment, which provides that "no person shall be deprived of property without due process of law;" while Senator Douglas and his peculiar adherents plant themselves upon the tenth amendment, providing that "the powers not granted by the Constitution are reserved to the states respectively and to the people."

Now, it so happens that these amendments were framed by the first Congress which sat under the Constitution—the identical Congress which passed the act already mentioned, enforcing the prohibition of slavery in the Northwestern Territory. Not only was it the same Congress, but they were the identical same individual men who, at the same session, and at the same time within the session, had under consideration, and in progress toward maturity, these constitutional amendments and this act prohibiting slavery in all the territory the nation then owned. The constitutional amendments were introduced before and passed after the act enforcing the ordinance of 1787; so that during the whole pendency of the act to enforce the ordinance, the constitutional amendments were also pending.

That Congress, consisting in all of seventy-six members, including sixteen of the framers of the original Constitution, as before stated, were pre-eminently our fathers who framed that part of the government under which we live which is now claimed as forbidding the Federal Government to control slavery in the Federal territories.

Is it not a little presumptuous in any one at this day

to affirm that the two things which that Congress deliberately framed, and carried to maturity at the same time, are absolutely inconsistent with each other? And does not such affirmation become impudently absurd when coupled with the other affirmation, from the same mouth, that those who did the two things alleged to be inconsistent understood whether they really were inconsistent better than we—better than he who affirms that they are inconsistent?

It is surely safe to assume that the "thirty-nine" framers of the original Constitution, and the seventy-six members of the Congress which framed the amendments thereto, taken together, do certainly include those who may be fairly called "our fathers who framed the government under which we live." And so assuming, I defy any man to show that any one of them ever in his whole life declared that, in his understanding, any proper division of local from Federal authority, or any part of the Constitution, forbade the Federal Government to control as to slavery in the Federal territories. I go a step farther. I defy any one to show that any living man in the whole world ever did, prior to the beginning of the present century, (and I might almost say prior to the beginning of the last half of the present century,) declare that, in his understanding, any proper division of local from Federal authority, or any part of the Constitution, forbade the Federal Government to control as to slavery in the Federal territories. To those who now so declare, I give, not only "our fathers who framed the government under which we live," but with them all other living men within the century in which it was framed, among whom to search, and they shall not be able to find the evidence of a single man agreeing with them.

Now, and here, let me guard a little against being misunderstood. I do not mean to say we are bound to follow implicitly in whatever our fathers did. To do so would be to discard all the lights of current experience —to reject all progress—all improvement. What I do say is, that if we would supplant the opinions and policy of our fathers in any case, we should do so upon evidence so conclusive, and argument so clear, that even their great authority, fairly considered and weighed, can not stand; and most surely not in a case whereof we ourselves declare they understood the question better than we.

If any man, at this day, sincerely believes that a proper division of local from Federal authority, or any part of the Constitution, forbids the Federal Government to control as to slavery in the Federal territories, he is right to say so, and to enforce his position by all truthful evidence and fair argument which he can. But he has no right to mislead others, who have less access to history and less leisure to study it, into the false belief that "our fathers, who framed the government under which we live," were of the same opinion—thus substituting falsehood and deception for truthful evidence and fair argument. If any man at this day sincerely believes "our fathers, who framed the government under which we live," used and applied principles, in other cases, which ought to have led them to understand that a proper division of local from Federal authority, or some part of the Constitution, forbids the Federal Government to control as to slavery in the Federal territories, he is right to say so. But he should, at the same time, brave the responsibility of declaring that, in his opinion, he understands their principles better than they did themselves; and especially should he not shirk that responsibility by asserting that they "understood the question just as well, and even better, than we do now."

But enough. Let all who believe that "our fathers, who framed the government under which we live, understood this question just as well, and even better, than we do now," speak as they spoke, and act as they acted upon it. This is all Republicans ask—all Republicans desire—in relation to slavery. As those fathers marked it, so let it be again marked, as an evil not to be extended, but to be tolerated and protected only because of and so far as its actual presence among us makes that toleration and protection a necessity. Let all the guarantees those fathers gave it be, not grudgingly, but fully and fairly maintained. For this Republicans contend, and with this, so far as I know or believe, they will be content.

And now, if they would listen—as I suppose they will not—I would address a few words to the Southern people.

I would say to them: You consider yourselves a reasonable and just people, and I consider that in the general qualities of reason and justice you are not inferior to any other people. Still, when you speak of us Republicans you do so only to denounce us as reptiles, or, at the best, as no better than outlaws. You will grant a hearing to pirates or murderers, but nothing like it to "Black Republicans." In all your contentions with one another, each of you deems an unconditional condemnation of "Black Republicanism" as the first thing to be attended to. Indeed, such condemnation of us seems to be an indispensable prerequisite—license, so to speak—among you, to be admitted or permitted to speak at all.

Now, can you, or not, be prevailed upon to pause and

to consider whether this is quite just to us, or even to yourselves?

Bring forward your charges and specifications, and then be patient long enough to hear us deny or justify.

You say we are sectional. We deny it. That makes an issue; and the burden of proof is upon you. You produce your proof; and what is it? Why, that our party has no existence in your section—gets no votes in your section. The fact is substantially true; but does it prove the issue? If it does, then, in case we should, without change of principle, begin to get votes in your section, we should thereby cease to be sectional. You can not escape this conclusion; and yet, are you willing to abide by it? If you are, you will probably soon find that we have ceased to be sectional, for we shall get votes in your section this very year. You will then begin to discover, as the truth plainly is, that your proof does not touch the issue. The fact that we get no votes in your section is a fact of your making, and not of ours. And if there be fault in that fact, that fault is primarily yours, and remains so until you show that we repel you by some wrong principle or practice. If we do repel you by any wrong principle or practice, the fault is ours; but this brings you to where you ought to have started—to a discussion of the right or wrong of our principle. If our principle, put in practice, would wrong your section for the benefit of ours, or for any other object, then our principle, and we with it, are sectional, and are justly opposed and denounced as such. Meet us, then, on the question of whether our principle, put in practice, would wrong your section: and so meet it as if it were possible that something may be said on our side. Do you accept the challenge? No? Then you really believe that the principle which our fathers, who framed the government under which we live, thought so clearly right as to adopt it, and indorse it again and again, upon their official oaths, is, in fact, so clearly wrong as to demand your condemnation without a moment's consideration.

Some of you delight to flaunt in our faces the warning against sectional parties given by Washington in his Farewell Address. Less than eight years before Washington gave that warning, he had, as President of the United States, approved and signed an act of Congress enforcing the prohibition of slavery in the Northwestern Territory, which act embodied the policy of the government upon that subject, up to and at the very moment he penned that warning; and about one year after he penned it, he wrote Lafayette that he considered that prohibition a wise measure, expressing, in the same connection, his hope that we should some time have a confederacy of free states.

Bearing this in mind, and seeing that sectionalism has since arisen upon this same subject, is that warning a weapon in your hands against us, or in our hands against you? Could Washington himself speak, would he cast the blame of that sectionalism upon us, who sustain his policy, or upon you who repudiate it? We respect that warning of Washington, and we commend it to you, together with his example pointing to the right application of it.

But you say you are conservative—eminently conservative—while we are revolutionary, destructive, or something of the sort. What is conservatism? Is it not adherence to the old and tried, against the new and untried? We stick to contend for the identical old policy, on the point of controversy, which was adopted by our fathers who framed the government under which we live; while you with one accord reject, and scout, and spit upon that old policy, and insist upon substituting something new. True, you disagree among yourselves as to what that substitute shall be. You have considerable variety of new propositions and plans, but you are unanimous in rejecting and denouncing the old policy of the fathers. Some of you are for reviving the foreign slave trade; some for a congressional slave code for the territories; some for Congress forbidding the territories to prohibit slavery within their limits; some for maintaining slavery in the territories through the judiciary; some for the "gur-reat pur-rinciple" that "if one man would enslave another, no third man should object," fantastically called "popular sovereignty;" but never a man among you in favor of Federal prohibition of slavery in Federal territories, according to the practice of our fathers who framed the government under which we live. Not one of all your various plans can show a precedent or an advocate in the century within which our government originated. Consider, then, whether your claim of conservatism for yourselves, and your charge of destructiveness against us, are based on the most clear and stable foundations.

Again, you say we have made the slavery question more prominent than it formerly was. We deny it. We admit that it is more prominent, but we deny that we made it so. It was not we, but you, who discarded the old policy of the fathers. We resisted, and still resist, your innovation; and thence comes the greater prominence of the question. Would you have that question reduced to its former proportions? Go back to that old policy. What has been will be again, under the same conditions. If you would have the peace of the old times, readopt the precepts and policy of the old times.

You charge that we stir up insurrections among your slaves. We deny it; and what is your proof? Harper's Ferry! John Brown! John Brown was no Republican; and you have failed to implicate a single Republican in his Harper's Ferry enterprise. If any member of our party is guilty in that matter, you know it or you do not know it. If you do know it, you are inexcusable to not designate the man and prove the fact. If you do not know it, you are inexcusable to assert it, and especially to persist in the assertion after you have tried and failed to make the proof. You need not be told that persisting in a charge which one does not know to be true, is simply malicious slander.

Some of you admit that no Republican designedly aided or encouraged the Harper's Ferry affair, but still insist that our doctrines and declarations necessarily lead to such results. We do not believe it. We know we hold to no doctrines, and make no declarations, which were not held to and made by our fathers who framed the government under which we live. You never dealt fairly by us in relation to this affair. When it occurred, some important state elections were near at hand, and you were in evident glee with the belief that, by charging the blame upon us you could get an advantage of us in those elections. The elections came, and your expectations were not quite fulfilled. Every Republican man knew that, as to himself at least, your charge was a slander, and he was not much inclined by it to cast his vote in your favor. Republican doctrines and declarations are accompanied with a continual protest against any interference whatever with your slaves, or with you about your slaves. Surely this does not encourage them to revolt. True, we do, in common with our fathers who framed the government under which we live, declare our belief that slavery is wrong; but the slaves do not hear us declare even this. For anything we say or do, the slaves would scarcely know there is a Republican party. I believe they would not, in fact, generally know it but for your misrepresentations of us in their hearing. In your political contests among yourselves, each faction charges the other with sympathy with Black Republicanism; and then, to give point to the charge, defines Black Republicanism to simply be insurrection, blood and thunder among the slaves.

Slave insurrections are no more common now than they were before the Republican party was organized. What induced the Southampton insurrection, twenty-eight years ago, in which at least three times as many lives were lost as at Harper's Ferry? You can scarcely stretch your very elastic fancy to the conclusion that Southampton was got up by Black Republicanism. In the present state of things in the United States, I do not think a general, or even a very extensive slave insurrection is possible. The indispensable concert of action cannot be attained. The slaves have no means of rapid communication; nor can incendiary free men, black or white, supply it. The explosive materials are everywhere in parcels; but there neither are, nor can be supplied, the indispensable connecting trains.

Much is said by Southern people about the affection of slaves for their masters and mistresses; and a part of it, at least, is true. A plot for an uprising could scarcely be devised and communicated to twenty individuals before some one of them, to save the life of a favorite master or mistress, would divulge it. This is the rule; and the slave revolution in Hayti was not an exception to it, but a case occurring under peculiar circumstances. The gunpowder plot of British history, though not connected with slaves, was more in point. In that case only about twenty were admitted to the secret; and yet one of them, in his anxiety to save a friend, betrayed the plot to that friend, and, by consequence, averted the calamity.

Occasional poisonings from the kitchen, and open or stealthy assassinations in the field, and local revolts extending to a score or so, will continue to occur as the natural results of slavery; but no general insurrection of slaves, as I think, can happen in this country for a long time. Whoever much fears, or much hopes, for such an event, will be alike disappointed.

In the language of Mr. Jefferson, uttered many years ago, "It is still in our power to direct the process of emancipation and deportation peaceably, and in such slow degrees, as that the evil will wear off insensibly; and their places be, *pari passu*, filled up by free white laborers. If, on the contrary, it is left to force itself on, human nature must shudder at the prospect held up."

Mr. Jefferson did not mean to say, nor do I, that the power of emancipation is in the Federal Government. He spoke of Virginia; and, as to the power of emancipation, I speak of the slaveholding states only.

The Federal Government, however, as we insist, has the power of restraining the extension of the institution —the power to insure that a slave insurrection shall never occur on any American soil which is now free from slavery.

John Brown's effort was peculiar. It was not a slave insurrection. It was an attempt by white men to get up a revolt among slaves, in which the slaves refused to participate. In fact, it was so absurd that the slaves, with all their ignorance, saw plainly enough it could not succeed. That affair, in its philosophy, corresponds with the many attempts, related in history, at the assassination of kings and emperors. An enthusiast broods over the oppression of a people till he fancies himself commissioned by Heaven to liberate them. He ventures the attempt, which ends in little else than in his own execution. Orsini's attempt on Louis Napoleon, and John Brown's attempt at Harper's Ferry, were, in their philosophy, precisely the same. The eagerness to cast blame on old England in the one case, and on New England in the other, does not disprove the sameness of the two things.

And how much would it avail you if you could, by the use of John Brown, Helper's book, and the like, break up the Republican organization? Human action can be modified to some extent, but human nature cannot be changed. There is a judgment and a feeling against slavery in this nation, which cast at least a million and a half of votes. You cannot destroy that judgment and feeling—that sentiment—by breaking up the political organization which rallies around it. You can scarcely scatter and disperse an army which has been formed into order in the face of your heaviest fire; but if you could, how much would you gain by forcing the sentiment which created it out of the peaceful channel of the ballot-box into some other channel? What would that other channel probably be? Would the number of John Browns be lessened or enlarged by the operation?

But you will break up the Union, rather than submit to a denial of your Constitutional rights.

That has a somewhat reckless sound; but it would be palliated, if not fully justified, were we proposing, by the mere force of numbers, to deprive you of some right, plainly written down in the Constitution. But we are proposing no such thing.

When you make these declarations, you have a specific and well understood allusion to an assumed Constitutional right of yours, to take slaves into the Federal Territories, and to hold them there as property. But no such right is specifically written in the Constitution. That instrument is literally silent about any such right. We, on the contrary, deny that such a right has any existence in the Constitution, even by implication.

Your purpose, then, plainly stated, is, that you will destroy the government unless you be allowed to construe and enforce the Constitution as you please, on all points in dispute between you and us. You will rule or ruin in all events.

This, plainly stated, is your language to us. Perhaps you will say the Supreme Court has decided the disputed constitutional question in your favor. Not quite so. But, waiving the lawyers' distinction between dictum and decision, the court have decided the question for you in a sort of way. The court have substantially said it is your constitutional right to take slaves into the Federal territories, and to hold them there as property.

When I say the decision was made in a sort of way, I mean it was made in a divided court, by a bare majority of the judges, and they not quite agreeing with one another in the reasons for making it; that it is so made as that its avowed supporters disagree with one another about its meaning; and that it was mainly based upon a mistaken statement of fact—the statement in the opinion that "the right of property in a slave is distinctly and expressly affirmed in the Constitution."

An inspection of the Constitution will show that the right of property in a slave is not distinctly and expressly affirmed in it. Bear in mind the judges do not pledge their judicial opinion that such right is implicitly affirmed in the Constitution ; but they pledge their veracity that it is distinctly and expressly affirmed there—"distinctly"—that is, not mingled with anything else—"expressly"—that is, in words meaning just that, without the aid of any inference, and susceptible of no other meaning.

If they had only pledged their judicial opinion, that such right is affirmed in the instrument by implication, it would be open to others to show that, either the word "slave" nor "slavery" is to be found in the Constitution, nor the word "property" even, in any connection with language alluding to the things slave or slavery, and that wherever, in that instrument, the slave is alluded to, he is called "a person ;" and wherever his master's legal right in relation to him is alluded to, it is spoken of as "service or labor due," as a "debt" payable in service or labor.

Also, it would be open to show, by cotemporaneous history, that this mode of alluding to slaves and slavery, instead of speaking of them, was employed on purpose to exclude from the Constitution the idea that there could be property in man.

To show all this is easy and certain.

When this obvious mistake of the judges shall be brought to their notice, is it not reasonable to expect that they will withdraw the mistaken statement, and reconsider the conclusion based upon it?

And then it is to be remembered that "our fathers, who framed the government under which we live"—the men who made the Constitution—decided this same constitutional question in our favor, long ago—decided it without a division among themselves, when making the decision ; without division among themselves about the meaning of it after it was made, and so far as any evidence is left, without basing it upon any mistaken statement of facts.

Under all these circumstances, do you really feel yourselves justified to break up this government, unless such a court decision as yours is shall be at once submitted to as a conclusive and final rule of political action?

But you will not abide the election of a Republican President. In that supposed event, you say, you will destroy the Union; and then, you say, the great crime of having destroyed it will be upon us?

That is cool. A highwayman holds a pistol to my ear, and mutters through his teeth, "Stand and deliver, or I shall kill you, and then you will be a murderer!"

To be sure, what the robber demanded of me—my money—was my own; and I had a clear right to keep it; but it was no more my own than my vote is my own; and the threat of death to me, to extort my money, and the threat of destruction to the Union, to extort my vote, can scarcely be distinguished in principle.

A few words now to Republicans. It is exceedingly desirable that all parts of this great confederacy shall be at peace, and in harmony, one with another. Let us Republicans do our part to have it so. Even though much provoked, let us do nothing through passion and ill temper. Even though the Southern people will not so much as listen to us, let us calmly consider their demands, and yield to them if, in our deliberate view of our duty, we possibly can. Judging by all they say and do, and by the subject and nature of their controversy with us, let us determine, if we can, what will satisfy them.

Will they be satisfied if the territories be unconditionally surrendered to them? We know they will not. In all their present complaints against us, the territories are scarcely mentioned. Invasions and insurrections are the rage now. Will it satisfy them if, in the future, we have nothing to do with invasions and insurrections? We know it will not. We so know because we know we never had anything to do with invasions and insurrections; and yet this total abstaining does not exempt us from the charge and the denunciation.

The question recurs, what will satisfy them? Simply this: We must not only let them alone, but we must, somehow, convince them that we do let them alone. This, we know by experience, is no easy task. We have been so trying to convince them from the very beginning of our organization, but with no success. In all our platforms and speeches, we have constantly protested our purpose to let them alone; but this has had no tendency to convince them. Alike unavailing to convince them is the fact that they have never detected a man of us in any attempt to disturb them.

These natural and apparently adequate means all failing, what will convince them? This, and this only: Cease to call slavery *wrong*, and join them in calling it *right*. And this must be done thoroughly—done in *acts* as well as in *words*. Silence will not be tolerated—we must place ourselves avowedly with them. Douglas's new sedition law must be enacted, and enforced, suppressing all declarations that slavery is wrong, whether made in politics, in presses, in pulpits, or in private. We must arrest and return their fugitive slaves with greedy pleasure. We must pull down our Free State Constitutions. The whole atmosphere must be disinfected from all taint of opposition to slavery, before they will cease to believe that all their troubles proceed from us.

I am quite aware they do not state their case precisely in this way. Most of them would probably say to us,

"Let us alone, do nothing to us, and say what you please about slavery." But we do let them alone—have never disturbed them—so that, after all, it is what we say which dissatisfies them. They will continue to accuse us of doing until we cease saying.

I am also aware they have not, as yet, in terms, demanded the overthrow of our Free State Constitutions. Yet those Constitutions declare the wrong of slavery with more solemn emphasis than do all other sayings against it; and when all other sayings shall have been silenced, the overthrow of these Constitutions will be demanded, and nothing be left to resist the demand. It is nothing to the contrary that they do not demand the whole of this just now. Demanding what they do, and for the reason they do, they can voluntarily stop nowhere short of this consummation. Holding, as they do, that slavery is morally right and socially elevating, they can not cease to demand a full national recognition of it, as a legal right and a social blessing.

Nor can we justifiably withhold this on any ground, save our conviction that slavery is wrong. If slavery is right, all words, acts, laws, and Constitutions against it, are themselves wrong, and should be silenced and swept away. If it is right, we can not justly object to its nationality—its universality; if it is wrong, they can not justly insist upon its extension—its enlargement. All they ask we could readily grant, if we thought slavery right; all we ask they could readily grant, if they thought it wrong.

Their thinking it right, and our thinking it wrong, is the precise fact upon which depends the whole controversy. Thinking it right, as they do, they are not to blame for desiring its full recognition, as being right; but, thinking it wrong, as we do, can we yield to them?

Can we cast our votes with their view, and against our own? In view of our moral, social, and political responsibilities, can we do this?

Wrong as we think slavery is, we can yet afford to let it alone where it is, because that much is due to the necessity arising from its actual presence in the nation; but can we, while our votes will prevent it, allow it to spread into the national territories, and to overrun us here in these free states?

If our sense of duty forbids this, then let us stand by our duty, fearlessly and effectively. Let us be diverted by none of those sophistical contrivances wherewith we are so industriously plied and belabored—contrivances such as groping for some middle ground between the right and the wrong, vain as the search for a man who should be neither a living man nor a dead man—such as a policy of "don't care" on a question about which all true men do care—such as Union appeals beseeching true Union men to yield to disunionists, reversing the Divine rule, and calling, not the sinners, but the righteous to repentance — such as invocations of Washington, imploring men to unsay what Washington said, and undo what Washington did.

Neither let us be slandered from our duty by false accusations against us, nor frightened from it by menaces of destruction to the government, nor of dungeons to ourselves. Let us have faith that right makes might; and in that faith let us, to the end, dare to do our duty as we understand it.

SPEECH

DELIVERED AT COLUMBUS, OHIO, SEPTEMBER, 1859.

Fellow-citizens of the State of Ohio: I can not fail to remember that I appear for the first time before an audience in this now great State—an audience that is accustomed to hear such speakers as Corwin, and Chase, and Wade, and many other renowned men; and remembering this, I feel that it will be well for you, as for me, that you should not raise your expectations to that standard to which you would have been justified in raising them had one of these distinguished men appeared before you. You would perhaps be only preparing a disappointment for yourselves, and, as a consequence of your disappointment, mortification to me. I hope, therefore, that you will commence with very moderate expectations; and perhaps, if you will give me your attention, I shall be able to interest you to a moderate degree.

Appearing here for the first time in my life, I have been somewhat embarrassed for a topic by way of introduction to my speech; but I have been relieved from that embarrassment by an introduction which the *Ohio Statesman* newspaper gave me this morning. In this paper, I have read an article, in which, among other statements, I find the following:

"In debating with Senator Douglas during the memorable contest of last fall, Mr. Lincoln declared in favor of negro suffrage, and attempted to defend that vile conception against the Little Giant."

I mention this now, at the opening of my remarks, for the purpose of making three comments upon it. The first I have already announced—it furnishes me an introductory topic; the second is to show that the gentleman is mistaken; thirdly, to give him an opportunity to correct it.

In the first place, in regard to this matter being a mistake. I have found that it is not entirely safe, when one is misrepresented under his very nose, to allow the misrepresentation to go uncontradicted. I therefore propose here, at the outset, not only to say that this is a misrepresentation, but to show conclusively that it is so; and you will bear with me while I read a couple of extracts from that very "memorable" debate with Judge Douglas last year, to which this newspaper refers. In the first pitched battle which Senator Douglas and myself had, at the town of Ottawa, I used the language which I will now read. Having been previously reading an extract, I continued as follows:

"Now, gentlemen, I don't want to read at any greater length, but this is the true complexion of all I have ever said in regard to the institution of slavery and the black race. This is the whole of it, and anything that argues me into his idea of perfect social and political equality with the negro, is but a specious and fastastic arrangement of words, by which a man can prove a horse-chestnut to be a chestnut horse. I will say here, while upon this subject, that I have no purpose directly or indirectly to interfere with the institution of slavery in the states where it exists. I believe I have no lawful right to do so, and I have no inclination to do so. I have no purpose to introduce political and social equality between the white and the black races. There is a physical difference between the two which, in my judgment, will probably forbid their ever living together upon the footing of perfect equality; and inasmuch as it becomes a necessity that there must be a difference, I, as well as Judge Douglas, am in favor of the race to which I belong having the superior position. I have never said anything to the contrary, but I hold that, notwithstanding all this, there is no reason in the world why the negro is not entitled to all the natural rights enumerated in the Declaration of Independence—the right of life, liberty, and the pursuit of happiness. I hold that he is as much entitled to these as the white man. I agree with Judge Douglas, he is not my equal in many respects—certainly not in color, perhaps not in moral or intellectual endowments. But in the right to eat the bread, without leave of anybody else, which his own hand earns, *he is my equal, and the equal of Judge Douglas, and the equal of every living man.*"

Upon a subsequent occasion, when the reason for making a statement like this recurred, I said:

"While I was at the hotel to-day, an elderly gentleman called upon me to know whether I was really in favor of producing perfect equality between the negroes and white people. While I had not proposed to myself on this occasion to say much on that subject, yet as the question was asked me, I thought I would occupy perhaps five minutes in saying something in regard to it. I will say, then, that I am not, nor ever have been, in favor of bringing about in any way the social and political equality of the white and black races—that I am not nor ever have been in favor of making voters or jurors of negroes, nor of qualifying them to hold office, or intermarry with white people; and I will say in addition to this, that there is a physical difference between the white and black races which I believe will forever forbid the two races living together on terms of social and political equality. And inasmuch as they can not so live, while they do remain together there must be the position of superior and inferior, and I, as much as any other man, am in favor of having the superior position assigned to the white race. I say upon this occasion I do not perceive that because the white man is to have the superior position, the negro should be denied everything. I do not understand that because I do not want a negro woman for a slave, I must necessarily want her for a wife. My understanding is that I can just let her alone. I am now in my fiftieth year, and I certainly never have had a black woman for either a slave or a wife. So it seems to me quite possible for us to get along without making either slaves or wives of negroes. I will add to this that I have never seen to my knowledge a man, woman, or child, who was in favor of producing perfect equality, social and political, between negroes and white men. I recollect of but one distinguished instance that I ever heard of so frequently as to be satisfied of its correctness—and that is the case of Judge Douglas's old friend, Colonel Richard M. Johnson. I will also add to the remarks I have made (for I am not going to enter at large upon this subject,) that I have never had the least apprehension that I or my friends would marry negroes, if there was no law to keep them from it; but as Judge Douglas and his friends seem to be in great apprehension that they might, if there were no law to keep them from it, I give him the most solemn pledge that I will, to the very last, stand by the law of the State, which forbids the marrying of white people with negroes."

There, my friends, you have briefly what I have, on former occasions, said upon the subject to which this newspaper, to the extent of its ability, has drawn the public attention. In it you not only perceive, as a probability, that in that contest I did not at any time say I was in favor of negro suffrage, but the absolute proof that twice, once substantially and once expressly, I declared against it. Having shown you this, there remains but a word of comment upon that newspaper article. It is this: that I presume the editor of that paper is an honest and truth-loving man, and that he will be greatly obliged to me for furnishing him thus early an opportunity to correct the misrepresentation he has made, before it has run so long that malicious people can call him a liar.

The Giant himself has been here recently. I have seen a brief report of his speech. If it were otherwise unpleasant to me to introduce the subject of the negro as a topic for discussion, I might be somewhat relieved by the fact that he dealt exclusively in that subject while he was here. I shall, therefore, without much hesitation or diffidence, enter upon this subject.

The American people, on the first day of January, 1854, found the African slave-trade prohibited by a law of Congress. In a majority of the states of this Union, they found African slavery, or any other sort of slavery, prohibited by State Constitutions. They also found a law existing, supposed to be valid, by which slavery was excluded from almost all the territory the United States then owned. This was the condition of the country, with reference to the institution of slavery, on the first of January, 1854. A few days after that, a bill was introduced into Congress, which ran through its regular course in the two branches of the National Legislature, and finally passed into a law in the month of May, by which the act of Congress prohibiting slavery from going into the Territories of the United States was repealed. In connection with the law itself, and, in fact, in the terms of the law, the then existing prohibition was not only repealed, but there was a declaration of a purpose on the part of Congress never thereafter to exercise any power that they might have, real or supposed, to prohibit the extension or spread of slavery. This was a very great change; for the law thus repealed was of more than thirty years' standing. Following rapidly upon the heels of this action of Congress, a decision of the Supreme Court is made, by which it is declared that Congress, if it desires to prohibit the spread of slavery into the territories, has no constitutional power to do so. Not only so, but that decision lays down principles, which, if pushed to their logical conclusion—I say pushed to their logical conclusion—would decide that the Constitutions of free states, forbidding slavery, are themselves unconstitutional. Mark me, I do not say the judge said this, and let no man say I affirm the judge used these words; but I only say it is my opinion that what they did say, if pressed to its logical conclusion, will inevitably result thus.

Looking at these things, the Republican party, as I understand its principles and policy, believe that there is great danger of the institution of slavery being spread out and extended, until it is ultimately made alike lawful in all the states of this Union; so believing, to prevent that incidental and ultimate consummation, is the original and chief purpose of the Republican organization. I say "chief purpose" of the Republican organization; for it is certainly true that if the national house shall fall into the hands of the Republicans, they will have to attend to all the other matters of national housekeeping, as well as this. The chief and real purpose of the Republican party is eminently conservative. It proposes nothing save and except to restore this government to its original tone in regard to this element of slavery, and there to maintain it, looking for no further change in reference to it, than that which the original framers of the government themselves expected and looked forward to.

The chief danger to this purpose of the Republican party is not just now the revival of the African slave trade, or the passage of a Congressional slave code, or the declaring of a second Dred Scott decision, making slavery lawful in all the states. These are not pressing us just now. They are not quite ready yet. The authors of these measures know that we are too strong for them; but they will be upon us in due time, and we will be grappling with them hand to hand, if they are not now headed off. They are not now the chief danger to the purpose of the Republican organization; but the most imminent danger that now threatens that purpose is that insidious Douglas popular sovereignty. This is the miner and sapper. While it does not propose to revive the African slave-trade, nor to pass a slave code, nor to make a second Dred Scott decision, it is preparing us for the onslaught and charge of these ultimate enemies when they shall be ready to come on, and the word of command for them to advance shall be given. I say this Douglas popular sovereignty—for there is a broad distinction, as I now understand it, between that article and a genuine popular sovereignty.

I believe there is a genuine popular sovereignty. I think a definition of genuine popular sovereignty, in the abstract, would be about this: That each man shall do precisely as he pleases with himself, and with all those things which exclusively concern him. Applied to government, this principle would be, that a General Government shall do all those things which pertain to it, and all the local governments shall do precisely as they please in respect to those matters which exclusively concern them. I understand that this government of the United States, under which we live, is based upon this principle; and I am misunderstood if it is supposed that I have any war to make upon that principle.

Now, what is Judge Douglas's popular sovereignty? It is, as a principle, no other than that, if one man chooses to make a slave of another man, neither that other man nor anybody else has a right to object. Applied in Government, as he seeks to apply it, it is this: If, in a new territory into which a few people are beginning to enter for the purpose of making their homes, they choose to either exclude slavery from their limits, or to establish it there, however one or the other may affect the persons to be enslaved, or the infinitely greater number of persons who are afterward to inhabit that territory, or the other members of the families of communities, of which they are but an incipient member, or the general head of the family of states as parent of all—however their action may affect one or the other of these, there is no power or right to interfere. That is Douglas's popular sovereignty applied.

He has a good deal of trouble with popular sovereignty. His explanations explanatory of explanations explained are interminable. The most lengthy, and, as I suppose, the most maturely considered of his long series of explanations, is his great essay in *Harper's Magazine*. I will not attempt to enter on any very thorough investigation of his argument, as there made and presented. I will nevertheless occupy a good portion of your time here in drawing your attention to certain points in it.

Such of you as may have read this document will have perceived that the judge, early in the document, quotes from two persons as belonging to the Republican party, without naming them, but who can readily be recognized as being Governor Seward, of New York, and myself.

It is true, that exactly fifteen months ago this day, I believe, I, for the first time, expressed a sentiment upon this subject, and in such a manner that it should get into print, that the public might see it beyond the circle of my hearers; and my expression of it at that time is the quotation that Judge Douglas makes. He has not made the quotation with accuracy, but justice to him requires me to say that it is sufficiently accurate not to change its sense.

The sense of that quotation condensed is this—that this slavery element is a durable element of discord among us, and that we shall probably not have perfect peace in this country with it, until it either masters the free principle in our government, or is so far mastered by the free principle as for the public mind to rest in the belief that it is going to its end. This sentiment, which I now express in this way, was, at no great distance of time, perhaps in different language, and in connection with some collateral ideas, expressed by Governor Seward. Judge Douglas has been so much annoyed by the expression of that sentiment that he has constantly, I believe, in almost all his speeches since it was uttered, been referring to it. I find he alluded to it in his speech here, as well as in the copy-right essay.

I do not now enter upon this for the purpose of making an elaborate argument to show that we were right in the expression of that sentiment. In other words, I shall not stop to say all that might properly be said upon this point; but I only ask your attention to it for the purpose of making one or two points upon it.

If you will read the copy-right essay, you will discover that Judge Douglas himself says a controversy between the American colonies and the government of Great Britain began on the slavery question in 1699, and continued from that time until the revolution; and, while he did not say so, we all know that it has continued with more or less violence ever since the revolution.

Then we need not appeal to history, to the declaration of the framers of the government, but we know from Judge Douglas himself that slavery began to be an element of discord among the white people of this country as far back as 1699, or one hundred and sixty years ago, or five generations of men—counting thirty years to a generation. Now it would seem to me that it might have occurred to Judge Douglas, or anybody who had turned his attention to these facts, that there was something in the nature of that thing, slavery, somewhat durable for mischief and discord.

There is another point I desire to make in regard to this matter, before I leave it. From the adoption of the Constitution down to 1820 is the precise period of our history when we had comparative peace upon this question—the precise period of time when we came nearer to having peace about it than any other time of that entire one hundred and sixty years, in which he says it began, or of the eighty years of our own Constitution. Then it would be worth our while to stop and examine into the probable reason of our coming nearer to having peace then than at any other time. This was the precise period of time in which our fathers adopted, and during which they followed, a policy restricting the spread of slavery, and the whole Union was acquiescing in it. The whole country looked forward to the ultimate extinction of the institution. It was when a policy had been adopted and was prevailing, which led all just and right-minded men to suppose that slavery was gradually coming to an end, and that they might be quiet about it, watching it as it expired.

I think Judge Douglas might have perceived that too, and whether he did or not, it is worth the attention of fair-minded men, here and elsewhere, to consider whether that is not the truth of the case. If he had looked at these two facts, that this matter has been an element of discord for one hundred and sixty years among this people, and that the only comparative peace we have had about it was when that policy prevailed in this government, which he now wars upon, he might then, perhaps, have been brought to a more just appreciation of what I said fifteen months ago—that "a house divided against itself can not stand. I believe that this government can not endure permanently half slave and half free. I do not expect the house to fall. I do not expect the Union to dissolve; but I do expect it will cease to be divided. It will become all one thing or all the other. Either the opponents of slavery will arrest the further spread of it, and place it where the public mind will rest in the belief that it is in the course of ultimate extinction; or its advocates will push it forward, until it shall become alike lawful in all the states, old as well as new, North as well as South." That was my sentiment at that time. In connection with it, I said, "We are now far into the fifth year, since a policy was inaugurated with the avowed object and confident promise of putting an end to slavery agitation. Under the operation of the policy, that agitation has not only not ceased, but has constantly augmented."

I now say to you here that we are advanced still further into the sixth year since that policy of Judge Douglas—that popular sovereignty of his, for quieting the slavery question—was made the national policy. Fifteen months more have been added since I uttered that sentiment, and I call upon you, and all other right-minded men, to say whether that fifteen months have belied or corroborated my words.

While I am here upon this subject, I cannot but express gratitude that this true view of this element of discord among us—as I believe it is—is attracting more and more attention. I do not believe that Governor Seward uttered that sentiment because I had done so before, but because he reflected upon this subject, and saw the truth of it. Nor do I believe, because Governor Seward or I uttered it, that Mr. Hickman, of Pennsylvania, in different language, since that time, has declared his belief in the utter antagonism which exists between the principles of liberty and slavery. You see we are multiplying.

Now, while I am speaking of Hickman, let me say, I know but little about him. I have never seen him, and know scarcely anything about the man; but I will say this much of him: Of all the anti-Lecompton Democracy that have been brought to my notice, he alone has the true, genuine ring of the metal. And now, without indorsing anything else he has said, I will ask this audience to give three cheers for Hickman. (The audience responded with three rousing cheers for Hickman.)

Another point in the copy-right essay to which I would ask your attention, is rather a feature to be extracted from the whole thing, than from any express declaration of it at any point. It is a general feature of that document, and indeed, of all of Judge Douglas's discussions of this question, that the territories of the United States, and the states of this Union, are exactly alike—that there is no difference between them at all—that the Constitution applies to the territories precisely as it does to the states—and that the United States Government, under the Constitution, may not do in a state what it may not do in a territory, and what it must do in a state, it must do in a territory. Gentlemen, is that a true view of the case? It is necessary for this squatter sovereignty; but is it true?

Let us consider. What does it depend upon? It depends altogether upon the proposition that the States must, without the interference of the General Government, do all those things that pertain *exclusively* to themselves—that are local in their nature, that have no connection with the General Government. After Judge Douglas has established this proposition, which nobody disputes or ever has disputed, he proceeds to assume, without proving it, that slavery is one of those little, unimportant, trivial matters which are of just about as much consequence as the question would be to me, whether my neighbor should raise horned cattle or plant tobacco; that there is no moral question about it, but that it is altogether a matter of dollars and cents; that when a new territory is opened for settlement, the first man who goes into it may plant there a thing which, like the Canada thistle or some other of those pests of the soil, can not be dug out by the millions of men who will come thereafter; that it is one of those little things that is so trivial in its nature that it has no effect upon anybody save the few men who first plant upon the soil; that it is not a thing which in any way affects the family of communities composing these states, nor any way endangers the General Government. Judge Douglas ignores altogether the very well known fact, that we have never had a serious menace to our political existence, except it sprang from this thing, which he chooses to regard as only upon a par with onions and potatoes.

Turn it, and contemplate it in another view. He says, that according to his popular sovereignty, the General Government may give to the territories governors, judges, marshals, secretaries, and all the other chief men to govern them, but they must not touch upon this other question. Why? The question of who shall be governor of a territory for a year or two, and pass away, without his track being left upon the soil, or an act which he did for good or for evil being left behind, is a question of vast national magnitude. It is so much opposed in its nature to locality, that the nation itself must decide it; while this other matter of planting slavery upon a soil—a thing which once planted can not be eradicated by the succeeding millions who have as much right there as the first comers, or if eradicated, not without infinite difficulty and a long struggle—he considers the power to prohibit it as one of these little, local, trivial things, that the nation ought not to say a word about; that it affects nobody save the few men who are there.

Take these two things and consider them together; present the question of planting a state with the institution of slavery by the side of a question of who shall be governor of Kansas for a year or two, and is there a man here—is there a man on earth—who would not say the governor question is the little one, and the slavery question is the great one? I ask any honest

Democrat if the small, the local, and the trivial and temporary question is not, who shall be governor? While the durable, the important and the mischievous one is, shall this soil be planted with slavery?

This is an idea, I suppose, which has arisen in Judge Douglas's mind from his peculiar structure. I suppose the institution of slavery really looks small to him. He is so put up by nature that a lash upon his back would hurt him, but a lash upon anybody else's back does not hurt him. That is the build of the man, and consequently he looks upon the matter of slavery in this unimportant light.

Judge Douglas ought to remember when he is endeavoring to force this policy upon the American people that while he is put up in that way a good many are not. He ought to remember that there was once in this country a man by the name of Thomas Jefferson, supposed to be a Democrat—a man whose principles and policy are not very prevalent among Democrats to-day, it is true; but that man did not take exactly this view of the insignificance of the element of slavery which our friend Judge Douglas does. In contemplation of this thing, we all know he was led to exclaim: "I tremble for my country when I remember that God is just!" We know how he looked upon it when he thus expressed himself. There was danger to this country—danger of the avenging justice of God in that little unimportant popular sovereignty question of Judge Douglas. He supposed there was a question of God's eternal justice wrapped up in the enslaving of any race of men, or any man, and that those who did so braved the arm of Jehovah—that when a nation thus dared the Almighty, every friend of that nation had cause to dread his wrath. Choose ye between Jefferson and

Douglas as to what is the true view of this element among us.

There is another little difficulty about this matter of treating the territories and states alike in all things, to which I ask your attention, and I shall leave this branch of the case. If there is no difference between them, why not make the territories states at once? What is the reason that Kansas was not fit to come into the Union when it was organized into a territory, in Judge Douglas's view? Can any of you tell any reason why it should not have come into the Union at once? They are fit, as he thinks, to decide upon the slavery question—the largest and most important with which they could possibly deal—what could they do by coming into the Union that they are not fit to do, according to his view, by staying out of it? O, they are not fit to sit in Congress and decide upon the rates of postage, or questions of *ad valorem* or specific duties on foreign goods, or live oak timber contracts; they are not fit to decide these vastly important matters, which are national in their import, but they are fit, "from the jump," to decide this little negro question. But, gentlemen, the case is too plain; I occupy too much time on this head, and I pass on.

Near the close of the copy-right essay, the Judge, I think, comes very near kicking his own fat into the fire. I did not think, when I commenced these remarks, that I would read from that article, but I now believe I will:

"This exposition of the history of these measures, shows conclusively that the authors of the Compromise Measures of 1850 and of the Kansas-Nebraska act of 1854, as well as the members of the Continental Congress of 1774, and the founders of our system of government subsequent to the Revolution, regarded the people of the territories and colonies as political communities, which were entitled to a free and exclusive power of legislation in their provisional Legislatures, where their representation could alone be preserved, in all cases of taxation and internal polity."

When the judge saw that putting in the word "slavery" would contradict his own history, he put in what he knew would pass as synonymous with it: "internal polity." Whenever we find *that* in one of his speeches, the substitute is used in this manner; and I can tell you the reason. It would be too bald a contradiction to say slavery, but "internal polity" is a general phrase, which would pass in some quarters, and which he hopes will pass with the reading community for the same thing:

"This right pertains to the people collectively, as a law-abiding and peaceful community, and not in the isolated individuals who may wander upon the public domain in violation of the law. It can only be exercised where there are inhabitants sufficient to constitute a government, and capable of performing its various functions and duties, a fact to be ascertained and determined by"—who do you think? Judge Douglas says, "By Congress!"

"Whether the number shall be fixed at ten, fifteen, or twenty thousand inhabitants, does not affect the principle."

Now I have only a few comments to make. Popular sovereignty, by his own words, does not pertain to the few persons who wander upon the public domain in violation of law. We have his words for that. When it does pertain to them, is when they are sufficient to be formed into an organized political community, and he fixes the minimum for that at 10,000, and the maximum at 20,000. Now I would like to know what is to be done with the 9,000? Are they all to be treated, until they are large enough to be organized into a political community, as wanderers upon the public land in violation of law? And if so treated and driven out, at what point of time would there ever be ten thousand? If they were not driven out, but remained there as trespassers upon the public land in violation of the law, can they establish slavery there? No—the judge says popular sovereignty don't pertain to them then. Can they exclude it then? No, popular sovereignty don't pertain to them then. I would like to know, in the case covered by the essay, what condition the people of the territory are in before they reach the number of ten thousand?

But the main point I wish to ask attention to is, that the question as to when they shall have reached a sufficient number to be formed into a regular organized community, is to be decided "by Congress." Judge Douglas says so. Well, gentlemen, that is about all we want. No, that is all the Southerners want. That is what all those who are for slavery want. They do not want Congress to prohibit slavery from coming into the new territories, and they do not want popular sovereignty to hinder it; and as Congress is to say when they are ready to be organized, all that the South has to do is to get Congress to hold off. Let Congress hold off until they are ready to be admitted as a state, and the South has all it wants in taking slavery into and planting it in all the territories that we now have, or hereafter may have. In a word, the whole thing, at a dash of the pen, is at last put in the power of Congress; for if they do not have this popular sovereignty until Congress organizes them, I ask if it at last does not come from Congress? If, at last, it amounts to anything at all, Congress gives it to them. I submit this rather for your reflection than for comment. After all that is said, at last, by a dash of the pen, everything that has gone before is undone, and he puts the whole question under the control of Congress. After fighting through more than three hours, if you undertake to read it, he at last places the whole matter under the control of that power which he had been contending against, and arrives at a result directly contrary to what he had been laboring to do. He at last leaves the whole matter to the control of Congress.

There are two main objects, as I understand it, of this Harper's Magazine essay. One was to show, if possible, that the men of our Revolutionary times were in favor of his popular sovereignty; and the other was to show that the Dred Scott decision had not entirely squelched out this popular sovereignty. I do not propose, in regard to this argument drawn from the history of former times, to enter into a detailed examination of the historical statements he has made. I have the impression that they are inaccurate in a great many instances. Sometimes in positive statement, but very much more inaccurate by the suppression of statements that really belong to the history. But I do not propose to affirm that this is so to any very great extent; or to enter into a very minute examination of his historical statements. I avoid doing so upon this principle—that if it were important for me to pass out of this lot in the least period of time possible, and I came to that fence and saw by a calculation of my known strength and agility that I could clear it at a bound, it would be folly for me to stop and consider whether I could or not crawl through a crack. So I say of the whole history, contained in his essay, where he endeavored to link the men of the Revolution to popular sovereignty. It only requires an effort to leap out of it—a single bound to be entirely successful. If you read it over, you will find that he quotes here and there from documents of the Revolutionary times, tending to show that the people of the colonies were desirous of regulating their own concerns in their own way; that the British Government should not interfere; that at one time they struggled with the British Government to be permitted to exclude the African slave-trade; if not directly, to be permitted to exclude it indirectly by taxation sufficient to discourage and destroy it. From these and many things of this sort, Judge Douglas argues that they were in favor of the people of our own territories excluding slavery if they wanted to, or planting it there if they wanted to, doing just as they pleased from the time they settled upon the territory. Now, however his history may apply, and whatever of his argument there may be that is sound and accurate or unsound and inaccurate, if we can find out what these men did themselves do upon this very question of slavery in the territories, does it not end the whole thing? If after all this labor and effort to show that the men of the Revolution were in favor of his popular sovereignty and his mode of dealing with slavery in the territories, we can show that these very men took hold of that subject, and dealt with it; we can see for ourselves *how* they dealt with it. It is not a matter of argument or inference, but we know what they thought about it.

It is precisely upon that part of the history of the country, that one important omission is made by Judge Douglas. He selects parts of the history of the United States upon the subject of slavery, and treats it as the whole, omitting from his historical sketch the legislation of Congress in regard to the admission of Missouri, by which the Missouri Compromise was established, and slavery excluded from a country half as large as the present United States. All this is left out of his history, and in nowise alluded to by him, so far as I can remember, save once, when he makes a remark, that upon his principle the Supreme Court were authorized to pronounce a decision that the act called the Missouri Compromise was unconstitutional. All that history has been left out. But this part of the history of the country was not made by the men of the Revolution.

There was another part of our political history made by the very men who were the actors in the Revolution, which has taken the name of the ordinance of '87. Let me bring that history to your attention. In 1784, I believe, this same Mr. Jefferson drew up an ordinance for the government of the country, upon which we now stand; or rather, a frame or draft of an ordinance for the government of this country, here in Ohio, our neighbors in Indiana, us who live in Illinois, our neighbors in Wisconsin, and Michigan. In that ordinance, drawn up not only for the government of that territory, but for the territories south of the Ohio River, Mr. Jefferson expressly provided for the prohibition of slavery. Judge Douglas says, and perhaps is right, that that provision was lost from that ordinance. I believe that is true. When the vote was taken upon it, a majority of all present in the Congress of the Confederation voted for it; but there were so many absentees that those voting for it did not make the clear majority necessary, and it was lost. But three years after that, the Congress of the Confederation were together again, and they adopted a new ordinance for the government of this Northwest Territory, not contemplating territory south of the river, for the states owning that territory had hitherto refrained from giving it to the General Government; hence, they made the ordinance to apply only to what the Government owned. In that, the provision excluding slavery *was inserted and passed unanimously*, or at any rate it passed and became a part of the law of the land. Under that ordinance we live. First here in Ohio you were a territory, then an enabling act was passed, authorizing you to form a Constitution and State Government, provided it was republican and not in conflict with the ordinance of '87. When you framed your Constitution and presented it for admission, I think you will find the legislation upon the subject will show that, 'Whereas you had formed a Constitution that was republican, and not in conflict with the Ordinance of '87," therefore, you were admitted upon equal footing with the original states. The same process in a few years was gone through with in Indiana, and so with Illinois, and the same substantially with Michigan and Wisconsin.

Not only did that ordinance prevail, but it was constantly looked to whenever a step was taken by a new territory to become a state. Congress always turned their attention to it, and in all their movements upon this subject, they traced their course by that ordinance of '87. When they admitted new states, they advertised them of this ordinance as a part of the legislation of the country. They did so because they had traced the ordinance of '87 throughout the history of this country. Begin with the men of the Revolution, and go down for sixty entire years, and until the last scrap of that territory comes into the Union in the form of the State of Wisconsin—everything was made to conform with the ordinance of '87, excluding slavery from that vast extent of country.

I omitted to mention in the right place that the Constitution of the United States was in process of being framed when that ordinance was made by the Congress of the Confederation; and one of the first acts of Congress itself, under the new Constitution itself, was to give force to that ordinance by putting power to carry it out in the hands of the new officers under the Constitution, in the place of the old ones, who had been legislated out of existence by the change in the Government from the Confederation to the Constitution. Not only so, but I believe Indiana once or twice, if not Ohio, petitioned the General Government for the privilege of suspending that provision and allowing them to have slaves. A report made by Mr. Randolph, of Virginia, himself a slaveholder, was directly against it, and the action was to refuse them the privilege of violating the ordinance of '87.

This period of history, which I have run over briefly, is, I presume, as familiar to most of this assembly as any other part of the history of our country. I suppose that few of my hearers are not as familiar with that part of history as I am, and I only mention it to recall your attention to it at this time. And hence I ask how extraordinary a thing it is that a man who has occupied a position upon the floor of the Senate of the United States, who is now in his third term, and who looks to see the government of this whole country fall into his own hands, pretending to give a truthful and accurate history of the slavery question in this country, should so entirely ignore the whole of that portion of our history—the most important of all. Is it not a most extraordinary spectacle, that a man should stand up and ask for any confidence in his statements, who sets out as he does with portions of history, calling upon the people to believe that it is a true and fair representation, when the leading part, and controlling feature, of the whole history is carefully suppressed?

But the mere leaving out is not the most remarkable feature of this most remarkable essay. His proposition is to establish that the leading men of the Revolution were for his great principle of non-intervention by the government in the question of slavery in the territories; while history shows that they decided in the cases actually brought before them, in exactly the contrary way, and he knows it. Not only did they so decide at that time, but they stuck to it during sixty years, through thick and thin, as long as there was one of the revolutionary heroes upon the stage of political action. Through their whole course, from first to last, they clung to freedom.

And now he asks the community to believe that the men of the Revolution were in favor of his great principle, when we have the naked history that they themselves dealt with this very subject-matter of his principle, and utterly repudiated his principle, acting upon a precisely contrary ground. It is as impudent and absurd as if a prosecuting attorney should stand up before a jury, and ask them to convict A as the murderer of B, while B was walking alive before them.

I say, again, if Judge Douglas asserts that the men of the revolution acted upon principles by which, to be consistent with themselves, they ought to have adopted his popular sovereignty, then, upon a consideration of his own argument, he had a right to make you believe that they understood the principles of government, but misapplied them—that he has arisen to enlighten the world as to the just application of this principle. He has a right to try to persuade you that he understands their principles better than they did, and, therefore, he will apply them now, not as they did, but as they ought to have done. He has a right to go before the community, and try to convince them of this; but he has no right to attempt to impose upon any one the belief that these men themselves approved of his great principle. There are two ways of establishing a proposition. One is by trying to demonstrate it upon reason; and the other is, to show that great men in former times have thought so and so, and thus to pass it by the weight of pure authority.

Now, if Judge Douglas will demonstrate somehow that this is popular sovereignty—the right of one man to make a slave of another, without any right in that other, or any one else to object—demonstrate it as Euclid demonstrated propositions—there is no objection. But when he comes forward, seeking to carry a principle by bringing to it the authority of men who themselves utterly repudiate that principle, I ask that he shall not be permitted to do it.

I see, in the judge's speech here, a short sentence in these words: "Our fathers, when they formed this government under which we live, understood this question just as well and even better than we do now." That is true; I stick to that. I will stand by Judge Douglas in that to the bitter end.

And now, Judge Douglas, come and stand by me, and truthfully show how they acted, understanding it better than we do. All I ask of you, Judge Douglas, is to stick to the proposition that the men of the Revolution understood this subject better than we do now, *and with that better understanding they acted better than you are trying to act now.*

I wish to say something now in regard to the Dred Scott decision, as dealt with by Judge Douglas. In that "memorable debate" between Judge Douglas and myself, last year, the judge thought fit to commence a process of catechising me, and at Freeport I answered his questions, and propounded some to him. Among others propounded to him was one that I have here now. The substance, as I remember it, is, "Can the people of a United States territory, under the Dred Scott decision, in any lawful way, against the wish of any citizen of the United States, exclude slavery from its limits, prior to the formation of a State Constitution?"

He answered that they could lawfully exclude slavery from the United States territories, notwithstanding the Dred Scott decision. There was something about that answer that has probably been a trouble to the judge ever since.

The Dred Scott decision expressly gives every citizen of the United States a right to carry his slaves into the United States territories. And now there was some inconsistency in saying that the decision was right, and saying, too, that the people of the territory could lawfully drive slavery out again. When all the trash, the words, the collateral matter, was cleared away from it—all the chaff was fanned out of it, it was a bare absurdity—*no less than that a thing may be lawfully driven away from where it has a lawful right to be.* Clear it of all the verbiage, and that is the naked truth of his proposition—that a thing may be lawfully driven from the place where it has a lawful right to stay.

Well, it was because the judge could n't help seeing this, that he has had so much trouble with it; and what I want to ask your especial attention to, just now, is to remind you, if you have not noticed the fact, that the judge does not any longer say that the people can exclude slavery. He does not say so in the copy-right essay; he did not say so in the speech that he made here; and, so far as I know, since his re-election to the Senate, he has never said, as he did at Freeport, that the people of the territories can exclude slavery. He desires that you, who wish the territories to remain free, should believe that he stands by that position, but he does not say it himself. He escapes, to some extent, the absurd position I have stated, by changing his language entirely.

What he says now, is something different in language, and we will consider whether it is not different in sense, too. It is now that the Dred Scott decision, or rather the Constitution under that decision, does not carry slavery into the territories beyond the power of the people of the territories *to control it as other property.* He does not say the people can drive it out, but they can control it as other property. The language is different; we should consider whether the sense is different. Driving a horse out of this lot is too plain a proposition to be mistaken about; it is putting him on the other side of the fence. Or it might be a sort of exclusion of him from the lot if you were to kill him, and let the worms devour him; but neither of these things is the same as "controlling him as other property." That would be to feed him, to pamper him, to ride him, to use and abuse him, to make the most money out of him "as other property;" but, please you, what do the men who are in favor of slavery want more than this? What do they really want, other than that slavery, being in the territories, shall be controlled as other property?

If they want anything else, I do not comprehend it. I ask your attention to this—first, for the purpose of pointing out the change of ground the judge has made, and, in the second place, the importance of the change—that that change is not such as to give you gentlemen who want his popular sovereignty the power to exclude the institution or drive it out at all. I know the judge sometimes squints at the argument that in controlling it as other property, by unfriendly legislation, they may control it to death, as you might in the case of a horse, perhaps, feed him so lightly and ride him so much that he would die. But when you come to legislative control, there is something more to be attended to. I have no doubt, myself, that if the territories should undertake to control slave property as other property—that is, control it in such a way that it would be the most valuable as property, and make it bear its just proportion in the way of burdens as property—really deal with it as property—the Supreme Court of the United States will say, "God speed you, and amen."

But I undertake to give the opinion, at least, that if the territories attempt, by any direct legislation, to drive the man, with his slave, out of the territory, or to decide that his slave is free because of his being taken in there, or to tax him to such an extent that he cannot keep him there, the Supreme Court will unhesitatingly decide all such legislation unconstitutional, as long as that Supreme Court is constructed as the Dred Scott Supreme Court is. The first two things they have already decided, except that there is a little quibble among the lawyers between the words *dicta* and decision. They have already decided a negro can not be made free by territorial legislation.

What is that Dred Scott decision? Judge Douglas labors to show that it is one thing, while I think it is altogether different. It is a long opinion, but it is all embodied in this short statement: "The Constitution of the United States forbids Congress to deprive a man of his property, without due process of law; the right of property in slaves is distinctly and expressly affirmed in that Constitution; therefore if Congress shall undertake to say that a man's slave is no longer his slave, when he crosses a certain line into a territory, that is depriving him of his property without due process of law, and is unconstitutional." There is the whole Dred Scott decision. They add that if Congress can not do so itself, Congress can not confer any power to do so, and hence any effort by the Territorial Legislature to do either of these things is absolutely decided against. It is a foregone conclusion by that court.

Now, as to this indirect mode by "unfriendly legislation," all lawyers here will readily understand that such a proposition can not be tolerated for a moment, because a Legislature can not indirectly do that which it can not accomplish directly. Then I say any legislation to control this property, as property, for its benefit as property, would be hailed by this Dred Scott Supreme Court, and fully sustained; but any legislation driving slave property out, or destroying it as property, directly or indirectly, will most assuredly, by that court, be held unconstitutional.

Judge Douglas says if the Constitution carries slavery into the territories, beyond the power of the people of the territories to control it as other property, then it follows logically that every one who swears to support the Constitution of the United States, must give that support to that property which it needs. And if the Constitution carries slavery into the territories, beyond the power of the people to control it as other property, then it also carries it into the states, because the Constitution is the supreme law of the land. Now, gentlemen, if it were not for my excessive modesty I would say that I told that very thing to Judge Douglas quite a year ago. This argument is here in print, and if it were not for my modesty, as I said, I might call your attention to it. If you read it, you will find that I not only made that argument, but made it better than he has made it since.

There is, however, this difference. I say now, and said then, there is no sort of question that the Supreme Court *has* decided that it is the right of the slaveholder to take his slave and hold him in the territory; and saying this, Judge Douglas himself admits the conclusion. He says if that is so, this consequence will follow; and because this consequence would follow, his argument is, the decision can not, therefore, be that way—"that would spoil my popular sovereignty, and it can not be possible that this great principle has been squelched out in this extraordinary way. It might be, if it were not for the extraordinary consequences of spoiling my humbug."

Another feature of the judge's argument about the Dred Scott case is, an effort to show that that decision deals altogether in declarations of negatives; that the Constitution does not affirm anything as expounded by the Dred Scott decision, but it only declares a want of power—a total absence of power, in reference to the territories. It seems to be his purpose to make the whole of that decision to result in a mere negative declaration of a want of power in Congress to do anything in relation to this matter in the territories. I know the opinion of the judges states that there is a total absence of power; but that is, unfortunately, not all it states; for the judges add that the right of property in a slave is distinctly and expressly affirmed in the Constitution. It does not stop at saying that the right of property in a slave is recognized in the Constitution, is declared to exist somewhere in the Constitution, but says it is *affirmed* in the Constitution. Its language is equivalent to saying that it is embodied and so woven into that instrument that it can not be detached without breaking the Constitution itself. In a word, it is a part of the Constitution.

Douglas is singularly unfortunate in his effort to make out that decision to be altogether negative, when the express language at the vital part is that this is distinctly affirmed in the Constitution. I think myself, and I repeat it here, that this decision does not merely carry slavery into the territories, but by its logical conclusion it carries it into the states in which we live. One provision of that Constitution is, that it shall be the supreme law of the land—I do not quote the language—any Constitution or law of any state to the contrary notwithstanding. This Dred Scott decision says that the right of property in a slave is affirmed in that Constitution, which is the supreme law of the land, any State Constitution or law notwithstanding. Then I say that to destroy a thing which is distinctly affirmed and supported by the supreme law of the land, even by a State Constitution or law, is a violation of that supreme law, and there is no escape from it. In my judgment there is no avoiding that result, save that the American people shall see that Constitutions are better construed than our Constitution is construed in that decision. They must take care that it is more faithfully and truly carried out than it is there expounded.

I must hasten to a conclusion. Near the beginning of my remarks, I said that this insidious Douglas popular sovereignty is the measure that now threatens the purpose of the Republican party, to prevent slavery from being nationalized in the United States. I propose to ask your attention for a little while to some propositions in affirmance of that statement. Take it just as it stands, and apply it as a principle; extend and apply that principle elsewhere, and consider where it will lead you. I now put this proposition, that Judge Douglas's popular sovereignty applied will reopen the African slave-trade; and I will demonstrate it by any variety of ways in which you can turn the subject or look at it.

The judge says that the people of the territories have the right, by his principle, to have slaves, if they want them. Then I say that the people in Georgia have the right to buy slaves in Africa, if they want them, and I defy any man on earth to show any distinction between the two things—to show that the one is either more wicked or more unlawful; to show, on original principles, that one is better or worse than the other; or to show by the Constitution, that one differs a whit from the other. He will tell me, doubtless, that there is no Constitutional provision against people taking slaves into the new territories, and I tell him that there is equally no Constitutional provision against buying slaves in Africa. He will tell you that a people, in the exercise of popular sovereignty, ought to do as they please about that thing, and have slaves if they want them; and I tell you that the people of Georgia are as much entitled to popular sovereignty and to buy slaves in Africa, if they want them, as the people of the territory are to have slaves if they want them. I ask any man, dealing honestly with himself, to point out a distinction.

I have recently seen a letter of Judge Douglas's, in which, without stating that to be the object, he doubtless endeavors to make a distinction between the two. He says he is unalterably opposed to the repeal of the laws against the African slave-trade. And why? He then seeks to give a reason that would not apply to his popular sovereignty in the territories. What is that reason? "The abolition of the African slave-trade is a compromise of the Constitution!" I deny it. There is no truth in the proposition that the abolition of the African slave-trade is a compromise of the Constitution. No man can put his finger on anything in the Constitution, or on the line of history, which shows it. It is a mere barren assertion, made simply for the purpose of getting up a distinction between the revival of the African slave-trade and his "great principle."

At the time the Constitution of the United States was adopted, it was expected that the slave-trade would be abolished. I should assert, and insist upon that, if Judge Douglas denied it. But I know that it was equally expected that slavery would be excluded from the territories, and I can show by history, that in regard to these two things, public opinion was exactly alike, while in regard to positive action, there was more done in the ordinance of '87 to resist the spread of slavery than was ever done to abolish the foreign slave-trade. Lest I be misunderstood, I say again, that at the time of the formation of the Constitution, public expectation was that the slave-trade would be abolished, but no more so than the spread of slavery in the territories should be restrained. They stand alike, except that in the ordinance of '87 there was a mark left by public opinion, showing that it was more committed against the spread of slavery in the territories than against the foreign slave-trade.

Compromise! What word of compromise was there about it? Why, the public sense was then in favor of the abolition of the slave-trade; but there was, at the time, a very great commercial interest involved in it, and extensive capital in that branch of trade. There were, doubtless, the incipient stages of improvement in the

South in the way of farming, dependent on the slave-trade, and they made a proposition to Congress to abolish the trade after allowing it twenty years, a sufficient time for the capital and commerce engaged in it to be transferred to other channels. They made no provision that it should be abolished in twenty years; I do not doubt that they expected it would be; but they made no bargain about it. The public sentiment left no doubt in the minds of any that it would be done away. I repeat, there is nothing in the history of those times in favor of that matter being a *compromise* of the Constitution. It was the public expectation at the time, manifested in a thousand ways, that the spread of slavery should also be restricted.

Then, I say, if this principle is established, that there is no wrong in slavery, and whoever wants it has a right to have it, is a matter of dollars and cents, a sort of question as to how they shall deal with brutes, that between us and the negro here, there is no sort of question, but at the South the question is between the negro and the crocodile. That is all. It is a mere matter of policy; there is a perfect right according to interest to do just as you please—when this is done, where this doctrine prevails, the miners and sappers will have formed public opinion for the slave-trade. They will be ready for Jeff. Davis, and Stephens, and other leaders of that company, to sound the bugle for the revival of the slave-trade, for the second Dred Scott decision, for the flood of slavery to be poured over the free states, while we shall be here tied down, and helpless, and run over like sheep.

It is to be a part and parcel of this same idea, to say to men who want to adhere to the Democratic party, who have always belonged to that party, and are only looking about for some excuse to stick to it, but nevertheless hate slavery, that Douglas's popular sovereignty is as good a way as any to oppose slavery. They allow themselves to be persuaded easily in accordance with their previous dispositions, into this belief, that it is about as good a way of opposing slavery as any, and we can do that without straining our old party ties or breaking up old political associations. We can do so without being called negro-worshipers. We can do that without being subjected to the jibes and sneers that are so readily thrown out in place of argument where no argument can be found. So let us stick to this popular sovereignty—this insidious popular sovereignty.

Now let me call your attention to one thing that has really happened, which shows this gradual and steady debauching of public opinion, this course of preparation for the revival of the slave-trade, for the territorial slave code, and the new Dred Scott decision that is to carry slavery into the free states. Did you ever, five years ago, hear of anybody in the world saying that the negro had no share in the Declaration of National Independence; that it did not mean negroes at all; and when "all men" were spoken of, negroes were not included?

I am satisfied that, five years ago, that proposition was not put upon paper by any living being anywhere. I have been unable at any time, to find a man in an audience who would declare that he had ever known of anybody saying so five years ago. But, last year, there was not a Douglas popular sovereign in Illinois who did not say it. Is there one in Ohio but declares his firm belief that the Declaration of Independence did not mean negroes at all? I do not know how this is; I have not been here much; but I presume you are very much alike everywhere. Then I suppose that all now express the belief that the Declaration of Independence never did mean negroes. I call upon one of them to say that he said it five years ago.

If you think that now, and did not think it then, the next thing that strikes me is to remark that there has been a *change* wrought in you, and a very significant change it is, being no less than changing the negro, in your estimation, from the rank of a man to that of a brute. They are taking him down, and placing him, when spoken of, among reptiles and crocodiles, as Judge Douglas himself expresses it.

Is not this change wrought in your minds a very important change? Public opinion in this country is everything. In a nation like ours, this popular sovereignty and squatter sovereignty have already wrought a change in the public mind to the extent I have stated. There is no man in this crowd who can contradict it.

Now, if you are opposed to slavery honestly, as much as anybody, I ask you to note that fact, and the like of which is to follow, to be plastered on, layer after layer, until very soon you are prepared to deal with the negro everywhere as with the brute. If public sentiment has not been debauched already to this point, a new turn of the screw in that direction is all that is wanting; and this is constantly being done by the teachers of this insidious popular sovereignty. You need but one or two turns further until your minds, now ripening under these teachings, will be ready for all these things, and you will receive and support, or submit to, the slave-trade, revived with all its horrors, a slave code enforced in our territories, and a new Dred Scott decision to bring slavery up into the very heart of the free North.

This, I must say, is but carrying out those words prophetically spoken by Mr. Clay, many, many years ago—I believe more than thirty years—when he told an audience that if they repress all tendencies to liberty and ultimate emancipation, they must go back to the era of our independence and muzzle the cannon which thundered its annual joyous return on the Fourth of July; they must blow out the moral lights around us; they must penetrate the human soul, and eradicate the love of liberty; but until they did these things, and others eloquently enumerated by him, they could not repress all tendencies to ultimate emancipation.

I ask attention to the fact that in a pre-eminent degree these popular sovereigns are at this work; blowing out the moral lights around us; teaching that the negro is no longer a man, but a brute; that the Declaration has nothing to do with him; that he ranks with the crocodile and the reptile; that man, with body and soul, is a matter of dollars and cents. I suggest to this portion of the Ohio Republicans, or Democrats, if there be any present, the serious consideration of this fact, that there is now going on among you a steady process of debauching public opinion on this subject. With this, my friends, I bid you adieu.

SPEECH

DELIVERED AT PEORIA, ILLINOIS, OCTOBER 16, 1854,

IN REPLY TO JUDGE DOUGLAS.

[From the *Daily* (Springfield) *Illinois Journal*, of October 21, 1854.]

On Monday, October 16, Senator DOUGLAS, by appointment, addressed a large audience at Peoria. When he closed, he was greeted with six hearty cheers, and the band in attendance played a stirring air. The crowd then began to call for LINCOLN, who, as Judge Douglas had announced, was, by agreement, to answer him. Mr. Lincoln then took the stand, and said :

I DO not rise to speak now, if I can stipulate with the audience to meet me here at half-past six or at seven o'clock. It is now several minutes past five, and Judge Douglas has spoken over three hours. If you hear me at all, I wish you to hear me through. It will take me as long as it has taken him. That will carry us beyond eight o'clock at night. Now every one of you who can remain that long, can just as well get his supper, meet me at seven, and remain one hour or two later. The judge has already informed you that he is to have an hour to reply to me. I doubt not but you have been a little surprised to learn that I have consented to give one of his high reputation and known ability this advantage of me. Indeed, my consenting to it, though reluctant, was not wholly unselfish; for I suspected, if it were understood, that the judge was entirely done, you Democrats would leave and not hear me; but by giving him the close, I felt confident you would stay for the fun of hearing him skin me.

[The audience signified their assent to the arrangement, and adjourned to seven o'clock P. M., at which time they reassembled, and Mr. Lincoln spoke substantially as follows :]

The repeal of the Missouri Compromise, and the propriety of its restoration, constitute the subject of what I am about to say.

As I desire to present my own connected view of this subject, my remarks will not be specifically an answer to Judge Douglas ; yet as I proceed, the main points he has presented will arise, and will receive such respectful attention as I may be able to give them.

I wish further to say that I do not propose to question the patriotism, or to assail the motives of any man or class of men, but rather to confine myself strictly to the naked merits of the question.

I also wish to be no less than national in all the positions I may take, and whenever I take ground which others have thought, or may think, narrow, sectional, and dangerous to the Union, I hope to give a reason, which will appear sufficient, at least to some, why I think differently.

And as this subject is no other than part and parcel of the larger general question of domestic slavery, I wish to MAKE and to KEEP the distinction between the EXISTING institution and the EXTENSION of it, so broad and so clear, that no honest man can misunderstand me, and no dishonest one successfully misrepresent me.

In order to a clear understanding of what the Missouri Compromise is, a short history of the preceding kindred subjects will perhaps be proper.

When we established our independence, we did not own or claim the country to which this compromise applies. Indeed, strictly speaking, the Confederacy then owned no country at all; the states respectively owned the country within their limits, and some of them owned territory beyond their strict state limits. Virginia thus owned the Northwestern Territory—the country out of which the principal part of Ohio, all Indiana, all Illinois, all Michigan, and all Wisconsin, have since been formed. She also owned (perhaps within her then limits) what has since been formed into the State of Kentucky. North Carolina thus owned what is now the State of Tennessee; and South Carolina and Georgia owned, in separate parts, what are now Mississippi and Alabama. Connecticut, I think, owned the little remaining part of Ohio—being the same where they now send Giddings to Congress, and beat all creation at making cheese.

These territories, together with the states themselves, constituted all the country over which the Confederacy then claimed any sort of jurisdiction. We were then living under the Articles of Confederation, which were superseded by the Constitution several years afterward. The question of ceding these territories to the General Government was set on foot. Mr. Jefferson—the author of the Declaration of Independence, and otherwise a chief actor in the Revolution; then a delegate in Congress; afterward, twice President; who was, is, and perhaps will continue to be, the most distinguished politician of our history; a Virginian by birth and continued residence, and withal a slaveholder—conceived the idea of taking that occasion to prevent slavery ever going into the Northwestern Territory. He prevailed on the Virginia Legislature to adopt his views, and to cede the territory, making the prohibition of slavery therein a condition of the deed. Congress accepted the cession with the condition; and in the first ordinance (which the acts of Congress were then called) for the government of the territory, provided that slavery should never be permitted therein. This is the famed "Ordinance of '87," so often spoken of.

Thenceforward for sixty-one years, and until, in 1848, the last scrap of this territory came into the Union as the State of Wisconsin, all parties acted in quiet obedience to this ordinance. It is now what Jefferson foresaw and intended—the happy home of teeming millions of free, white, prosperous people, and no slave among them.

Thus, with the author of the Declaration of Independence, the policy of prohibiting slavery in new territory originated. Thus, away back of the Constitution, in the pure, fresh, free breath of the Revolution, the State of Virginia and the National Congress put that policy in practice. Thus, through more than sixty of the best years of the Republic, did that policy steadily work to its great and beneficent end. And thus, in those five states, and five millions of free, enterprising people, we have before us the rich fruits of this policy.

But *now*, new light breaks upon us. Now Congress declares this ought never to have been, and the like of it must never be again. The sacred right of self-government is grossly violated by it. We even find some men, who drew their first breath, and every other breath of

* Mr. Lincoln authorizes the correction of the error into which the report here falls, with regard to the prohibition being made a condition of the deed. It was *not* a condition.

their lives, under this very restriction, now live in dread of absolute suffocation, if they should be restricted in the "sacred right" of taking slaves to Nebraska. That *perfect* liberty they sigh for—the liberty of making slaves of other people—Jefferson never thought of; their own fathers never thought of; they never thought of themselves, a year ago. How fortunate for them they did not sooner become sensible of their great misery! O, how difficult it is to treat with respect such assaults upon all we have ever really held sacred.

But to return to history. In 1803 we purchased what was then called Louisiana, of France. It included the present states of Louisiana, Arkansas, Missouri, and Iowa; also the territory of Minnesota, and the present bone of contention, Kansas and Nebraska. Slavery already existed among the French at New Orleans; and to some extent, at St. Louis. In 1812, Louisiana came into the Union as a slave state, without controversy. In 1818 or '19, Missouri showed signs of a wish to come in with slavery. This was resisted by Northern members of Congress; and thus began the first great slavery agitation in the nation. This controversy lasted several months, and became very angry and exciting; the House of Representatives voting steadily for the prohibition of slavery in Missouri, and the Senate voting as steadily against it. Threats of breaking up the Union were freely made; and the ablest public men of the day became seriously alarmed. At length a compromise was made, in which, as in all compromises, both sides yielded something. It was a law passed on the 6th day of March, 1820, providing that Missouri might come into the Union *with* slavery, but that in all the remaining part of the territory purchased of France, which lies north of thirty-six degrees and thirty minutes north latitude, slavery should never be permitted. This provision of law *is the*

Missouri Compromise. In excluding slavery north of the line, the same language is employed as in the ordinance of '87. It directly applied to Iowa, Minnesota, and to the present bone of contention, Kansas and Nebraska. Whether there should or should not be slavery South of that line, nothing was said in the law. But Arkansas constituted the principal remaining part, south of the line; and it has since been admitted as a slave state, without serious controversy. More recently, Iowa, north of the line, came in as a free state, without controversy. Still later, Minnesota, north of the line, had a territorial organization without controversy. · Texas, principally south of the line, and west of Arkansas, though originally within the purchase from France, had, in 1819, been traded off to Spain, in our treaty for the acquisition of Florida. It had thus become a part of Mexico. Mexico revolutionized, and became independent of Spain. American citizens began settling rapidly with their slaves in the Southern part of Texas. Soon they revolutionized against Mexico, and established an independent government of their own, adopting a Constitution, with slavery, strongly resembling the Constitutions of our slave states. By still another rapid move, Texas, claiming a boundary much further west than when we parted with her in 1819, was brought back to the United States, and admitted into the Union as a slave state. Then there was little or no settlement in the northern part of Texas, a considerable portion of which lay north of the Missouri line; and in the resolutions admitting her into the Union, the Missouri restriction was expressly extended westward across her territory. This was in 1845, only nine years ago.

Thus originated the Missouri Compromise; and thus has it been respected down to 1845. And even four years later, in 1489, our distinguished senator, in a public address, held the following language in relation to it:

"The Missouri Compromise had been in practical operation for about a quarter of a century, and had received the sanction and approbation of men of all parties in every section of the Union. It had allayed all sectional jealousies and irritations, growing out of this vexed question, and harmonized and tranquilized the whole country. It had given to Henry Clay, as its prominent champion, the proud soubriquet of the 'Great Pacificator,' and by that title, and for that service, his political friends had repeatedly appealed to the people to rally under his standard, as a Presidential candidate, as the man who had exhibited the patriotism and the power to suppress an unholy and treasonable agitation, and preserve the Union. He was not aware that any man, or any party from any section of the Union, had ever urged as an objection to Mr. Clay, that he was the great champion of the Missouri Compromise. On the contrary, the effort was made by the opponents of Mr. Clay, to prove that he was not entitled to the exclusive merit of that great patriotic measure; and that the honor was equally due to others, as well as to him, for securing its adoption—that it had its origin in the hearts of all patriotic men, who desired to preserve and perpetuate the blessings of our glorious Union—an origin akin to that of the Constitution of the United States, conceived in the same spirit of fraternal affection, and calculated to remove forever the only danger, which seemed to threaten, at some distant day, to sever the social bond of Union. All the evidences of public opinion at that day seemed to indicate that this Compromise had been canonized in the hearts of the American people, as a sacred thing, which no ruthless hand would ever be reckless enough to disturb."

I do not read this extract to involve Judge Douglas in an inconsistency. If he afterward thought he had been wrong, it was right for him to change—I bring this forward merely to show the high estimate placed on the Missouri Compromise by all parties up to so late as the year 1849.

But going back a little, in point of time. Our war with Mexico broke out in 1846. When Congress was about adjourning that session, President Polk asked them to place two millions of dollars under his control, to be used by him in the recess, if found practicable and expedient, in negotiating a treaty of peace with Mexico, and acquiring some part of her territory. A bill was duly gotten up for the purpose, and was progressing swimmingly in the House of Representatives, when a member by the name of David Wilmot, a Democrat from Pennsylvania, moved as an amendment, "Provided, that in any territory thus acquired, there shall never be slavery."

This is the origin of the far-famed "Wilmot Proviso." It created a great flutter; but it stuck like wax, was voted into the bill, and the bill passed with it through the House. The Senate, however, adjourned without final action on it, and so both appropriation and proviso were lost, for the time. The war continued, and at the next session the President renewed his request for the appropriation, enlarging the amount, I think, to three millions. Again came the proviso, and defeated the measure. Congress adjourned again, and the war went on. In December, 1847, the new Congress assembled. I was in the lower House that term. The "Wilmot Proviso," or the principle of it, was constantly coming up in some shape or other, and I think I may venture to say I voted for it at least forty times, during the short term I was there. The Senate, however, held it in check, and it never became a law. In the spring of 1848 a treaty of peace was made with Mexico, by which we obtained that portion of her country which now constitutes the territories of New Mexico and Utah, and the present State of California. By this treaty the "Wilmot Proviso" was defeated, in so far as it was intended to be a condition of the acquisition of territory. Its friends, however, were still determined to find some way to restrain slavery from getting into the new country. This new acquisition lay directly west of our old purchase from France, and extended west to the Pacific Ocean—and was so situated that if the Missouri line should be extended straight west, the new country would be divided by such extended line, leaving some north and some south of it. On Judge Douglas's motion, a bill, or provision of a bill, passed the Senate to so extend the Missouri line. The Proviso men in the House, including myself, voted it down, because, by implication, it gave up the southern part to slavery, while we were bent on having it *all* free.

In the fall of 1848, the gold mines were discovered in California. This attracted people to it with unprecedented rapidity, so that on, or soon after the meeting of the new Congress in December, 1849, she already had a population of nearly a hundred thousand, had called a convention, formed a State Constitution, excluding slavery, and was knocking for admission into the Union. The Proviso men, of course, were for letting her in, but the Senate, always true to the other side, would not consent to her admission. And there California stood, kept *out* of the Union, because she would not let slavery *into* her borders. Under all the circumstances, perhaps this was not wrong. There were other points of dispute connected with the general question of slavery, which equally needed adjustment. The South clamored for a more efficient fugitive slave law. The North clamored for the abolition of a peculiar species of slave-trade in the District of Columbia, in connection with which, in view from the windows of the Capitol, a sort of negro livery-stable, where droves of negroes were collected, temporarily kept, and finally taken to Southern markets, precisely like droves of horses, had been openly maintained for fifty years. Utah and New Mexico needed territorial governments; and whether slavery should or should not be prohibited within them was another question. The indefinite western boundary of Texas was to be settled. She was a slave state, and consequently the farther west the slavery men could push her boundary, the more slave country they secured; and the farther east the slavery opponents could thrust the boundary back, the less slave ground was secured. Thus this was just as clearly a slavery question as any of the others.

These points all needed adjustment; and they were all held up, perhaps wisely, to make them help to adjust one another. The Union now, as in 1820, was thought to be in danger; and devotion to the Union rightfully inclined men to yield somewhat, in points, where nothing else could have so inclined them. A compromise was finally effected. The South got their new fugitive slave law; and the North got California (by far the best part of our acquisition from Mexico) as a free state. The South got a provision that New Mexico and Utah, *when admitted as states*, may come in *with* or *without* slavery as they may then choose; and the North got the slave-trade abolished in the District of Columbia. The North got the western boundary of Texas thrown farther back eastward than the South desired; but, in turn, they gave Texas ten millions of dollars, with which to pay her old debts. This is the Compromise of 1850.

Preceding the Presidential election of 1852, each of the great political parties, Democrats and Whigs, met in convention, and adopted resolutions indorsing the Compromise of '50, as a "finality," a final settlement, so far as these parties could make it so, of all slavery agitation. Previous to this, in 1851, the Illinois Legislature had indorsed it.

During this long period of time, Nebraska had remained substantially an uninhabited country, but now emigration to, and settlement within it began to take place. It is about one-third as large as the present United States, and its importance so long overlooked, begins to come into view. The restriction of slavery by the Missouri Compromise directly applies to it; in fact, was first made, and has since been maintained expressly for it. In 1853, a bill to give it a territorial government passed the House of Representatives, and, in the hands of Judge Douglas, failed of passing only for want of time. This bill contained no repeal of the Missouri Compromise. Indeed, when it was assailed because it did contain such repeal, Judge Douglas defended it in its existing form. On January 4th, 1854, Judge Douglas introduces a new bill to give Nebraska territorial government. He accompanies this bill with a report, in which last, he expressly recommends that the Missouri Compromise shall neither be affirmed nor repealed.

Before long the bill is so modified as to make two territories instead of one, calling the southern one Kansas.

Also, about a month after the introduction of the bill, on the judge's own motion, it is so amended as to declare the Missouri Compromise inoperative and void; and, substantially, that the people who go and settle there may establish slavery, or exclude it, as they may see fit. In this shape, the bill passed both branches of Congress and became a law.

This is the *repeal* of the Missouri Compromise. The foregoing history may not be precisely accurate in every particular; but I am sure it is sufficiently so, for all the use I shall attempt to make of it; and in it we have before us the chief material enabling us to judge correctly whether the repeal of the Missouri Compromise is right or wrong.

I think, and shall try to show, that it is wrong; wrong in its direct effect, letting slavery into Kansas and Nebraska, and wrong in its prospective principle, allowing it to spread to every other part of the wide world, where men can be found inclined to take it.

This *declared* indifference, but as I must think, covert *real* zeal for the spread of slavery, I can not but hate. I hate it because of the monstrous injustice of slavery itself. I hate it because it deprives our republican example of its just influence in the world; enables the enemies of free institutions, with plausibility to taunt us as hypocrites; causes the real friends of freedom to doubt our sincerity; and especially because it forces so many really good men among ourselves into an open war with the very fundamental principles of civil liberty, criticising the Declaration of Independence, and insisting that there is no right principle of action but *self-interest.*

Before proceeding, let me say I think I have no prejudice against the Southern people. They are just what we would be in their situation. If slavery did not now exist among them, they would not introduce it. If it did now exist among us, we should not instantly give it up. This I believe of the masses North and South. Doubtless there are individuals, on both sides, who would not hold slaves under any circumstances, and others who would gladly introduce slavery anew, if it were out of existence. We know that some Southern men do free their slaves, go north, and become tip-top abolitionists; while some Northern ones go south, and become most cruel slave-masters.

When Southern people tell us they are no more responsible for the origin of slavery than we are, I acknowledge the fact. When it is said that the institution exists, and that it is very difficult to get rid of it in any satisfactory way, I can understand and appreciate the saying. I surely will not blame them for not doing what I should not know how to do myself. If all earthly power were given me, I should not know what to do, as to the existing institution. My first impulse would be to free all the slaves, and send them to Liberia—to their own native land. But a moment's reflection would convince me, that whatever of high hope (as I think there is) there may be in this in the long run, its sudden execution is impossible. If they were all landed there in a day, they would all perish in the next ten days, and there are not surplus shipping and surplus money enough to carry them there in many times ten days. What then? Free them all, and keep them among us as underlings? Is it quite certain that this betters their condition? I think I would not hold one in slavery, at any rate; yet the point is not clear enough for me to denounce people upon. What next? Free them, and make them politically and socially our equals? My own feelings will not admit of this; and if mine would, we well know that those of the great mass of white people will not. Whether this feeling accords with justice and sound judgment, is not the sole question, if indeed, it is any part of it. A universal feeling, whether well or ill-founded, can not be safely disregarded. We can not, then, make them equals. It does seem to me that systems of gradual emancipation might be adopted; but for their tardiness in this, I will not undertake to judge our brethren of the South.

When they remind us of their constitutional rights, I acknowledge them, not grudgingly, but fully and fairly; and I would give them any legislation for the reclaiming of their fugitives, which should not in its stringency be more likely to carry a free man into slavery, than our ordinary criminal laws are to hang an innocent one.

But all this, to my judgment, furnishes no more excuse for permitting slavery to go into our own free territory, than it would for reviving the African slave-trade by law. The law which forbids the bringing of slaves *from* Africa, and that which has so long forbidden the taking of them *into* Nebraska, can hardly be distinguished on any moral principle; and the repeal of the former could find quite as plausible excuses as that of the latter.

The arguments by which the repeal of the Missouri Compromise is sought to be justified, are these:

First. That the Nebraska country needed a territorial government.

Second. That in various ways, the public had repudiated that Compromise, and demanded the repeal, and therefore should not now complain of it.

And, lastly. That the repeal establishes a principle which is intrinsically right.

I will attempt an answer to each of them in its turn.

First, then. If that country was in need of a territorial organization, could it not have had it as well without as with the repeal? Iowa and Minnesota, to both of which the Missouri restriction applied, had, without its repeal, each in succession, territorial organizations.

And even the year before, a bill for Nebraska itself, was within an ace of passing, without the repealing clause; and this in the hands of the same men who are now the champions of repeal. Why no necessity then for the repeal? But still later, when this very bill was first brought in, it contained no repeal. But, say they, because the people had demanded, or rather commanded the repeal, the repeal was to accompany the organization, whenever that should occur.

Now, I deny that the public ever demanded any such thing—ever repudiated the Missouri Compromise—ever commanded its repeal. I deny it, and call for the proof. It is not contended, I believe, that any such command has ever been given in express terms. It is only said that it was done *in principle*. The support of the Wilmot Proviso is the first fact mentioned, to prove that the Missouri restriction was repudiated *in principle*, and the second is, the refusal to extend the Missouri line over the country acquired from Mexico. These are near enough alike to be treated together. The one was to exclude the chances of slavery from the whole new acquisition by the lump, and the other was to reject a division of it, by which one half was to be given up to those chances. Now, whether this was a repudiation of the Missouri line, *in principle*, depends upon whether the Missouri law contained any *principle* requiring the line to be extended over the country acquired from Mexico. I contend it did not. I insist that it contained no general principle, but that it was, in every sense, specific. That its terms limit it to the country purchased from France, is undenied and undeniable. It could have no principle beyond the intention of those who made it. They did not intend to extend the line to country which they did not own. If they intended to extend it, in the event of acquiring additional territory, why did they not say so? It was just as easy to say, that "in all the country west of the Mississippi which we now own *or may hereafter acquire*, there shall never be slavery," as to say what they did say; and they would have said it, if they had meant it. An intention to extend the law is not only not mentioned in the law, but is not mentioned in any cotemporaneous history. Both the law itself and the history of the times are a blank as to any *principle* of extension; and by neither the known rules for construing statutes and contracts, nor by common sense, can any such *principle* be inferred.

Another fact showing the specific character of the Missouri law—showing that it intended no more than it expressed; showing that the line was not intended as a universal dividing line between free and slave territory, present and prospective, north of which slavery could never go—is the fact that, by that very law, Missouri came in as a slave state, *north* of the line. If that law contained any prospective *principle*, the whole law must be looked to in order to ascertain what the *principle* was. And by this rule, the South could fairly contend that inasmuch as they got one slave state north of the line at the inception of the law, they have the right to have another given them *north* of it occasionally, now and then, in the indefinite westward extension of the line. This demonstrates the absurdity of attempting to deduce a prospective *principle* from the Missouri Compromise line.

When we voted for the Wilmot Proviso, we were voting to keep slavery out of the whole Mexican acquisition; and little did we think we were thereby voting to let it *into* Nebraska, lying several hundred miles distant.

When we voted against extending the Missouri line, little did we think we were voting to destroy the old line, then of near thirty years' standing.

To argue that we thus repudiated the Missouri Compromise is no less absurd than it would be to argue that because we have so far forborne to acquire Cuba, we have thereby, *in principle*, repudiated our former acquisitions, and determined to throw them out of the Union. No less absurd than it would be to say that, because I may have refused to build an addition to my house, I thereby have decided to destroy the existing house! And if I catch you setting fire to my house, you will turn upon me, and say I INSTRUCTED you to do it!

The most conclusive argument, however, that, while voting for the Wilmot Proviso, and while voting against the EXTENSION of the Missouri line, we never thought of disturbing the original Missouri Compromise, is found in the fact that there was then, and still is, an unorganized tract of fine country, nearly as large as the State of Missouri, lying immediately West of Arkansas, and South of the Missouri Compromise line; and that we never attempted to prohibit slavery as to it. I wish particular attention to this. It adjoins the original Missouri Compromise line by its Northern boundary; and consequently is part of the country into which, by implication, slavery was permitted to go by that Compromise. There it has lain open ever since, and there it still lies; and yet no effort has been made at any time to wrest it from the South. In all our struggles to prohibit slavery within our Mexican acquisitions, we never so much as lifted a finger to prohibit it as to this tract. Is not this entirely conclusive that, at all times, we have held the Missouri Compromise as a sacred thing, even when against ourselves as well as when for us?

Senator Douglas sometimes says the Missouri line itself, was, *in principle*, only an extension of the line of the ordinance of '87 — that is to say, an extension of the Ohio river. I think this is weak enough on its face. I will remark, however, that, as a glance at the map will show, the Missouri line is a long way farther South than the Ohio, and that if our Senator, in proposing his extension, had stuck to the *principle* of jogging southward, perhaps it might not have been voted down so readily.

But next it is said that the Compromises of '50, and the ratification of them by both political parties in '52, established a *new principle*, which required the repeal of the Missouri Compromise. This, again, I deny. I deny it, and demand the proof. I have already stated fully what the Compromises of '50 are. The particular part of those measures from which the virtual repeal of the Missouri Compromise is sought to be inferred, (for it is admitted they contain nothing about it, in express terms,) is the provision in the Utah and New Mexico laws, which permits them, when they seek admission into the Union as states, to come in with or without slavery, as they shall then see fit. Now I insist this provision was made for Utah and New Mexico, and for no other place whatever. It had no more direct reference to Nebraska than it had to the territories of the moon. But, say they, it had reference to Nebraska, *in principle.* Let us see. The North consented to this provision, not because they considered it right in itself, but because they were compensated—paid for it.

They, at the same time, got California into the Union as a free state. This was far the best part of all they had struggled for by the Wilmot Proviso. They also got the area of slavery somewhat narrowed in the settlement of the boundary of Texas. Also, they got the slave-trade abolished in the District of Columbia.

For all these desirable objects, the North could afford to yield something; and they did yield to the South the Utah and New Mexico provision. I do not mean that the whole North, or even a majority, yielded, when the law passed; but enough yielded, when added to the vote of the South, to carry the measure. Now can it be pretended that the *principle* of this arrangement requires us to permit the same provision to be applied to Nebraska, *without any equivalent at all?* Give us another free state; press the boundary of Texas still further back; give us another step toward the destruction of slavery in the District, and you present us a similar case. But ask us not to repeat, for nothing, what you paid for in the first instance. If you wish the thing again, pay again. That is the *principle* of the Compromises of '50, if indeed they had any principles beyond their specific terms—it was the system of equivalents.

Again, if Congress, at that time, intended that all future territories should, when admitted as states, come in with or without slavery, at their own option, why did it not say so? With such an universal provision, all know the bills could not have passed. Did they, then—could they—establish a *principle* contrary to their own intention? Still further; if they intended to establish the principle that wherever Congress had control, it should be left to the people to do as they thought fit with slavery, why did they not authorize the people of the District of Columbia, at their option, to abolish slavery within their limits?

I personally know that this has not been left undone because it was unthought of. It was frequently spoken of by members of Congress, and by citizens of Washington, six years ago; and I heard no one express a doubt that a system of gradual emancipation, with compensation to owners, would meet the approbation of a large majority of the white people of the District. But without the action of Congress they could say nothing; and Congress said "No." In the measures of 1850, Congress had the subject of slavery in the District expressly on hand. If they were then establishing the *principle* of allowing the people to do as they please with slavery, why did they not apply the *principle* to that people?

Again, it is claimed that by the Resolutions of the Illinois Legislature, passed in 1851, the repeal of the Missouri Compromise was demanded. This I deny also. Whatever may be worked out by a criticism of the language of those resolutions, the people have never understood them as being any more than an indorsement of the Compromises of 1850; and a release of our Senators from voting for the Wilmot Proviso. The whole people are living witnesses, that this only was their view. Finally, it is asked, "If we did not mean to apply the Utah and New Mexico provision to all future territories, what did we mean when we, in 1852, indorsed the Compromises of 1850?"

For myself, I can answer this question most easily. I meant not to ask a repeal or modification of the fugitive slave law. I meant not to ask for the abolition of slavery in the District of Columbia. I meant not to resist the admission of Utah and New Mexico, even should they ask to come in as slave states. I meant nothing about additional territories, because, as I understood, we then had no territory whose character as to slavery was not already settled. As to Nebraska, I regarded its character as being fixed, by the Missouri Compromise, for thirty years—as unalterably fixed as that of my own home in Illinois. As to new acquisitions, I said, "Sufficient unto the day is the evil thereof." When we make new acquisitions, we will, as heretofore, try to manage them somehow. That is my answer; that is what I meant and said; and I appeal to the people to say each for himself, whether that was not also the universal meaning of the free states.

And now, in turn, let me ask a few questions. If, by any or all these matters, the repeal of the Missouri Compromise was commanded, why was not the command sooner obeyed? Why was the repeal omitted in the Nebraska bill of 1853? Why was it omitted in the original bill of 1854? Why, in the accompanying report, was such a repeal characterized as a departure from the course pursued in 1850? And its continued omission recommended?

I am aware Judge Douglas now argues that the subsequent express repeal is no substantial alteration of the bill. This argument seems wonderful to me. It is as if one should argue that white and black are not different. He admits, however, that there is a literal change in the bill, and that he made the change in deference to other Senators, who would not support the bill without. This proves that those other Senators thought the change a substantial one, and that the judge thought their opinions worth deferring to. His own opinions, therefore, seem not to rest on a very firm basis, even in his own mind; and I suppose the world believes, and will continue to believe, that precisely on the substance of that change this whole agitation has arisen.

I conclude, then, that the public never demanded the repeal of the Missouri Compromise.

I now come to consider whether the repeal, with its avowed principles, is intrinsically right. I insist that it is not. Take the particular case. A controversy had arisen between the advocates and opponents of slavery, in relation to its establishment within the country we had purchased of France. The southern, and then best part of the purchase, was already in as a slave state. The controversy was settled by also letting Missouri in as a slave state; but with the agreement that within all the remaining part of the purchase, north of a certain line, there should never be slavery. As to what was to be done with the remaining part south of the line nothing was said; but perhaps the fair implication was, that it should come in with slavery, if it should so choose. The southern part, except a portion heretofore mentioned, afterward did come in with slavery, as the State of Arkansas. All these many years, since 1820, the northern part had remained a wilderness. At length, settlements began in it also. In due course, Iowa came in as a free state, and Minnesota was given a territorial government, without removing the slavery restriction. Finally, the sole remaining part, north of the line—Kansas and Nebraska—was to be organized; and it is proposed, and carried, to blot out the old dividing line of thirty-four years' standing, and to open the whole of that country to the introduction of slavery. Now this, to my mind, is manifestly unjust. After an angry and dangerous controversy, the parties made friends by dividing the bone of contention. The one party first appropriates her own share, beyond all power to be disturbed in the possession of it, and then seizes the share of the other party. It is as if two starving men had divided their only loaf; the one had hastily swallowed his half, and then grabbed the other's half just as he was putting it to his mouth.

Let me here drop the main argument, to notice what

I consider rather an inferior matter. It is argued that slavery will not go to Kansas and Nebraska, *in any event.* This is a *palliation*—a *lullaby.* I have some hope that it will not; but let us not be too confident. As to climate, a glance at the map shows that there are five slave states—Delaware, Maryland, Virginia, Kentucky, and Missouri, and also the District of Columbia, all north of the Missouri Compromise line. The census returns of 1850, show that, within these, there are eight hundred and sixty-seven thousand two hundred and seventy-six slaves—being more than one-fourth of all the slaves in the nation.

It is not climate, then, that will keep slavery out of these territories. Is there anything in the peculiar nature of the country? Missouri adjoins these territories by her entire western boundary, and slavery is already within every one of her western counties. I have even heard it said that there are more slaves in proportion to whites in the northwestern county of Missouri, than within any other county in the state. Slavery pressed entirely up to the old western boundary of the state, and when, rather recently, a part of that boundary at the northwest was moved out a little farther west, slavery followed on quite up to the new line. Now when the restriction is removed, what is to prevent it from going still farther? Climate will not—no peculiarity of the country will—nothing in *nature* will. Will the disposition of the people prevent it? Those nearest the scene are all in favor of the extension. The Yankees, who are opposed to it, may be most numerous; but, in military phrase, the battle-field is too far from their base of operations.

But it is said, there now is no law in Nebraska on the subject of slavery, and that, in such case, taking a slave there operates his freedom. That *is* good book law, but is not the rule of actual practice. Wherever slavery is it has been first introduced without law. The oldest laws we find concerning it, are not laws introducing it, but *regulating* it as an already existing thing. A white man takes his slave to Nebraska now. Who will inform the negro that he is free? Who will take him before court to test the question of his freedom? In ignorance of his legal emancipation, he is kept chopping, splitting, and plowing. Others are brought and move on in the same track. At last, if ever the time for voting comes on the question of slavery, the institution already, in fact, exists in the country, and can not well be removed. The fact of its presence, and the difficulty of its removal, will carry the vote in its favor. Keep it out until a vote is taken, and a vote in favor of it can not be got in any population of forty thousand on earth, who have been drawn together by the ordinary motives of emigration and settlement. To get slaves into the territory simultaneously with the whites, in the incipient stages of settlement, is the precise stake played for, and won, in this Nebraska measure.

The question is asked us: "If slaves will go in, notwithstanding the general principle of law liberates them, why would they not equally go in against positive statute law—go in, even if the Missouri restriction were maintained!" I answer, because it takes a much bolder man to venture in with his property in the latter case than in the former; because the positive Congressional enactment is known to, and respected by all, or nearly all; whereas the negative principle that *no* law is free law, is not much known except among lawyers. We have some experience of this practical difference. In spite of the ordinance of '87, a few negroes were brought into Illinois, and held in a state of *quasi* slavery, not enough, however, to carry a vote of the people in favor of the institution, when they came to form a Constitution. But, in the adjoining Missouri country, where there was no ordinance of '87—was no restriction—they were carried ten times, nay, a hundred times, as fast, and actually made a slave state. This is fact—naked fact.

Another *lullaby* argument is, that taking slaves to new countries does not increase their number—does not make any one slave who otherwise would be free. There is some truth in this, and I am glad of it; but it is not *wholly* true. The African slave-trade is not yet effectually suppressed; and if we make a reasonable deduction for the white people among us who are foreigners, and the descendants of foreigners, arriving here since 1808, we shall find the increase of the black population outrunning that of the white, to an extent unaccountable, except by supposing that some of them, too, have been coming from Africa. If this be so, the opening of new countries to the institution increases the demand for, and augments the price of slaves, and so does, in fact, make slaves of freemen, by causing them to be brought from Africa and sold into bondage.

But however this may be, we know the opening of new countries to slavery tends to the perpetuation of the institution, and so does keep men in slavery who would otherwise be free. This result we do not FEEL like favoring, and we are under no legal obligation to suppress our feelings in this respect.

Equal justice to the South, it is said, requires us to consent to the extension of slavery to new countries. That is to say, inasmuch as you do not object to my takking my hog to Nebraska, therefore I must not object to you taking your slave. Now, I admit that this is perfectly logical, if there is no difference between hogs and negroes. But while you thus require me to deny the humanity of the negro, I wish to ask whether you of the South, yourselves, have ever been willing to do as much? It is kindly provided, that of all those who come into the world, only a small percentage are natural tyrants. That percentage is no larger in the slave states than in the free. The great majority South, as well as North, have human sympathies, of which they can no more divest themselves, than they can of their sensibility to physical pain. These sympathies in the bosoms of the Southern people manifest, in many ways, their sense of the wrong of slavery, and their consciousness that, after all, there is humanity in the negro. If they deny this, let me address them a few plain questions. In 1820, you joined the North, almost unanimously, in declaring the African slave-trade piracy, and in annexing to it the punishment of death. Why did you do this? If you did not feel that it was wrong, why did you join in providing that men should be hung for it? The practice was no more than bringing wild negroes from Africa to sell to such as would buy them. But you never thought of hanging men for catching and selling wild horses, wild buffaloes, or wild bears.

Again: you have among you a sneaking individual of the class of native tyrants, known as the "SLAVE-DEALER." He watches your necessities, and crawls up to buy your slave, at a speculating price. If you can not help it, you sell to him; but if you can help it, you drive him from your door. You despise him utterly. You do not recognize him as a friend, or even as an honest man. Your children must not play with his; they may rollick freely with the little negroes, but not with the "slave-dealer's" children. If you are obliged to deal with him, you try to get through the job, without so much as touching him. It is common with you to join hands with the men you meet; but with the slave-dealer you avoid the ceremony--instinctively shrinking from the snaky contact. If he grows rich and retires from business, you still remember him, and still keep up the ban of non-intercourse upon him and his family. Now, why is this? You do not so treat the man who deals in corn, cattle, or tobacco.

And yet again: There are in the United States and territories, including the District of Columbia, 433,643 free blacks. At $500 per head, they are worth over two hundred millions of dollars. How comes this vast amount of property to be running about, without owners? We do not see free horses, or free cattle, running at large. How is this? All these free blacks are the descendants of slaves, or have been slaves themselves; and they would be slaves now, but for SOMETHING which has operated on their white owners, inducing them at vast pecuniary sacrifices to liberate them. What is that SOMETHING? Is there any mistaking it? In all these cases, it is your sense of justice and human sympathy, continually telling you that the poor negro has some natural right to himself—that those who deny it, and make mere merchandise of him, deserve kickings, contempt, and death.

And now, why will you ask us to deny the humanity of the slave, and estimate him as only the equal of the hog? Why ask us to do what you will not do yourselves? Why ask us to do for *nothing* what two hundred millions of dollars could not induce you to do?

But one great argument in the support of the repeal of the Missouri Compromise is still to come. That argument is "the sacred right of self-government." It seems our distinguished Senator has found great difficulty in getting his antagonists, even in the Senate, to meet him fairly on this argument. Some poet has said:

> "Fools rush in where angels fear to tread."

At the hazard of being thought one of the fools of this quotation, I meet that argument—I rush in—I take that bull by the horns.

I trust I understand and truly estimate the right of self-government. My faith in the proposition that each man should do precisely as he pleases with all which is exclusively his own, lies at the foundation of the sense of justice there is in me. I extend the principle to communities of men, as well as to individuals. I so extend it, because it is politically wise, as well as naturally just; politically wise in saving us from broils about matters which do not concern us. Here, or at Washington, I would not trouble myself with the oyster laws of Virginia, or the cranberry laws of Indiana.

The doctrine of self-government is right—absolutely and eternally right—but it has no just application as here attempted. Or perhaps I should rather say that whether it has such just application, depends upon whether a negro *is not* or *is* a man. If he is *not* a man, in that case he who *is* a man, may, as a matter of self-government, do just what he pleases with him. But if the negro *is* a man, is it not to that extent a total destruction of self-government to say that he too shall not govern *himself?* When the white man governs himself, that is self-government; but when he governs himself, and also governs *another* man, that is *more* than self-government—that is despotism. If the negro is a *man*, why, then, my ancient faith teaches me that "all men are created equal;" and that there can be no moral right in connection with one man's making a slave of another.

Judge Douglas frequently, with bitter irony and sarcasm, paraphrases our argument by saying: "The white people of Nebraska are good enough to govern themselves, *but they are not good enough to govern a few miserable negroes!*"

Well, I doubt not that the people of Nebraska are, and will continue to be as good as the average of people elsewhere. I do not say the contrary. What I do say is, that no man is good enough to govern another man, *without that other's consent.* I say this is the leading principle, the sheet-anchor of American Republicanism. Our Declaration of Independence says:

> "We hold these truths to be self-evident: That all men are created equal; that they are endowed by their Creator with certain inalienable rights; that among these are life, liberty, and the pursuit of happiness. That to secure these rights, governments are instituted among men, DERIVING THEIR JUST POWERS FROM THE CONSENT OF THE GOVERNED."

I have quoted so much at this time merely to show that, according to our ancient faith, the just powers of governments are derived from the consent of the governed. Now, the relation of master and slave is *pro tanto* a total violation of their principle. The master not only governs the slave without his consent, but he governs him by a set of rules altogether different from those which he prescribes for himself. Allow ALL the governed an equal voice in the government; and that, and that only, is self-government.

Let it not be said I am contending for the establishment of political and social equality between the whites and blacks. I have already said the contrary. I am not now combating the argument of NECESSITY, arising from the fact that the blacks are already among us; but I am combating what is set up as MORAL argument for allowing them to be taken where they have never yet been—arguing against the extension of a bad thing, which, where it already exists, we must of necessity manage as we best can.

In support of his application of the doctrine of self-government, Senator Douglas has sought to bring to his aid the opinions and examples of our Revolutionary fathers. I am glad he has done this. I love the sentiments of those old-time men, and shall be most happy to abide by their opinions. He shows us that when it was in contemplation for the colonies to break off from Great Britain, and set up a new government for themselves, several of the states instructed their delegates to go for the measure, PROVIDED EACH STATE SHOULD BE ALLOWED TO REGULATE ITS DOMESTIC CONCERNS IN ITS OWN WAY. I do not quote; but this in substance. This was right. I see nothing objectionable in it. I also think it probable that it had some reference to the existence of slavery among them. I will not deny that it had. But had it any reference to the carrying of slavery into NEW COUNTRIES? That is the question, and we will let the fathers themselves answer it.

This same generation of men, and mostly the same individuals of the generation who declared this principle, who declared independence, who fought the war of the Revolution through, who afterward made the Constitution under which we still live—these same men passed the ordinance of '87, declaring that slavery should never go to the Northwest Territory. I have no doubt Judge Douglas thinks they were very inconsistent in this. It is a question of discrimination between them and him.

But there is not an inch of ground left for his claiming that their opinions, their example, their authority, are on his side in this controversy.

Again, is not Nebraska, while a territory, a part of us? Do we not own the country? And if we surrender the control of it, do we not surrender the right of self-government? It is part of ourselves? If you say we shall not control it, because it is ONLY part, the same is true of every other part; and when all the parts are gone, what has become of the whole? What is then left of us? What use for the General Government, when there is nothing left for it to govern?

But you say this question should be left to the people of Nebraska, because they are more particularly interested. If this be the rule, you must leave it to each individual to say for himself whether he will have slaves. What better moral right have thirty-one citizens of Nebraska to say, that the thirty-second shall not hold slaves, than the people of the thirty-one states have to say that slavery shall not go into the thirty-second state at all?

But if it is a sacred right for the people of Nebraska to take and hold slaves there, it is equally their sacred right to buy them where they can buy them cheapest; and that, undoubtedly, will be on the coast of Africa, provided you will consent not to hang them for going there to buy them. You must remove this restriction, too, from the sacred right of self-government. I am aware, you say, that taking slaves from the States to Nebraska, does not make slaves of freemen; but the African slave-trader can say just as much. He does not catch free negroes and bring them here. He finds them already slaves in the hands of their black captors, and he honestly buys them at the rate of about a red cotton handkerchief a head. This is very cheap and it is a great abridgment of the sacred right of self-government to hang men for engaging in this profitable trade.

Another important objection to this application of the right of self-government, is, that it enables the first FEW to deprive the succeeding MANY of a free exercise of the right of self-government. The first few may get slavery IN, and the subsequent many can not easily get it OUT. How common is the remark now in the slave states: "If we were only clear of our slaves, how much better it would be for us." They are actually deprived of the privilege of governing themselves as they would, by the action of a very few in the beginning. The same thing was true of the whole nation at the time our Constitution was formed.

Whether slavery shall go into Nebraska, or other new territories, is not a matter of exclusive concern to the people who may go there. The whole nation is interested that the best use shall be made of these territories. We want them for the homes of free white people. This they can not be, to any considerable extent, if slavery shall be planted within them. Slave states are places for poor white people to remove FROM; not to remove TO. New free states are the places for poor people to go to, and better their condition. For this use the nation needs these territories.

Still further; there are constitutional relations between the slave and free states, which are degrading to the latter. We are under legal obligations to catch and return their runaway slaves to them, a sort of dirty, disagreeable job which I believe, as a general rule, the slaveholders will not perform for one another. Then again, in the control of the government—the management of the partnership affairs—they have greatly the advantage of us. By the Constitution each state has two Senators, each has a number of Representatives, in proportion to the number of its people, and each has a number of Presidential electors, equal to the whole number of its Senators and Representatives together. But in ascertaining the number of the people for this purpose, five slaves are counted as being equal to three whites. The slaves do not vote; they are only counted and so used, as to swell the influence of the white people's votes. The practical effect of this is more aptly shown by a comparison of the states of South Carolina and Maine. South Carolina has six Representatives, and so has Maine; South Carolina has eight Presidential electors, and so has Maine. This is precise equality so far; and of course they are equal in Senators, each having two. Thus in the control of the government, the two states are equals precisely. But how are they in the number of their white people? Maine has 581,813, while South Carolina has 274,567; Maine has twice as many as South Carolina, and 32,679 over. Thus, each white man in South Carolina is more than the double of any man in Maine. This is all because South Carolina, besides her free people, has 384,984 slaves. The South Carolinian has precisely the same advantage over the white man in every other free state, as well as in Maine. He is more than the double of any one of us in this crowd. The same advantage, but not to the same extent, is held by all the citizens of the slave states, over those of the free; and it is an absolute truth without an exception, that there is no voter in any slave state, but who has more legal power in the government than any voter in any free state. There is no instance of exact equality; and the disadvantage is against us the whole chapter through. This principle in the aggregate, gives the slave states in the present Congress, twenty additional representatives, being seven more than the whole majority by which they passed the Nebraska bill.

Now all this is manifestly unfair; yet I do not mention it to complain of it, in so far as it is already settled. It is in the Constitution, and I do not for that cause, or any other cause, propose to destroy, or alter, or disregard the Constitution. I stand to it, fairly, fully, and firmly.

But when I am told I must leave it altogether to OTHER PEOPLE to say whether new partners are to be bred up and brought into the firm, on the same degrading terms against me, I respectfully demur. I insist that whether I shall be a whole man, or only the half of one, in comparison with others, is a question in which I am somewhat concerned; and one which no other man can have a sacred right of deciding for me. If I am wrong in this—if it really be a sacred right of self-government, in the man who shall go to Nebraska, to decide whether he will be the EQUAL of me or the DOUBLE of me, then, after he shall have exercised that right, and thereby shall have reduced me to a still smaller fraction of a man than I already am, I should like for some gentleman, deeply skilled in the mysteries of sacred rights, to provide himself with a microscope, and peep about, and find out, if he can, what has become of my sacred rights! They will surely be too small for detection with the naked eye.

Finally, I insist that if there is ANYTHING which it is the duty of the WHOLE PEOPLE to never intrust to any hands but their own, that thing is the preservation and perpetuity of their own liberties and institutions. And if they shall think, as I do, that the extension of slavery endangers them, more than any or all other causes, how recreant to themselves if they submit the question, and with it the fate of their country, to a mere handful of men, bent only on temporary self-interest. If this question of slavery extension were an insignificant one—one having no power to do harm—it might be shuffled aside in this way; but being, as it is, the great Behemoth of danger, shall the strong gripe of the nation be loosened upon him, to intrust him to the hands of such feeble keepers?

I have done with this mighty argument of self-government. Go, sacred thing! Go, in peace.

But Nebraska is urged as a great Union-saving measure. Well, I, too, go for saving the Union. Much as I hate slavery, I would consent to the extension of it rather than see the Union dissolved, just as I would consent to any GREAT evil to avoid a GREATER one. But when I go to Union-saving, I must believe, at least, that the means I employ have some adaptation to the end. To my mind, Nebraska has no such adaptation.

"It hath no relish of salvation in it."

It is an aggravation, rather, of the only one thing which ever endangers the Union. When it came upon us, all was peace and quiet. The nation was looking to the forming of new bonds of union, and a long course of peace and prosperity seemed to lie before us. In the whole range of possibility, there scarcely appears to me to have been anything out of which the slavery agitation could have been revived, except the very project of repealing the Missouri Compromise. Every inch of territory we owned, already had a definite settlement of the slavery question, by which all parties were pledged to abide. Indeed, there was no uninhabited country on the continent which we could acquire; if we except some extreme northern regions which are wholly out of the question.

In this state of affairs, the Genius of Discord himself could scarcely have invented a way of again getting us by the ears, but by turning back, and destroying the peace measures of the past. The councils of that Genius seem to have prevailed; the Missouri Compromise was repealed; and here we are, in the midst of a new slavery agitation, such, I think, as we have never seen before. Who is responsible for this? Is it those who resist the measure; or those who, causelessly, brought it forward, and pressed it through, having reason to know, and, in fact, knowing it must and would be so resisted? It could not but be expected by its author, that it would be looked upon as a measure for the extension of slavery, aggravated by a gross breach of faith.

Argue as you will, and long as you will, this is the naked FRONT and ASPECT of the measure. And in this aspect, it could not but produce agitation. Slavery is founded in the selfishness of man's nature—opposition to it, in his love of justice. These principles are an eternal antagonism; and when brought into collision so fiercely as slavery extension brings them, shocks, and throes, and convulsions must ceaselessly follow. Repeal the Missouri Compromise—repeal all compromise—repeal the Declaration of Independence—repeal all past history—you still can not repeal human nature. It still will be the abundance of man's heart that slavery extension is wrong; and out of the abundance of his heart his mouth will continue to speak.

The structure, too, of the Nebraska bill is very peculiar. The people are to decide the question of slavery for themselves; but WHEN they are to decide, or HOW they are to decide, or whether when the question is once decided, it is to remain so, or is to be subject to an indefinite succession of new trials, the law does not say. Is it to be decided by the first dozen settlers who arrive there? or is it to await the arrival of a hundred? Is it to be decided by a vote of the people? or a vote of the Legislature? or, indeed, by a vote of any sort? To these questions, the law gives no answer. There is a mystery about this; for when a member proposed to give the Legislature express authority to exclude slavery, it was hooted down by the friends of the bill. This fact is worth remembering. Some Yankees, in the East, are sending emigrants to Nebraska, to exclude slavery from it; and, so far as I can judge, they expect the question to be decided by voting in some way or other. But the Missourians are awake too. They are within a stone's throw of the contested ground. They hold meetings, and pass resolutions, in which not the slightest allusion to voting is made. They resolve that slavery already exists in the territory; that more shall go there; that they, remaining in Missouri, will protect it; and that Abolitionists shall be hung or driven away. Through all this, bowie-knives and six-shooters are seen plainly enough; but never a glimpse of the ballot-box.

And, really, what is to be the result of this? Each party WITHIN, having numerous and determined backers WITHOUT, is it not probable that the contest will come to blows and bloodshed? Could there be a more apt invention to bring about collision and violence, on the slavery question, than this Nebraska project is? I do not charge or believe that such was intended by Congress; but if they had literally formed a ring, and placed champions within it to fight out the controversy, the fight could be no more likely to come off than it is. And if this fight should begin, is it likely to take a very peaceful Union-saving turn? Will not the first drop of blood, so shed, be the real knell of the Union?

The Missouri Compromise ought to be restored. For the sake of the Union, it ought to be restored. We ought to elect a House of Representatives which will vote its restoration. If, by any means, we omit to do this, what follows? Slavery may or may not be established in Nebraska. But whether it be or not, we shall have repudiated—discarded from the councils of the nation—the SPIRIT of COMPROMISE; for who, after this, will ever trust in a national compromise? The spirit of mutual concession—that spirit which first gave us the Constitution, and which has thrice saved the Union—we shall have strangled and cast from us forever. And what shall we have in lieu of it? The South, flushed with triumph and tempted to excesses; the North, betrayed as they believe, brooding on wrong and burning for revenge. One side will provoke, the other resent. The one will taunt, the other defy; one aggresses, the other retaliates. Already a few in the North defy all Constitutional restraints, resist the execution of the fugitive slave law, and even menace the institution of slavery in the states where it exists. Already a few in the South claim the Constitutional right to take to and hold slaves in the free states—demand the revival of the slave-trade—and demand a treaty with Great Britain, by which fugitive slaves may be reclaimed from Canada. As yet they are but few on either side. It is a grave question for the lovers of the Union, whether the final destruction of the Missouri Compromise, and with it the spirit of all compromise, will or will not embolden and embitter each of these, and fatally increases the number of both.

But restore the compromise, and what then? We thereby restore the national faith, the national confidence, the national feeling of brotherhood. We thereby reinstate the spirit of concession and compromise—that spirit which has never failed us in past perils, and which may be safely trusted for all the future. The South ought to join in doing this. The peace of the nation is as dear to them as to us. In memories of the past and hopes of the future, they share as largely as we. It would be, on their part, a great act—great in its spirit, and great in its effect. It would be worth to the nation a hundred years' purchase of peace and prosperity. And what of sacrifice would they make? They only surrender to us what they gave us for a consideration long, long ago; what they have not now asked for, struggled, or cared for; what has been thrust upon them, not less to their own astonishment than to ours.

But it is said we can not restore it; that though we elect every member of the lower House, the Senate is still against us. It is quite true that, of the Senators who passed the Nebraska bill, a majority of the whole Senate will retain their seats in spite of the elections of this and the next year. But if, at these elections, their several constituencies shall clearly express their will against Nebraska, will these Senators disregard their will? Will they neither obey, nor make room for those who will?

But even if we fail to technically restore the compromise, it is still a great point to carry a popular vote in favor of the restoration. The moral weight of such a vote can not be estimated too highly. The authors of Nebraska are not at all satisfied with the destruction of the compromise—an indorsement of this PRINCIPLE they proclaim to be the great object. With them, Nebraska alone is a small matter—to establish a principle for FUTURE USE is what they particularly desire.

That future use is to be the planting of slavery wherever in the wide world local and unorganized opposition can not prevent it. Now, if you wish to give them this indorsement, if you wish to establish this principle, do so. I shall regret it, but it is your right. On the contrary, if you are opposed to the principle—intend to give it no such indorsement—let no wheedling, no sophistry, divert you from throwing a direct vote against it.

Some men, mostly Whigs, who condemn the repeal of the Missouri Compromise, nevertheless hesitate to go for its restoration, lest they be thrown in company with the Abolitionist. Will they allow me, as an old Whig, to tell them, good-humoredly, that I think this is very silly? Stand with anybody that stands RIGHT. Stand with him while he is right, and PART with him when he goes wrong. Stand WITH the Abolitionist in restoring the Missouri Compromise, and stand AGAINST him when he attempts to repeal the fugitive slave law. In the latter case you stand with the Southern disunionist. What of that? you are still right. In both cases you are right. In both cases you oppose the dangerous extremes. In both you stand on middle ground, and hold the ship level and steady. In both you are national, and nothing less than national. This is the good old Whig ground. To desert such ground because of any company, is to be less than a Whig—less than a man—less than an American.

I particularly object to the NEW position which the avowed principle of this Nebraska law gives to slavery in the body politic. I object to it because it assumes that there CAN be MORAL RIGHT, in the enslaving of one man by another. I object to it as a dangerous dalliance for a free people—a sad evidence that, feeling prosperity, we forget right—that liberty, as a principle, we have ceased to revere. I object to it, because the fathers of the republic eschewed and rejected it. The argument of "necessity," was the only argument they ever admitted in favor of slavery; and so far, and so far only, as it carried them did they ever go. They found the institution existing among us, which they could not help, and they cast blame upon the British king for having permitted its introduction. BEFORE the Constitution they prohibited its introduction into the Northwestern Territory, the only country we owned then free from it. AT the framing and adoption of the Constitution, they forebore to so much as mention the word "slave," or "slavery," in the whole instrument. In the provision for the recovery of fugitives, the slave is spoken of as a "PERSON HELD TO SERVICE OR LABOR." In that prohibiting the abolition of the African slave-trade for twenty years, that trade is spoken of as "The migration or importation of such persons as any of the states NOW EXISTING shall think proper to admit," etc. These are the only provisions alluding to slavery. Thus the thing is hid away in the Constitution, just as an afflicted man hides away a wen or cancer, which he dares not cut out at once, lest he bleed to death; with the promise, nevertheless, that the cutting may begin at the end of a certain time. Less than this our fathers COULD not do; and MORE they WOULD not do. Necessity drove them so far, and further they would not go. But this is not all. The earliest Congress under the Constitution took the same view of slavery. They hedged and hemmed it in to the narrowest limits of necessity.

In 1794, they prohibited an out-going slave-trade—that is, the taking of slaves FROM the United States to sell.

In 1798, they prohibited the bringing of slaves from

Africa INTO the Mississippi Territory—this territory then comprising what are now the states of Mississippi and Alabama. This was TEN YEARS before they had the authority to do the same thing as to the states existing at the adoption of the Constitution.

In 1800, they prohibited AMERICAN CITIZENS from trading in slaves between foreign countries, as, for instance, from Africa to Brazil.

In 1803, they passed a law in aid of one or two slave state laws, in restraint of the internal slave-trade.

In 1807, in apparent hot haste, they passed the law nearly a year in advance, to take effect the first day of 1808—the very first day the Constitution would permit—prohibiting the African slave-trade by heavy pecuniary and corporal penalties.

In 1820, finding these provisions ineffectual, they declared the slave-trade piracy, and annexed to it the extreme penalty of death. While all this was passing in the General Government, five or six of the original slave states had adopted systems of gradual emancipation; by which the institution was rapidly becoming extinct within these limits.

Thus we see the plain, unmistakable spirit of that age, toward slavery, was hostility to the PRINCIPLE, and toleration ONLY BY NECESSITY.

But now it is to be transformed into a "sacred right." Nebraska brings it forth, places it on the high road to extension and perpetuity; and with a pat on its back, says to it, "Go, and God speed you." Henceforth it is to be the chief jewel of the nation—the very figure-head of the ship of state. Little by little, but steadily as man's march to the grave, we have been giving up the OLD for the NEW faith. Near eighty years ago we began by declaring that all men are created equal; but now from that beginning we have run down to the other declaration, that for SOME men to enslave OTHERS is a "sacred right of self-government." These principles can not stand together. They are as opposite as God and Mammon; and whoever holds to the one must despise the other. When Pettit, in connection with his support of the Nebraska bill, called the Declaration of Independence "a self-evident lie," he only did what consistency and candor require all other Nebraska men to do. Of the forty odd Nebraska Senators who sat present and heard him, no one rebuked him. Nor am I apprised that any Nebraska newspaper, or any Nebraska orator, in the whole nation, has ever yet rebuked him. If this had been said among Marion's men, Southerners though they were, what would have become of the man who said it? If this had been said to the men who captured André, the man who said it would probably have been hung sooner than André was. If it had been said in old Independence Hall, seventy-eight years ago, the very door-keeper would have throttled the man, and thrust him into the street.

Let no one be deceived. The spirit of seventy-six and the spirit of Nebraska are utter antagonisms; and the former is being rapidly displaced by the latter.

Fellow-countrymen: Americans, South as well as North, shall we make no effort to arrest this? Already the liberal party throughout the world express the apprehension "that the one retrograde institution in America is undermining the principles of progress, and fatally violating the noblest political system the world ever saw." This is not the taunt of enemies, but the warning of friends. Is it quite safe to disregard it—to despise it? Is there no danger to liberty itself, in discarding the earliest practice, and first precept of our ancient faith? In our greedy chase to make profit of the negro, let us beware lest we "cancel and tear to pieces" even the white man's charter of freedom.

Our republican robe is soiled, and trailed in the dust. Let us re-purify it. Let us turn and wash it white, in the spirit, if not the blood, of the Revolution. Let us turn slavery from its claims of "moral right" back upon its existing legal rights, and its arguments of "necessity." Let us return it to the position our fathers gave it, and there let it rest in peace. Let us readopt the Declaration of Independence, and with it the practices and policy which harmonize with it. Let North and South—let all Americans—let all lovers of liberty everywhere—join in the great and good work. If we do this, we shall not only have saved the Union, but we shall have so saved it as to make, and to keep it, forever worthy of the saving. We shall have so saved it, that the succeeding millions of free happy people, the world over, shall rise up and call us blessed, to the latest generations.

At Springfield, twelve days ago, where I had spoken substantially as I have here, Judge Douglas replied to me—and as he is to reply to me here, I shall attempt to anticipate him, by noticing some of the points he made there. He commenced by stating I had assumed all the way through that the principle of the Nebraska bill would have the effect of extending slavery. He denied that this was INTENDED or that this EFFECT would follow.

I will not reopen the argument upon this point. That such WAS the intention, the world believed at the start, and will continue to believe. This was the COUNTENANCE of the thing; and both friends and enemies instantly recognized it as such. That countenance can not now be changed by argument. You can as easily argue the color out of the negro's skin. Like the "bloody hand," you may wash it, and wash it, the red witness of guilt still sticks, and stares horribly at you.

Next he says, Congressional intervention never prevented slavery anywhere—that it did not prevent it in the Northwestern Territory, nor in Illinois—that, in fact, Illinois came into the Union as a slave state—that the principle of the Nebraska bill expelled it from Illinois, from several old states, from everywhere.

Now this is mere quibbling all the way through. If the ordinance of '87 did not keep slavery out of the Northwest Territory, how happens it that the northwest shore of the Ohio River is entirely free from it, while the southeast shore, less than a mile distant, along nearly the whole length of the river, is entirely covered with it?

If that ordinance did not keep it out of Illinois, what was it that made the difference between Illinois and Missouri? They lie side by side, the Mississippi river only dividing them; while their early settlements were within the same latitude. Between 1810 and 1820, the number of slaves in Missouri INCREASED 7,211; while in Illinois, in the same ten years, they DECREASED 51. This appears by the census returns. During nearly all of that ten years, both were territories—not states.

During this time, the ordinance forbade slavery to go into Illinois; and NOTHING forbade it to go into Missouri. It DID go into Missouri, and did NOT go into Illinois. That is the fact. Can any one doubt as to the reason of it?

But, he says, Illinois came into the Union as a slave state. Silence, perhaps, would be the best answer to this flat contradiction of the known history of the country. What are the facts upon which this bold assertion is based?

When we first acquired the country, as far back as 1787, there were some slaves within it, held by the French inhabitants of Kaskaskia. The territorial legislation admitted a few negroes from the slave states, as indentured servants. One year after the adoption of the first State Constitution, the whole number of them was—what do you think? Just 117—while the aggregate free population was 55,094—about 470 to 1. Upon this state of facts, the people framed their Constitution, prohibiting the further introduction of slavery, with a sort of guarantee to the owners of the few indentured servants, giving freedom to their children to be born thereafter, and making no mention whatever of any supposed slave for life. Out of this small matter, the judge manufactures his argument that Illinois came into the Union as a slave state. Let the facts be the answer to the argument.

The principles of the Nebraska bill, he says, expelled slavery from Illinois. The principle of that bill first planted it here—that is, it first came because there was no law to prevent it—first came before we owned the country; and finding it here, and having the ordinance of '87 to prevent its increasing, our people struggled along, and finally got rid of it as best they could.

But the principle of the Nebraska bill abolished slavery in several of the old states. Well, it is true that several of the old states, in the last quarter of the last century, did adopt systems of gradual emancipation, by which the institution has finally become extinct within their limits; but it MAY or MAY NOT be true that the principle of the Nebraska bill was the cause that led to the adoption of these measures. It is now more than fifty years since the last of these states adopted its system of emancipation.

If the Nebraska bill is the real author of the benevolent works, it is rather deplorable that it has for so long a time ceased working altogether. Is there not some reason to suspect that it was the principle of the REVOLUTION, and not the principle of the Nebraska bill, that led to emancipation in these old states? Leave it to the people of those old emancipating states, and I am quite certain they will decide that neither that nor any other good thing ever did or ever will come of the Nebraska bill.

In the course of my main argument, Judge Douglas interrupted me to say that the principle of the Nebraska bill was very old; that it originated when God made man, and placed good and evil before him, allowing him to choose for himself, being responsible for the choice he should make. At the time, I thought this was merely playful; and I answered it accordingly. But in his reply to me, he renewed it as a serious argument. In seriousness, then, the facts of this proposition are not true as stated. God did not place good and evil before man, telling him to make his choice. On the contrary, he did tell him there was one tree, of the fruit of which he should not eat, upon pain of certain death. I should scarcely wish so strong a prohibition against slavery in Nebraska.

But this argument strikes me as not a little remarkable in another particular—in its strong resemblance to the old argument for the "Divine right of kings." By the latter, the king is to do just as he pleases with his white subjects, being responsible to God alone. By the former, the white man is to do just as he pleases with his black slaves, being responsible to God alone. The two things are precisely alike; and it is but natural that they should find similar arguments to sustain them.

I had argued that the application of the principle of self-government, as contended for, would require the revival of the African slave-trade—that no argument could be made in favor of a man's right to take slaves to Nebraska, which could not be equally well made in favor of his right to bring them from the coast of Africa. The judge replied that the Constitution requires the suppression of the foreign slave-trade; but does not require the prohibition of slavery in the territories. That is a mistake, in point of fact. The Constitution does NOT require the action of Congress in either case; and it does AUTHORIZE it in both. And so, there is still no difference between the cases.

In regard to what I had said of the advantage the slave states have over the free, in the matter of representation, the judge replied that we, in the free states, count five free negroes as five white people, while in the slave states they count five slaves as three whites only; and that the advantage, at last, was on the side of the free states.

Now, in the slave states, they count free negroes just as we do; and it so happens that, besides their slaves, they have as many free negroes as we have, and thirty-three thousand over. Thus, their free negroes more than balance ours; and their advantage over us, in consequence of their slaves, still remains as I stated it.

In reply to my argument, that the Compromise Measures of 1850 were a system of equivalents, and that the provisions of no one of them could fairly be carried to other subjects, without its corresponding equivalent being carried with it, the judge denied outright that these measures had any connection with, or dependence upon each other. This is mere desperation. If they had no connection, why are they always spoken of in connection? Why has he so spoken of them a thousand times? Why has he constantly called them a SERIES of measures? Why does everybody call them a compromise? Why was California kept out of the Union, six or seven months, if it was not because of its connection with the other measures? Webster's leading definition of the verb, "to compromise," is, "to adjust and settle a difference, by mutual agreement, with concessions of claims by the parties." This conveys precisely the popular understanding of the word "compromise."

We knew, before the judge told us, that these measures passed separately, and in distinct bills; and that no two of them were passed by the votes of precisely the same members. But we also know, and so does he know, that no one of them could have passed both branches of Congress, but for the understanding that the others were to pass also. Upon this understanding, each got votes, which it could have got in no other way. It is this fact that gives to the measures their true character; and it is the universal knowledge of this fact, that has given them the name of "Compromises," so expressive of that true character.

I had asked, "If in carrying the provisions of the Utah and New Mexico laws to Nebraska, you could clear away other objection, how can you leave Nebraska 'perfectly free' to introduce slavery BEFORE she forms a Constitution, during her territorial government? while the Utah and New Mexico laws only authorized it WHEN they form Constitutions, and are admitted into the Union?" To this Judge Douglas answered that the Utah and New Mexico laws, also authorized it BEFORE; and to prove this, he read from one of their laws, as follows:

"That the legislative power of said territory shall extend to all rightful subjects of legislation, consistent with the Constitution of the United States and the provisions of this act."

Now it is perceived from the reading of this, that there is nothing express upon the subject; but that the authority is sought to be implied merely, for the general provision of "all rightful subjects of legislation." In reply to this I insist, as a legal rule of construction, as well as the plain popular view of the matter, that the EXPRESS provision for Utah and New Mexico coming in with slavery if they choose, when they shall form Constitutions, is an EXCLUSION of all implied authority on the same subject; that Congress having the subject distinctly in their minds, when they made the express provision, they therein expressed their WHOLE meaning on that subject.

The judge rather insinuated that I had found it convenient to forget the Washington territorial law passed in 1853. This was a division of Oregon, organizing the northern part as the Territory of Washington. He asserted, that, by this act, the ordinance of '87, theretofore existing in Oregon, was repealed; that nearly all the members of Congress voted for it, beginning in the House of Representatives, with Charles Allen, of Massachusetts, and ending with Richard Yates, of Illinois; and that he could not understand how those who now oppose the Nebraska bill, so voted there, unless it was because it was then too soon after both the great political parties had ratified the Compromises of 1850, and the ratification therefore too fresh to be then repudiated.

Now I had seen the Washington act before; and I have carefully examined it since; and I aver that there is no repeal of the ordinance of '87, or of any prohibition of slavery in it. In express terms, there is absolutely nothing in the whole law upon the subject; in fact, nothing to lead a reader to THINK of the subject. To my judgment it is equally free from everything from which repeal can be legally implied; but, however this may be, are men now to be intrapped by a legal implication, extracted from covert language, introduced, perhaps, for the very purpose of intrapping them? I sincerely wish every man could read this law quite through, carefully watching every sentence, and every line, for a repeal of the ordinance of '87, or anything equivalent to it.

Another point on the Washington act. If it was intended to be modeled after the Utah and New Mexico acts, as Judge Douglas insists, why was it not inserted in it, as in them, that Washington was to come in with or without slavery as she may choose at the adoption of her Constitution? It has no such provision in it; and I defy the ingenuity of man to give a reason for the omission, other than that it was not intended to follow the Utah and New Mexico laws in regard to the question of slavery.

The Washington act not only differs vitally from the Utah and New Mexico acts; but the Nebraska act differs vitally from both. By the latter act the people are left "perfectly free" to regulate their own domestic concerns, etc.; but in all the former, all their laws are to be submitted to Congress, and if disapproved are to be null. The Washington act goes even further; it absolutely prohibits the territorial legislation by very strong and guarded language, from establishing banks, or borrowing money on the faith of the territory. Is this the sacred right of self-government we hear vaunted so much? No, sir; the Nebraska bill finds no model in the acts of

'50, or the Washington act. It finds no model in any law from Adam till to-day. As Phillips says of Napoleon, the Nebraska act is grand, gloomy, and peculiar; wrapped in the solitude of its own originality, without a model and without a shadow upon the earth.

In the course of his reply, Senator Douglas remarked, in substance, that he had always considered this government was made for the white people and not for the negroes. Why, in point of mere fact, I think so too. But in this remark of the judge there is a significance, which I think is the key to the great mistake (if there is any such mistake) which he has made in this Nebraska measure. It shows that the judge has no very vivid impression that the negro is a human; and consequently has no idea that there can be any moral question in legislating about him. In his view, the question of whether a new country shall be slave or free, is a matter of as utter indifference, as it is whether his neighbor shall plant his farm with tobacco, or stock it with horned cattle. Now whether this view is right or wrong, it is very certain that the great mass of mankind take a totally different view. They consider slavery a great moral wrong; and their feeling against it is not evanescent, but eternal. It lies at the very foundation of their sense of justice, and it can not be trifled with. It is a great and durable element of popular action, and, I think, no statesman can safely disregard it.

Our Senator also objects that those who oppose him in this measure do not entirely agree with one another. He reminds me that in my firm adherence to the Constitutional rights of the slave states, I differ widely from others who are co-operating with me in opposing the Nebraska bill; and he says it is not quite fair to oppose him in this variety of ways. He should remember that he took us by surprise—astounded us—by this measure. We were thunderstruck and stunned; and we reeled and fell in utter confusion. But we rose each fighting, grasping whatever he could first reach—a scythe—a pitch-fork—a chopping-ax, or a butcher's cleaver. We struck in the direction of the sound; and we are rapidly closing in upon him. He must not think to divert us from our purpose by showing us that our drill, our dress, and our weapons, are not entirely perfect and uniform. When the storm shall be past, he shall find us still Americans; no less devoted to the continued union and prosperity of the country than heretofore.

Finally, the judge invokes against me the memory of Clay and of Webster. They were great men, and men of great deeds. But where have I assailed them? For what is it that their life-long enemy shall now make profit by assuming to defend them against me, their life-long friend? I go against the repeal of the Missouri Compromise; did they ever go for it? They went for the Compromises of 1850; did I ever go against them? They were greatly devoted to the Union; to the small measure of my ability was I ever less so? Clay and Webster were dead before this question arose; by what authority shall our Senator say they would espouse his side of it, if alive? Mr. Clay was the leading spirit in making the Missouri Compromise; is it very credible that if now alive, he would take the lead in the breaking of it? The truth is that some support from Whigs is now a necessity with the judge, and for this it is that the names of Clay and Webster are now invoked. His old friends have deserted him in such numbers as to leave too few to live by. He came to his own, and his own received him not; and lo! he turns unto the Gentiles.

A word now as to the judge's desperate assumption that the Compromises of 1850 had no connection with one another; that Illinois came into the Union as a slave state; and some other similar ones. This is no other than a bold denial of the history of the country. If we do not know that the Compromises of 1850 were dependent on each other; if we do not know that Illinois came into the Union as a free state—we do not know anything. If we do not know these things, we do not know that we ever had a Revolutionary war, or such a chief as Washington. To deny these things is to deny our national axioms—or dogmas at least; and it puts an end to all argument. If a man will stand up, and assert, and repeat, and reassert, that two and two do not make four, I know nothing in the power of argument that can stop him. I think I can answer the judge so long as he sticks to the premises; but when he flies from them, I can not work an argument into the consistency of a maternal gag, and actually close his mouth with it. In such a case I can only commend him to the seventy thousand answers just in from Pennsylvania, Ohio, and Indiana.

LIFE AND SPEECHES

OF

HANNIBAL HAMLIN.

BY

JOHN L. HAYES.

LIFE OF HANNIBAL HAMLIN.

To form an accurate opinion of the character of an individual, it is necessary to estimate that of the people from which he has sprung, and among whom he has lived. The people of Maine, descended from the English Puritans and merchant adventurers, have preserved in an eminent degree the characteristic traits impressed by their origin, prominent among which are a devotion to the doctrines of popular liberty, and the spirit of commercial enterprise. Possessing a country where the necessities of soil and climate demand unceasing exertion, and where the bounties of nature are offered only to toil, they feel the nature and dignity of labor, and are sensitive as to its rights. Less exclusively devoted to agriculture than the people of any other state, they seek their wealth in the forest and on the sea. Trained by their perilous toil, like the pioneers of the West, they are hardy, athletic, self-reliant, and brave. As Maine surpasses all the other states in the tonnage of her shipping and the extent of maritime privileges, the character of her people is strongly marked by their commercial relations. Commerce, as it depends upon the benefits derived from mutual exchanges with distant countries, is opposed to exclusiveness and local prejudice. Thus, with the intelligence, refinement, and wealth which commerce has given to this maritime state, and with the deep conviction of the value of their own system of free labor, we find among the people of Maine a most intimate knowledge and appreciation of the men, institutions, and rights of the other states, and a devoted attachment to the Union as the source of national and commercial prosperity.

Such are the people from whom has sprung the individual who now occupies the proud position of candidate for the Vice-Presidency of the United States, and such the people who, by making him for more than twenty years the recipient of their highest honors, have declared him to be a true representative of their sentiments and character.

HANNIBAL HAMLIN, the subject of this sketch, is the son of Cyrus Hamlin and Anna Livermore, and was born in Paris, the shire town of the county of Oxford, in Maine, on the 27th of August, 1809. Cyrus Hamlin, a physician by profession, upon removing from his native State, Massachusetts, first settled in the town of Livermore, where he married a daughter of Deacon Elijah Livermore, a principal proprietor of that town, and connected with the distinguished family of that name in New Hampshire. While in Livermore, Dr. Hamlin built the dwelling-house in which were born the three brothers Washburne, now so worthily representing three states in Congress.

On the formation of the county of Oxford, Dr. Hamlin received the responsible appointment of Clerk of the Courts of the county, and upon the separation of Maine from Massachusetts, was appointed High Sheriff of the county, which office he held for several years. He died in 1828, aged about 58, universally respected for his probity, benevolence, and Christian character, having been for many years a member of the Baptist Church.

Dr. Hamlin's father, the grandfather of Hannibal, resided in Massachusetts, and before the Revolution commanded a company of Minute Men, in which five of his sons were enrolled. One of them served during the Revolutionary war, and was a member of the Society of Cincinnati.

Hannibal was the sixth and youngest son of seven children, and is not the only one of his family who has held a prominent position in his State, one of whom, Hon. Elijah Hamlin, an elder brother, residing at Bangor, having been a member of the Legislature and Senate of Maine, and also land agent of the State, and having been a candidate of his party for the positions of member of Congress and Governor of Maine.

Hannibal Hamlin received his early instruction at a private school in Paris, and at a public academy in Hebron, an adjoining town. It was his intention to obtain a collegiate education, and he was nearly fitted for college, at the age of sixteen, when an elder brother, who it was designed should reside at home and carry on the farm, failed in health and left to pursue the study of medicine. The usage of the country required that one, at least, of the sons of the family should remain at the homestead, and Hannibal left his studies at the academy, relinquished the prospects of a collegiate career, and took his place with the laborers on the home farm.

For two years, he worked there with the steadiness of a man, when, at his father's instance, and upon the assurance that his assistance could be dispensed with, he determined to commence the study of the law. Quitting home, he read law in the office of his older brother, Elijah, in the eastern part of the State, when his father's death again broke up his plans. The only property left by his father was the farm, which was given to his mother, and filial duty left him no alternative but to remain and take charge of the farm, where he labored unremittingly for two years after his father's death.

Great as the sacrifice required in the abandonment of a professional career must have seemed to an ambitious young man, it was doubtless a blessing in disguise. The seclusion of a rural life developed, without doubt, his reflective faculties, and the necessity of daily toil gave that contempt for personal indulgence, and that energy of will which have since distinguished the public man. The long days of manual toil were not unrelieved by intellectual rest. His father's private library, and the well-selected books of the "social library," one of the "institutions" of Maine, afforded reading which may have been more profitable for his general culture than the technical studies of a profession.

The happy influences of nature ministered also to his culture. The county, in which he resided, presents landscape scenery of great magnificence. Lofty mountains, of massive granite, may be seen rising abruptly, one behind the other, in solemn grandeur, in the distance, while glorious views are opened of deep-wooded valleys, and small but beautiful lakes, lying in amphitheaters of hills.

Freedom has its birth-place in mountain homes, and the future advocate of freedom may have felt the inspiration of such scenery, so well expressed by the words of one of Maine's most gifted sons :

"As long as yonder firs shall spread
Their green arms o'er the mountain's head,
As long as yonder cliff shall stand,
Where join the ocean and the land,

> Shall those cliffs and mountains be
> Proud retreats for liberty."—UPHAM.

An incident in the life of young Hamlin, during the period of his home labors, illustrates the practical training to which the young men of New England are subjected. When Hannibal was about nineteen years old, his father having bought a township of land on Dead river, for lumbering purposes, and being unable to complete the survey in the fall, intrusted the work to his son. The township was distant about twelve miles from any settlement, and covered with the primeval forest. On the last of March, the young man took his compass and chain, and started for the woods on snow-shoes, with a party under his charge, himself "sacking," as it is called in woodman's phrase, his part of the necessary provisions on his back. He remained in the woods over a month, sleeping wherever the night overtook them, often in the gorges of the mountains upon the snow, with a depth of seven feet beneath him.

Another example will occur to all of a young man, whose first training for a life of practical labor, which has blessed his country and the world, was made as a surveyor.

In the spring of 1830, shortly before arriving at his majority, Mr. Hamlin, in company with a young man who has since attained an honorable public position, Horatio King, at present First Assistant Postmaster-General of the United States, bought, on credit, a Democratic paper published in Paris, called the *Jeffersonian*, a name indicative of the school of politics of which Mr. Hamlin has been so faithful a disciple and teacher. While connected with the paper, Mr. Hamlin, although constantly furnishing the contributions of his pen, both in prose and verse, stood regularly at the case, and set the types with his own hands. This editorial experience was an important part of the education of the future statesman, as it compelled him to study constitutional and political history, and gave a definiteness to his political opinions, which is best secured by writing under responsibility to the public eye.

In the fall of 1830, Mr. Hamlin sold out his interest in the *Jeffersonian* to his partner, and following the advice of his mother, recommenced the study of the law with Hon. Joseph G. Cole, of Paris, afterward a judge of the Circuit Court. He subsequently entered the office of Messrs. Fessenden, Deblois & Fessenden, of Portland, and it is an interesting coincidence, that the younger partner of that firm is now the distinguished colleague of Mr. Hamlin in the Senate of the United States.

After reading law the required term—three years—Mr. Hamlin was admitted to the bar in his native county, and at once entered upon the responsibilities of his profession, as, on the day of his admission, he was retained in an important case, argued it to the jury, and obtained a verdict. In April, 1833, he removed to Hampden, a town with about four thousand inhabitants, and a village of fifteen hundred, situated on the Penobscot river, six miles below the city of Bangor, where he now resides.

Mr. Hamlin entered at once on an extensive practice in his profession, his reputation soon being established as a faithful and able lawyer. His business habits, and the talent displayed as a public speaker at the bar, where he, from the first, argued his own causes, and as a lecturer and speaker in Lyceums, and other popular assemblies, as well as the earnestness and distinctness of his political opinions, soon attracted the attention of the dominant party, and within three years from the time of his taking up his residence among them, his fellow-citizens elected him to a seat in the lower house of the Legislature.

He was a member of the State Legislature of Maine for the years 1836, '37, '38, '39, and '40. He became at once a prominent member of the House, and one of the leaders of his party, assuming a leading part in all the principal debates, and was also one of the most active business men in the body. He was Speaker of the House for the years 1837, '39, and '40, being only twenty-seven years of age when first elected Speaker, and at the close of each year received the unanimous vote of thanks of the House for the manner in which he discharged his duties.

In 1840 he was candidate for Congress, during the Harrison tornado, and was defeated in a poll of some fifteen thousand, by less than two hundred votes. It is worthy of notice, that in that election, he canvassed the district with his opponent, Hon. Elisha H. Allen, this being the first instance, it is believed, in which it was ever done in New England.

In 1843, the election having been postponed one year, in consequence of a new apportionment of the census, Mr. Hamlin was again a candidate, running against his former competitor, and was elected by about a thousand majority.

In 1844, Mr. Hamlin was again elected to the House of Representatives, and, during this Congress, was Chairman of the Committee on Elections, and a member of the Committee on Naval Affairs. On returning home, in March, 1847, on completion of his service in the House, his town had not elected a Representative to the State Legislature, it requiring a majority of all the votes, and Mr. Hamlin being put in nomination, was elected and served in 1847.

In May, 1848, Gov. Fairfield, then Senator from Maine, having deceased, Mr. Hamlin was elected to the Senate of the United States, to fill the unexpired term of four years, and was re-elected on the 25th of July, 1851, after encountering the bitter hostility of the then pro-slavery Democrats, they refusing to vote for him to the last, notwithstanding he was the regular nominee.

The *Augusta Age*, the then official paper of its party—the Democratic organ, of August 27, 1850, thus congratulated its party upon the election of Mr. Hamlin to the Senate:

"Hon. Hannibal Hamlin, the regular Democratic nominee for United States Senator, was elected in both Houses of the Legislature, on Thursday last.

"We congratulate the Democracy of the State upon the result. We rejoice that the question has been finally disposed of in a manner conformable to the wishes and expectations of a great majority of the Democratic party of Maine.

"The failure to elect Mr. Hamlin at an earlier period in the session, was occasioned by the refusal of *a small portion of the Democratic members to support him*, the pretext of their opposition BEING THE OPINIONS HE ENTERTAINED UPON THE SUBJECT OF THE EXTENSION OF SLAVERY, and the determination which he cherished of obeying the resolutions of instruction passed by the last Legislature in relation to that subject.

"After repeated attempts to effect an election had been made without success, several members of the free-soil party, believing that there was an attempt on the part of the Democrats opposed to Mr. Hamlin, to *cut him down*, IN CONSEQUENCE OF HIS OPPOSITION TO THE INTRODUCTION OF SLAVERY INTO TERRITORY NOW FREE, although not concurring with him in political opinions, voluntarily gave him their votes, amounting to ten in the House of Representatives and three in the Senate, which secured his election. It was certainly an act of magnanimity, which can not fail to be appreciated, and particularly as it was a free-will offering (from men who are in an opposing political organization) to Mr. Hamlin, FOR HIS FIRM ADHERENCE TO PRINCIPLES

HELD IN COMMON BY THEM WITH THE GREAT MASS OF THE PEOPLE OF THE NORTH, IRRESPECTIVE OF PARTY DISTINCTIONS."

Mr. Hamlin served in the Senate and acted with the Democratic party until 1854, voting, however, uniformly against all projects for slavery extension. He then gave public notice in the Senate of the reasons why he would no longer co-operate with the party, and resigned his position as Chairman of the Committee on Commerce.

In June, 1856, he was nominated by the Republicans in Maine as candidate for Governor, the Democratic party having carried the State the year before, and being then in power. He entered upon the canvass in July, and addressed public meetings nearly a hundred times. He was elected by eighteen thousand majority, over two opponents, and twenty-three thousand majority over his Democratic opponent; more than double the majority that was ever given in a contested election.

On the 7th of January, 1857, he resigned his seat in the Senate, and was, on the same day, inaugurated Governor.

On the 16th of the same month, he was re-elected United States Senator for six years; and on the 20th of February following, resigned the office of Governor, and returned to Washington on the 4th of March.

It may be said, with strict truth, that during the whole period of his congressional life, Mr. Hamlin has pre-eminently distinguished himself as a prompt, efficient, and intelligent business man. His first object was to discharge the business demands made upon him by his own constituents. He never received a business letter without promptly answering it.

All parties in Maine demanded his services, and have always accorded to him the highest credit for the promptness and fidelity displayed in the charge of their interests. The heads of the Treasury, including such men as Secretary Guthrie, Acting and Assistant Secretaries Hodge and Washington, and Governor Anderson, Commissioner of Customs, have declared him to be the best business man in the Senate.

Mr. Hamlin has been a member of that most important Committee, that on Commerce, during his whole term in the Senate, and was chairman seven years.

In addition to the vast number of minor matters relating to his own constituents and State which he took care of, as chairman of his committee, he had the supervision of all the great questions and measures affecting the commerce of the country, both domestic and foreign, which were acted upon by that committee, no bill being reported which he did not fully understand by personal investigation.

Among the important measures instituted and reported by that committee, were those relating to the improvement of harbors, rivers, and lakes, the whole system of light-houses, the protection of passengers on steam and sailing vessels, the location and establishment of custom-houses, the fixing of ports of entry and delivery, and measures connected with the coast survey, besides a multitude of other measures of less importance connected with commerce in all its ramifications.

The very important act "For the better security of lives of passengers on board of vessels impelled in whole or in part by steam," passed in August, 1852, was reported to the Senate by Mr. Davis, of Massachusetts, but was prepared by Mr. Hamlin and Mr. Davis jointly, and was sustained by Mr. Hamlin in several speeches in the Senate. During all the time subsequent to the passage of the bill, while Mr. Hamlin was chairman, all the amendatory acts in relation to that subject have been reported and supported by him, and he has now charge of the bill passed by the House on the same subject. All the members of the Board of Supervising Inspectors, appointed under these laws, will bear testimony to the laborious investigation and practicability displayed by Mr. Hamlin in connection with this important matter.

The bill regulating the liability of shipowners, was reported by Mr. Hamlin, at the second session of the Thirty-first Congress, and was carried through the Senate mainly by his efforts. This bill placed American navigation on the same footing with British navigation, and was deemed, by American merchants, of very great importance. So important was it considered by the New York merchants, that they tendered him a public dinner as a testimonial of their appreciation of his services, which, however, he declined.

The codification of the whole revenue laws, prepared under Secretary Guthrie, was made in pursuance of a resolution introduced by Mr. Hamlin in the Senate, January 19, 1853, who subsequently obtained an appropriation of ten thousand dollars for the same.

It was by the efforts of Mr. Hamlin that appropriations were made for the construction of the various custom-houses, which have been built within the last few years—to wit: at Wheeling, Cincinnati, St. Louis, Bangor, Belfast, Portsmouth, Galveston, Georgetown, Milwaukie, Norfolk, Chicago, and more than twenty other points in different parts of the country. It was a proviso of his that the cost of construction should, in all cases, be limited to the amount appropriated.

Mr. Hamlin had made two elaborate speeches on the fisheries, as connected with the commerce and naval service of the country. He has also sustained the ocean mail service as auxiliary to the commerce of the country. An important report was made by him exhibiting the commercial relations between this country and Brazil.

He has always been a friend to a general system of improvement of harbors and rivers, and besides reporting many bills, has made several speeches in defense of the system.

The provision of law which grants pensions to the widows of Revolutionary soldiers since 1800, was the work of Mr. Hamlin.

While a member of the House, Mr. Hamlin made a speech giving notice to the British Government to terminate the joint occupancy of the Territory of Oregon.

This was a progressive and, it may be said, prophetic speech. In this, he indicated a Pacific Railroad, and predicted the establishment of great commercial states on the shores of the Pacific.

He was an early friend of a graduation in the price of public lands. He was not, at that time, a supporter of the homestead bill, but has been, for several years past, earnestly and decidedly so.

Mr. Hamlin was in favor of the bill appropriating land for agricultural colleges, and another bill making appropriations for the benefit of the indigent insane. He was an earnest advocate of the admission of California, and made the first elaborate speech in the Senate in favor of its admission.

Mr. Hamlin voted with his party for the tariff of 1846, although he never hesitated to express his personal preference for a system of specific duties.

The question arising in the House on the 5th of January, 1843, in relation to the twenty-first rule prohibiting the reception of abolition petitions, after some remarks by Mr. Black, who said he hoped the House would adopt the amendment which he had proposed, to instruct the Committee on Rules to report to the House that rule by which abolitionists would be debarred from intruding on them their incendiary doctrines, the effect and operation of which were most damnable. He desired the vote to be recorded by yeas and nays; and he relied confidently upon a democratic majority to sustain his motion. Mr. Hamlin, after declaring that the time, as he trusted, had gone by (if it ever existed) when the galvanic starts, and fits, and deep intonations of any gentleman could produce an impression in that hall, and that *he* should vote irrespective of all such influences, on this and every other question, according to the dictates of right and wrong, notwithstanding the *defiance* of the gentleman from Georgia; proceeded to say that he should vote against the rule, because he believed that the right of petition was not an abstraction, but a clear, plain, and sacred Constitutional right, neither to be denied or infringed upon. Such being its character it was one which could not be controlled by this or any other legislative body without a Constitutional violation. It was a Constitutional right disconnected with the opinions of any body of men. When the House said in advance that they would not receive petitions upon any particular subject, they undertook to prejudge, and they did prejudge the matter, and to exclude individuals from privileges which Constitutionally belonged to them. It was confounding our *duty* of receiving with the *right* to act after reception. He very well understood that the action of the House upon petitions after they were received, was to fully and clearly be determined by a majority. The right to petition was a distinct question; the power of the House to reject or refuse the prayer is another and distinct proposition.

If the right of the people to have their petitions *received*, is dependent upon the will of the majority, then there was no question, over which a majority, perhaps arbitrary and tyrannical, might not exercise that right; and the right of petition becomes then, not the right of a Constitution, but a right dependent upon the will of a majority. * * * He was not disposed to argue these questions. The conclusions which he drew from them were irresistible to his own mind. For the reasons stated, or rather upon these principles, as stated, he must vote against the twenty-first rule, and in favor of receiving such petitions as were presented.

On the 23d of January, 1845, the House having resolved itself into a Committee of the Whole, and having under consideration the joint resolutions for the re-annexation of Texas to the Union, Mr. Hamlin made a speech which is imperfectly and partially reported in the *Congressional Globe.* He observed, that he entertained but little hope that any suggestions that he might offer in this oft-discussed question would produce much impression within these walls. Yet the intrinsic importance of the question before the House, and its extensive influence on the most momentous interests of the country, would, he hoped, plead his excuse if he occupied his "brief hour within that hall."

We possessed a country favored of Heaven, extending from the frozen regions of the North, to the fair, and rich, and smiling lands beneath the southern sun, and spreading from the Atlantic ocean, which had for centuries dashed with unceasing wave upon our eastern seaboard, back, back to the Pacific, whose more gentle murmurs broke upon our western shores. We had a country which embraced every climate of the globe, and which brought forth, in rich abundance, almost every natural product known to the world. Over all this glory the light of knowledge and the purer light of Christianity shed their blended rays, while a mild system of municipal laws spread the shield of its protection over the homes of a happy people. Now, it must be manifest at a glance, that a government extended over so wide a space, and embracing interests so multifarious, and men so widely separated from each other, not merely in local habitation, but in feelings, sentiments, and habits, must of necessity be founded on compromise; and such was, in fact, the basis of our free republican government, reposing upon the confidence of its people. He invoked the legislators of such a country to come up to the important question before them, with impulses and feelings worthy of its importance and of their own high station, and with views wide and enlarged, as was that extended domain over which the voice of Providence, speaking through the voices of a free people, had made them for a time the rulers.

The gentleman who had preceded Mr. Hamlin had ably discussed those Constitutional provisions under which it was now claimed that he should act. It was not, therefore, his intention specially to present any views he might entertain as to the Constitutionality or unconstitutionality of the act to which they were invoked. He would merely say this, that from a cool, calm, and deliberate view of the question, he had arrived at a conclusion which would justify him in giving his ready sanction to the proposed annexation of Texas. All he desired was such provisions and restrictions as should present it in the form of a national, and not a sectional question, but alike just and fair to all. With these conditions and restrictions, Mr. Hamlin was prepared to go for immediate annexation. He should, indeed, have preferred that this measure should have been left to the incoming administration, which, as it had received the confidence of the people in advance, would vindicate their choice by proving themselves worthy of it. The present administration, as every one knew, enjoyed the confidence of no party, and the respect of but few men, and he had therefore hoped that a measure of such importance would have been reserved for an administration which would justly possess the confidence of the nation. But the question was now before them; it was there, and it was now their duty to examine it. This great and important national question had been dragged down, down, down, from its own proper sphere, to a wretched, contemptible one for extending and perpetuating slavery. Yes, he repeated it, the attempt had been made by certain gentlemen to degrade it from its nationality into a question for promoting one narrow sectional interest—the strengthening of slave power. Mr. Hamlin proposed to examine it as it had been presented to the Senate and to the nation by the *present* administration, in its correspondence. He should endeavor to trace its history from the first incipient step until it had at length reached this hall, and the position it now occupied there. He should treat it as a question of the reannexation of Texas, and not merely of the Texan territory, for there was a broad distinction between annexing a foreign government and admitting a territory which had belonged to us before. Mr. Hamlin was well aware that with a view to great and important national purposes, a union of this territory of Texas with our own had been desired by almost all the administrations of government from the days of Mr. Jefferson. In that desire Mr. Hamlin heartily concurred. Let it come now, as it would have come then, and he should be satisfied. What had been the origin of this idea of re-annexing a sovereign power to the Union? It had originated, if the published correspondence told the truth, in a letter from a gentleman of Baltimore, suggesting that the British Government cherished the design of effecting the abolition of slavery in Texas. Such had been the language of the late lamented Secretary Upsher; and he called the attention of our agents in Texas to the designs thus attributed to the British ministry. Such had been the original cause of the invitation to Texas to negotiate for a Union. Was there any force in this consideration that should engage our Government to look so favorably on the plan, while, on the other hand, we were gravely told that the official denial of the British Government that she did not design to interfere with that institution, was entitled to no confidence; and that we must not look at the course in which the question was presented in the correspondence of our Government? He thought otherwise. If our Government had deemed a *mere rumor* of sufficient importance to justify them in entering into negotiations with a foreign power, should they not regard the correspondence furnished them as demanding an examination for the purpose of seeing upon what ground the present administration had based its acts? What consistency! when our Government, on mere rumor, could enter into a foreign negotiation, yet Congress was not to examine even the correspondence of our own official agents. The President, in communicating the correspondence to the House, had indeed elevated it above that degrading position, yet the correspondence told, in language not to be misunderstood, the first main course urged and subsequently sustained by the present Secretary of State. Mr. Hamlin would trace the course of this correspondence. He need not read it, for it must be familiar to the minds of gentlemen. Having begun, in consequence of allegations contained in a private letter, we had next the same argument of Mr. Calhoun, asking for the action of Congress in the annexation of Texas. And for what? Because he greatly feared lest slavery should be abolished in Texas.

Mr. Hamlin would invite the attention of gentlemen especially to a labored article of the Secretary, and let them say whether its whole aim was not to justify, uphold, and defend slavery as *right in principle*, and whether he did not demand Texas for the avowed purpose of extending, strengthening, and perpetuating it. Was that a national aspect of this great question? Was it not stooping down from a high-sounding prologue to a most contemptible farce?

They had been told that the Government was alarmed from an apprehended interference by foreign Governments in this matter, and here Mr. Hamlin was happy to agree with gentlemen on all sides of the House. He would ask no power on the habitable globe to say what this republic might or ought to do. She was her own judge, and her own adviser, yielding to the dictates of no power on earth. He trusted that that would be her course in regard to the national honor and the national dignity at home. He entertained no doubt that it would be.

Next came the official correspondence of the State Department, and the instructions prepared for our minister to France. The language of those instructions was so very apposite to sustain the position Mr. Hamlin had taken that he would beg the attention of the Committee while he read a few extracts.

The letter was a labored defense of slavery, and the alleged design of the British Government to abolish slavery in Texas is seized upon to aid in favor of annexation. This was what he said:

"But, to descend to particulars: it is certain that while England, like France, desires the independence of Texas, with the view to commercial connections, it is not less so that one of the leading motives of England for desiring it, is the hope that, through her diplomacy and influence, negro slavery may be abolished there, and ultimately by consequence in the United States, and throughout the whole of this continent. That its ultimate abolition throughout the entire continent is an object ardently desired by her, we have decisive proof in the declaration of the Earl of Aberdeen, delivered to this department, and of which you will find a copy among the documents transmitted to Congress with the Texan treaty. That she desires its abolition in Texas, and has used her influence and diplomacy to effect it there, the same document, with the correspondence of this department with Mr. Packenham, also to be found among the documents, furnishes proof not less conclusive. That one of the objects of abolishing it there, is to facilitate its abolition in the United States, and throughout the continent, is manifest from the declaration of the abolition party and societies, both in this country and in England. In fact, there is good reason to believe that the scheme of abolishing it in Texas, with the view to its abolition in the United States, and over the continent, originated with the prominent members of the party in the United States, and was first broached by them in the (so-called) World's Convention, held in London in the year 1840, and through its agency brought to the notice of the British Government."

Then follows the argument of the Secretary to show why England designs to aid in the abolition of slavery in Texas, that she can better control the monopoly of the tropical productions. The whole scope of the argument tended to prove or assert that abolition in Texas should not be permitted by our Government. His conclusion, then, must be that it must be annexed for that cause. So he understood it.

"It is unquestionable that she regards the abolition of slavery in Texas as a most important step toward this great object of policy, so much the aim of her solicitude and exertions; and the defeat of the annexation of Texas to our Union as indispensable to the abolition of slavery there. She is too sagacious not to see what a fatal blow it would give to slavery in the United States, and how certainly its abolition with us would abolish it over the whole continent, and thereby give her a monopoly in the productions of the great tropical staples, and the command of the commerce, navigation, and manufactures of the world, with an established naval ascendency and political preponderance. To this continent the blow would be calamitous beyond description. It would destroy, in a great measure, the cultivation and production of the great tropical staples, amounting annually in value to nearly $300,000,000—the fund which stimulates and upholds almost every other branch of its industry, commerce, navigation, and manufactures. The whole, by their joint influence, are rapidly spreading population, wealth, improvement, and civilization over the whole continent, and vivifying, by their overflow, the industry of Europe; thereby increasing its population, wealth, and advance in the arts, in power, and in civilization."

What! was it true that the slave institution, in this country, was the great upholder of the power of this republic, and the great means of spreading civilization over the world? Was it on such a correspondence, and on such doctrines that gentlemen of that House were solicited to vote in the affirmative, and to consummate this union between Texas and the United States? When this correspondence was given to the world, and they should return home, and tell their constituents that they had voted for annexation, on such principles, and with such an aim, would they not be pronounced recreant to their duty, and traitors to their country?

Mr. Hamlin denied this reasoning, and the conclusion. If Government were thus bound to extend its dominion for such a purpose, it made what was entirely a domestic affair, one of a national character. The General Government had no right to interfere in it. If it could *extend* for a supposed beneficial purpose, it could *restrict*, if it believed it would produce the same or a beneficial effect. It was an attempt to make a national question out of what related solely to the states; and those who assumed to give it that character, would be swift indeed to prevent the action of Congress in another and different direction. The question of annexation was fully and clearly national, not one where Government should act for a cause over which he had no right to interfere.

But the matter stopped not here. What had been said by the Chairman of the Committee of Foreign Affairs, (Mr. C. J. Ingersoll,) when he had first presented this subject for the action of Congress. Mr. Hamlin would beg leave to read some sentences of the gentleman's speech, as it had been given in the report of the *Intelligencer*, word for word, and letter for letter.

He had suggested this plan of carrying out the treaty as well in committee as in the House, for these reasons: 1st. The measure was a bargain; it was an arrangement made with another nation, and the plan had been matured by respectable agents attending here on the part of the government of Texas, and empowered by it *ad hoc;* he therefore took it for granted that this plan was the most acceptable to that government, and he therefore gave it the preference. He went a step further: this was not only a Texas question; it was, moreover, a Southern question; and, as he meant to speak here with all the freedom and frankness which he supposed to become a gentleman, he would say that as a Southern question he considered it, and was ready to defer to Southern sentiment in regard to it. And was not this fair? When the question of the Northeastern boundary was agitated in Congress, had it not finally been settled by the expressed wishes of the two States immediately interested, viz., Massachusetts and Maine. The other States acquiesced. The measure could not have commanded a majority in the Senate, if all the Senators had been governed by their own particular wishes and views in regard to it; but they considered that if Massachusetts and Maine were satisfied with the arrangement, they ought not to resist it. So, in the present case, Mr. Ingersoll considered this, as he had said, not only as a Texas question, but as a Southern question, as a boundary question, and as a slavery question. He should speak without reserve. If that portion of the people of the Union whose existence depended on the existence of slavery, and who were the most deeply and immediately interested in this Texas question, preferred the treaty plan, Mr. Ingersoll was prepared to acquiesce. He admitted, indeed, that it was a national question; but so was our Maine boundary a national question; and there was such a thing as conforming a national question to local views. The former Secretary of State, a man of most honorable, lofty, and patriotic sentiments, (he referred to the late lamented Mr, Secretary Upshur,) who had originated this treaty, and his successor, another Southern gentleman, who carried it into effect, had been actuated, no doubt, by such Southern sentiments as they in the North were not exactly prepared to appreciate; but Mr. Ingersoll should not, therefore, reject the measure.

Who, then, has made this question subservient to a particular object? Those who had done so, certainly could not complain of others who would consult the wishes and opinions of all sections, and acquire it in such a way as would permit those who disagree on certain questions, to occupy it in portions as each should prefer. They could not with Banquo say:

> "Nay, shake not thy gory locks at me!
> Thou canst not say I did it."

To all these doctrines Mr. Hamlin entered his earnest, solemn protest. They were monstrous, and not for a moment to be entertained.

Here was the history of this measure as presented in our official correspondence, and as traced to the House. It was conceded that the treaty reported from the Committee on Foreign Affairs, was prepared by Mr. Upshur, as a "Southern measure." The doctrines laid down by the gentleman of Pennsylvania, (Mr. Ingersoll,) could not be admitted. If another republic was to come in this Union, it were right and just that all sections, in their views and sentiments, should be consulted, and the admission made in accordance to all, as near as possible. One section should be equally consulted and regarded in its interests and feelings with another. It was to these views to which he had referred, that Mr. Hamlin objected, and all he desired was to so place the matter before the country, as not to sanction or approve them. How was the responsibility of indorsing these opinions to be avoided, if the measure were consummated in such a way as to secure the object named, he could not see. Gentlemen did not, he was sure, design to annex Texas for such a purpose; and it was proper to be careful that their acts should not effect what they did not intend.

He could refer to other authorities elsewhere, placing the question, and urging its adoption on the same principles. He could cite the language used by honorable gentlemen upon that floor, but it was his design mainly to examine the false attitudes in which it had presented itself in the official correspondence, and how it had been introduced into the House. All he desired was to put the measure upon that position which would disconnect it from the basis upon which it had been falsely placed. Instead of carrying it out and consummating the act in that way, it should be upon grounds which would give all the states the territory in such a manner as would accommodate the whites and institutions of different sections. He would vote for either proposition thus guarded and just.

How was the question directly before the House:

First. Was the treaty from the Committee of Foreign Affairs, which had been rejected by the Senate, article for article, word for word, and letter for letter.

Second. The resolution, which was a literal copy of the treaty, and as an amendment to that was the resolution of the gentleman from Ohio, (Mr. Weller,) and as an amendment to the amendment was the proposition of the gentleman from Illinois, (Mr. Douglas.)

Would not the adoption of either of these secure all that has been desired by those who have put it on the ground of a sectional character. The question upon either of the amendments, as he fully understood it, would be admitting the territory and securing slave institutions in it all, or very nearly all. He could see no other conclusion which could be drawn.

It was very true that the amendment of the gentleman from Illinois, (Mr. Douglas,) excluded it from north of thirty-six degrees thirty minutes north latitude. It was said by many that no part of Texas lay north of that line, and according to the map it was a small strip not susceptible of forming even one state. The rest of Texas has slavery guaranteed to it by its Constitution, and intelligent gentlemen frankly admitted that it would demand an admission as a state, with the same institutions upon an implied guarantee.

Some gentlemen had said to the opponents of the measure on the ground of slavery: "Let the abstract question first be settled, and let the rest remain an open question, and we can arrange the details afterward." Mr. Hamlin had been and now was willing to go for that; he would cheerfully vote to settle the abstract question first without including any details, if they would only leave all else open and settle the details afterward. But how stood the matter in fact? Mr. Hamlin should be very glad to find that they had not been mistaken. Would they let the question of slavery remain an open question? He feared not. The moment that was insisted on, they opposed it with all their power. He asked gentlemen to answer him this question directly and plainly: If Texas should be admitted without the exclusion of slavery, would they not afterward say that those who had voted for the abstract question stood *pledged* to the whole territory, as it was when admitted? And would they not be *reproached* with a violation of faith, should they afterward insist on the exclusion of slavery from any portion of the territory? Would it not be said that they had bound themselves by every sacred tie that could bind a man? And would they not be taunted with more severity than they ever had been before should they then refuse to the South all it should demand?

If gentlemen really meant what they said verbally, let them employ language in the resolution which pledged them to that effect, and Mr. Hamlin was prepared to go for the measure. He honestly avowed what he intended. He stated his position without reserve, and he was ready to march up to his duty, come what might.

They had been told on all sides that this Texas question had been settled by the people in the recent Presidential election. To the decisions of his countrymen Mr. Hamlin was prepared ever to bow, because his doctrine was that the people of a nation, the great mass of the common intelligence, was always right: he did not mean to intimate that the public mind could never be deceived, but he did most firmly believe that the motives and impulses of the people, taken as a body, were always right, and therefore he was ready to bow to their opinion whenever expressed. And was the great majority of the American people in favor of annexation? He believed they were, and so was he decidedly; but that that majority had prescribed the manner of the annexation, and the details of the measure, he no more believed than he did that there had been no election at all. How had the question been presented to the people? In one section of the country it had been presented in one way, and in another section in another; in one portion of the Union the details had been omitted, and in others perhaps they might have been avowed. For himself, his colleagues would all testify with what industry and zeal he had labored in behalf of the Democratic party in the late election. His colleagues, too, know that Mr. Hamlin's exertions had not been limited by his own district, but had been extended through various parts of the state. He had met his own constituents face to face, and he knew how he presented it to them. And now he asked how this Texas question had been presented to the people of the North? Had they not been told that our government throughout was essentially a government of compromises? and that this question, like all others, was to be settled on fair principles of compromise? And were they not told that the arrangement would, in the end, admit more free than slave states into the Union? Undeniably they were. All the Democratic papers in New England which advocated the measure, that he saw, had placed it on that ground. There might be here and there a rare exception, but in general they quoted the language of Mr. Clay. They were honest in taking this position, and backed up this opinion by evidence drawn from the lips of the opponents of the measure. Mr. Hamlin had said to thousands of his constituents the same, and now demanded that gentlemen who had thus presented the measure should follow it out on the same ground. He now asked no more. What did the resolutions from the New Hampshire Legislature declare? and on what basis did they rest? Had it not been that more free states than slave states would be admitted, it would be a quibble to say that the reference was to states not found out of that territory; the reference was obviously to Texas and to Texas alone. Let the resolution speak for itself:

"*Resolved*, That we believe with Mr. Clay, 'that the reannexation of Texas will add more free than slave states to the Union, and that it would be unwise to refuse a permanent acquisition, which will exist as long as the globe remains, on account of a temporary institution.'"

If he was not mistaken this was nearly the language used by Mr. Clay in one of his letters, when he spoke of the territory as being so situated, that it would or could make more free than slave states. Such, certainly, was his expressed opinion and argument.

And now, what did they ask? What was the request of a portion of the decided friends of annexation? It was no more nor less than this, that gentlemen would meet them on the ground of mutual concession, and would take Texas in such a manner as to comply with Northern principles and sentiments, as well as with Southern feelings and interests. Was this asking too much? But Mr. Hamlin would go further. A proposition had been made in the other end of the Capitol, and that, too, by a Southern senator, (Mr. Hayward,) which spoke volumes for his heart as a man, and still more for his head as a statesman. Mr. Hamlin would strike out that provision in the joint resolution which required the action of the treaty power, as he deemed that unnecessary, and might endanger the measure. Here was a fair compromise, giving an equal number of free and slave states, and for it would gladly vote. Mr. Hamlin had no disposition to discuss either the merits or demerits of slavery; the eloquent Pinckney had done this far better than Mr. Hamlin could do. They were Southern lips which had in substance said of slavery, "that the green earth of God was scorched wherever its footsteps were seen." They had declared that slavery was marked by the curse both of God and man. For himself Mr. Hamlin took it as but one of many evils inflicted upon us in our colonial state by the British government. He left it to time and to God to control, to limit, or to abolish it as he deemed best. And now he would ask of the South whether they could say that their Northern friends asked more than they were willing to concede? Were they not willing to settle this matter on the principles of compromise? He was, because he believed that Northern as well as Southern interests, that the commerce, the agriculture, and especially the manufactures of the North, together with the industry of the country generally, would all be benefited by the proposed union. At the same time he believed this would prove a great benefit to the South, by giving them possession of a country eminently adapted to the production of our great staple commodities, more especially of cotton, of which they could enjoy a monopoly. These Mr. Hamlin considered as great national views, all going to justify the scheme of annexation. As for the military argument, he did not look upon that as worth a great deal. He regarded the mutual benefits which would result alike to the whole Union.

But then the North requested that if they aided their Southern brethren in making this acquisition they should themselves participate in it. Let them have an equal portion of the territory which they might populate and improve with the vigorous sinews and the strong arms of freemen.

A portion of the advocates of this measure contended that this was a national question, but there were others who had treated it as sectional, who did not cease to say that it was a Southern question and must be controlled by the South alone. Mr. Hamlin viewed it as a national question. He advocated it as such alone; and that it might be so, the North requested and expected that a fair proportion of Texan territory should be exempted from slavery, so that their emigrants might be enabled to go there and share in the benefits of the new acquisition. Wherever they had heretofore gone, they had subdued the forests and turned the unbroken wilderness into fruitful fields. If they became disgusted with the benefits and results of free labor, let them be left at liberty to exchange it for the labor of slaves if they could. Mr. Hamlin believed he hazarded nothing in saying that the day was far distant when any community that had made the experiment, and seen the effects of free labor on their prosperity, could ever be induced to introduce and establish slavery in its place. It could never be done.

Once more, he said, Let this question be settled now; let it be known, at once, whether any part of the Territory of Texas was to be resigned to slave-labor alone. If there was to be a partition line, let it be designated at once, so that settlers from the North might know where to go; and let it be a just line. It is admitted that a portion of the territory is adapted to free labor. That, too, is the part yet unsettled, and may be converted into free states without affecting the rights of persons now in Texas. An equal or fair division can be made, and not molest or disturb what may be secured to the citizens of that republic. Why are not they willing to do what is admitted to be in accordance with the character of the country; and let the citizens of one section of our Union enjoy the benefits of a part of the territory without coming in conflict with an institution which they neither desire nor would be connected with.

He would ask the attention of gentlemen to two points: If it was insisted on that he was under a wrong impression on this question, how easy was it to bring that question to a test, by meeting their friends on fair and equal terms; if gentlemen said that terms and details should remain an open question, then let them insert an "exclusion to a conclusion," and he would say at once, Let Texas come in. Let the North be but fairly met, and he would vote for her admission with cheerfulness.

But there was another matter connected with this question which Mr. Hamlin had designed to examine. He referred to the jeers and the taunts which had been thrown out, in the course of this debate, upon the North. When he first heard language of this kind, the natural impulse of his heart rose instantly, prompting him to hurl back all such reproaches, and meet them in the same spirit in which they came; but reflection had chastened him on that subject; Southern gentlemen should not provoke a retort from him. This was a question which it did not become a statesman to narrow down into an angry contest of mutual recrimination. No! he should pass by the taunts and the jeers by which it would seem that gentlemen sought to provoke even their Northern allies, as he would the idle wind; and, if it was any consolation to gentlemen to discuss a great national question in that spirit, he had no reproaches to cast upon them. No! he remembered the history of the South too well; he did not choose to forget that, in other days, the South had stood by the North, shoulder to shoulder, and had shed her gushing blood, like rain-drops, in many a hard-fought field. The sands of many a battle-plain had been fertilized by her best blood; and if her sons did now forget the feelings and the principles of their fathers, if that devoted patriotism and broad and general love of country, which led them into every pass of danger, and sustained them under every trying privation, had forsaken the bosom of their sons, he could only contemplate such a spectacle with a sigh. If the North had acted wickedly, he offered for her no apology—that wickedness was not the crime of her *people:* it belonged to her politicians alone. Mr. Hamlin had neither reproaches to cast nor defense to offer, for the folly or wickedness which, at times, had been committed by political men. Sure he was that the hardy sons of the ice-bound region of New England had poured out their blood without stint, to protect the homes of the South, and to avenge her wrongs; their bones were even now bleaching beneath the sun on many a Southern hill, and the monuments of their brave devotion might still be traced wherever their country's flag had floated in the battle-field, or on the breeze, upon the lakes, the ocean, and the land.

> "New England's dead—New England's dead,
> On every field they lie;
> On every field made red
> With bloody victory.
>
> "Their bones are on our Northern hills,
> And on the Southern plain,
> By brook and river, mount and rills,
> And in the sounding main."

"I glory," cried Mr. Hamlin, "in New England and New England's institutions. There she stands, with her free schools and her free labor, her fearless enterprise, her indomitable energy. With her rocky hills, her torrent streams, her green valleys, her heavenward pointed spires; there she stands, a moral monument, around which the gratitude of her country binds the wreath of fame, while protected freedom shall repose forever at its base.

"I meet not my Southern brethren with the brand of discord, but with the olive-branch of peace. I meet them in the spirit of harmony; I desire to meet them on even ground—on ground alike respectful to the North and to the South, and I invoke them to perform this great national act in such a manner that Southern and Northern hands may unite in raising the stars and stripes of our beloved Union; and that Southern and Northern hearts may rejoice together to behold them floating forever over the rich and fertile Texan plains. I ask, will not gentlemen meet us here? Will they not rescue this measure alike from danger and reproach, and put it in a shape to gratify us all? I entreat them to look at the question in all the lights of cool reflection, before they finally reject a compromise which, while it secures them an inestimable benefit, does equal justice to all sections and all interests of the Union."

On the 14th of January, 1847, the question arising on the bill to establish the territorial government of Oregon, Mr. Hamlin made the speech in the House before referred to, in which, among other things, he said:

"Before proceeding to an examination of the matters which I propose to discuss, I invoke the attention of this House to the manner in which this debate has been conducted upon the other side. Had a stranger within these walls listened to the discussion, he would readily have supposed that we of the free states were waging an unholy crusade against the Southern population of this confederacy; that we were laying unholy and polluted hands upon the sacred rights guaranteed by the Constitution to the Southern states; that we were disregarding their sacred rights, and almost trampling upon their domestic altars. Sir, is this so? I have not yet listened to the first man who has addressed this House, upon this side, who would trample upon, or trifle with, a solitary right of any one of the states of this Union. On the other hand, there has been but one spontaneous and uniform declaration that we will stand by them in weal and in woe.

"In the discussion of this matter, then, gentlemen are

not to escape on these collateral issues. They are not to raise the smoke of their own creating, and vanish behind it. No man proposes to disturb a single right guaranteed by the Constitution to any one of the states. On the other hand, we pledge ourselves, here and hereafter, that we will stand by them as one common brotherhood, engaged in one common cause. No, sir; we design no such thing; we counsel no such thing, and we will not concur in any such thing. As members of this great confederacy, however, we do ask and demand that in all things submitted to our deliberation, we shall have the right to speak, and speak with manly boldness and firmness, to defend and maintain the rights of the constituents we represent on this floor. We ask no more, we will take no less."

Further on he says: "The question submitted to us—and it is a question not to be winked out of sight—is, are we to acquire other and foreign territory, either for the purpose or with the consent of the people of this Union, that it may be converted into slave territory? Never, sir; never, to the end of time, with my aid and with my assistance, shall that acquisition take place. While I desire to see the union of California to these States, it must come *free*, or not at all. And now, I say, with the gentlemen from South Carolina, (Messrs. Burt and Rhett,) *now* is the time when we are to meet this question fairly, and talk openly and boldly to each other, that there may be no misunderstanding between us hereafter. Gentlemen have perfectly understood, if nothing were said or done now, slavery would be sure to advance and run over the territories which we might acquire There could be no mistake about that fact. Suffer this time to go by, and give the acquiescence of silence, and the conclusion was foregone. *A silent acquiescence is equal to an affirmative vote in favor of slavery;* and to avoid the issue now is equally responsible. And while we vote with cheerfulness for all supplies, men and money, to prosecute the war with the utmost vigor, and while *all* should rally for the country in this crisis; while there should be no holding back, at the same time, we are bound to declare that we will not permit the institution of slavery to exist in any territory which may result as an incident of the war."

After speaking of the failure to secure the rights of free labor in the acquisition of Texas, he says:

"But, sir, I discard, at once and forever, all talk about a compromise, on any parallel of latitude which can be named by man. To any proposition for taking territory now free, and sending there the shackles and manacles of slavery, I never will consent; never. No; cause the declaration to be placed on record on your journals, that it may be seen by those who shall come after us, and who shall be better able to carry out the doctrines we lay down. * * * I will go for no compromise whatever."

Annunciating the proposition which he would pass affirmatively, a proposition which should declare to the world that no territory now free shall ever come into the Union as slave territory, or be made slave territory, he says:

"But, sir, suppose we fail, suppose we are not able to pass that declaratory act; we give you notice, that this is the ground upon which we plant ourselves, and it is the ground to be supported by other, by abler and better men, who shall hereafter come here as representatives of the North. At the North, sir, there is but one public sentiment on this subject. I do not mean to say by this that you may not here and there find a case of a shackled press muttering its dissent against the doctrines of freemen; that you may not here and there find a *doughface*, with fetters on his lips, uttering his faint protest against it. But it is the doctrine of the North; it is the doctrine she will march up to. She will live up to it in all coming time. And we give you notice, that you may not hereafter say we have taken you by surprise; we give you notice, even if we are not able to carry it out now, that we shall have no shackles upon us when we come to vote for the admission of states to be formed out of this territory."

In conclusion, Mr. Hamlin said:

"A few more words and I have done. And in reference to the stale, worn-out cry of dissolution of this Union, the time was when even my nerves were a little disturbed by it. That time has long since passed, and gentlemen of timid, weak nerves are now rallying around the standard, on the free side of the question, who were wont to rally on the other side. This cry of dissolution of the Union has become too old to be repeated, or to be entitled to much weight and confidence, iterated and reiterated as it is on every major and minor question. The Union can not be dissolved. The mutual interests and benefits enjoyed by the different sections would not permit it. The great West was bound to the South by its commerce, and could not be separated while its mighty rivers rolled to the Gulf of Mexico. The North and the South, too, were equally bound by their commerce and exchange of productions. These were all ligaments that could not be rent or ruptured. The talk of it was folly, as well as madness. These great ties to which he had alluded, superadded to the patriotic devotion of our people to our government, would render our Union impregnable forever. A dissolution of this great and mighty republic, erected by the wisdom of our fathers, cemented by their blood! and for what? Spread it out, that the public eye may gaze upon it; proclaim it, that the public ear may hear it; utter it from the groaning press, and thunder it from the pulpit:—A dissolution of the Union *because* we will not extend the institution of negro slavery! Sir, the man who would utter that sentiment, should blush when it falls from his lips. Dissolve this great and mighty republic for this miserable pretext. I agree with the gentleman from Indiana (Mr. Petitt) that it is not the doctrine of the great and patriotic South. She has rallied—except the time when she was about to go to the death for sugar—she has rallied for this Union. She will stand by it, when others may desert it; stand by it in all coming time, and will regret that her sons proclaimed it to the world, in this nineteenth century, in this, the freest country on earth, that we are to dissolve this fair fabric for the miserable reason that we will not extend the institution which is a curse to all the states in which it exists. * * *

"In whatever may be the action and course of Northern Representatives here, the great mass of the Northern people have but one impulse beating in their bosoms—to stand by this Union through good and evil report—to rally around the blessed stars and stripes of our glorious Confederacy wherever they float—to peril their lives and pour out their blood and treasure, if need be, in its defense; but to the institution of slavery they say, 'Thus far hast thou gone—no further shalt thou go.'"

We can not, in justice to Mr. Hamlin, omit any portion of the important speech, before referred to, made by him in the Senate of the United States, July 22d, 1848, on the bill reported from the Select Committee to establish territorial governments in Oregon, New Mexico, and California, known as the Compromise Bill. Mr. Hamlin said: "I am admonished, Mr. President, by the whisperings within these walls, that we are to be pressed to a decision of this great question at the present sitting. If, therefore, I would offer any suggestions, which will control my vote and command my action, I must embrace the present as the only opportunity.

"The question which we are now called upon to decide is of momentous importance. Yet from its decision I have no disposition to shrink. It is, indeed, startling, that in the middle of the nineteenth century—in this model Republic, with the sun of liberty shining upon us, and while the governments of Europe are tottering to their base, from the lights reflected from our own, and while they are striking down the shackles of tyranny over the minds of men—we have been gravely discussing the proposition, whether we will not create, by law, the institution of human slavery in territories now free. Such, in direct terms, has been the question which we have had before us; such is the issue, in fact, now. Sophistry can not evade it—metaphysics can not escape it. If there have been those who have heretofore believed a discussion of this matter premature, all, or nearly all, have declared a willingness to meet the issue when it should be practically presented. That crisis is now upon us, and, as men faithfully representing the constituencies who have sent us here, we must meet it. I had hoped—nay, I had believed—that there were those common grounds of concession, union, and harmony, dictated by a lofty patriotism, upon which all would meet, and by which we would settle this vexed question. Of all things, I have been desirous that we might be able to arrive at such a decision of this matter as would quiet the public mind, and be just to all the people of all the states.

"The character of the debate, connected directly with this subject, within the last few weeks, must necessarily associate itself with the question immediately before us for our decision. This bill sprang from that discussion. They are one and the same. That was a bill for the establishment of a government for the Territory of Oregon. This includes also the Territories of California and New Mexico. As there is no connection in these matters, I had hoped to have seen each bill presented by itself—to stand upon its own merits, or fall upon its demerits. The Senate has decided that they shall not be separated, and we must meet it as it is presented. I will state the reasons why I am compelled to withhold from it my vote.

"We have acquired the territories over which this bill extends. They are embraced within the Union, and it now becomes our duty to legislate for them. It is proper and just that we should extend over them the laws of our country, and adopt such other legislation as the case shall demand. It is a solemn and responsible trust committed to our hands. We are about to shape and mold the character of these territories, which in time shall become a mighty empire. Their destiny is in our hands; the responsibility is upon us. Whether that country shall present all the elements of a free government, in which man is elevated as an intellectual and moral being, or whether the despotism of slavery shall imprint its soil, are matters depending entirely upon us. Let wisdom guide us in the path of duty, and let not the light of the past be lost upon us in our action. We must act; it now presents a point from which no man can shrink. The issue can not be avoided; and let no one imagine that an intelligent public can doubt as to the character of that issue. No matter in what form presented, it will be clearly understood. True, the bill, like the proposition discussed by the Senate, does not profess to establish slavery by law. It leaves it to extend itself by the "silent operation" of the law, *without restriction*. It does not guarantee it; but will it not permit it? and, after it has found an existence, will it not demand a guarantee? Thus, without inhibition, will it not become certain and fixed by the process of time? Is it too much that freedom of the soil shall be asked and demanded from this aggressive march of slavery? I solemnly believe that this bill will allow of the extension of slavery, as certainly as if it created it in express words. The bill, as I understand it, concedes practically all that the ultra doctrines of the South demand, or will, in its operations, end in that. Let us, then, erect a barrier to this tide of moral evil.

"With such a bill as this, I can not hesitate to give the aid of my voice and my vote to arrest it. To know and understand the views of those who sustain it, will enable us to judge of its merits. The public mind will be startled through all the North; it will thrill through all the country like an electric shock, that the acquisition of territory from a foreign power necessarily subjects it to the institution of slavery—that the flag of this Union carries that institution with it wherever it floats. This is a new principle in the doctrines of slavery propagandism. It is not the doctrine of the founders of the republic. Democracy has been called progressive, but my word for it, she goes along in the old-fashioned stage-coach style, while this doctrine of slavery propagandism has mounted the railroad cars, if it has not assumed the speed of electricity. I repeat, that it will startle the North when it is known that it is gravely discussed here that the Constitution of the United States, whenever it extends over territory which we may acquire, carries with it and establishes the institution; that it in fact abrogates the laws of the free, and gives, instead, the power of servitude. This is a doctrine of a later day. It is not the doctrine that accords with the sterling patriotism of the founders of our republic. Far from it! While such are the views of aggressive slavery which are promulgated here, it makes our path of duty as clear as sunlight. We must prevent this tide, by positive law, from spreading over our free soil. This extraordinary demand of this power leaves us but one course to pursue. We shall be faithless to ourselves—faithless to those we represent—faithless to our country, the age in which we live, and the principles of Christianity, if we falter. We have but to press on; and if, from any or various influences which shall be brought to bear against us, we shall not succeed, or shall suffer a partial defeat, yet—

"'Truth crushed to earth shall rise again—
The eternal years of God are hers;
While Error, wounded, writhes in pain,
And dies amid its worshipers.'

"While I do not admit the force or justice of these demands, so pertinaciously insisted upon, yet they must be met, or they will be certain to prevail. In my judgment these doctrines are not deduced from the Constitution, but are in derogation of its letter and spirit; that instrument is, in all its terms, and in all its scope, an antislavery instrument. It was conceived, it was enacted, it was approved by the States of this Union, not in the spirit of extension or creation of slavery, but in a spirit which looked to the future emancipation of the slave in this country. It looked not to the extension of the institution, but to the time when this anomaly in our system of government should cease to exist.

"I do not propose to follow gentlemen who have discussed this point at length, nor do I propose to detain the Senate with the views and opinions which I entertain, and which I have drawn from the Constitution, and which have brought my mind to a different conclusion. It is necessary, however, that I state briefly my views; that I state the points without attempting to elaborate them. I deny, then, utterly and entirely, this new doctrine which has been presented to us, that the Constitution of the United States contains within its provisions a power to extend and establish over territory now free, the institution of slavery. If I understand the argument upon which it is based, it is simply this: that these territories are the property of the people of the United States; that, as such, they are open to settlement by all the people of the United States; and that, as the Constitution recognized the institution of slavery at its adoption, it therefore authorizes the institution in those territories which belong to the United States, and in which the people of the United States may wish to reside with their slaves. The Constitution does *recognize* slavery as existing, but it does not *create* or *establish* it. Article 1, section 2, says:

"'Representatives and direct taxes shall be apportioned among the several states which may be included within the Union, according to their respective numbers, which shall be determined by adding to the whole number of free persons, including those bound to service for a term of years, and excluding Indians not taxed, three-fifths of all other persons.'

"This, surely, is not establishing slavery by the Constitution; it makes slaves a basis of representation and taxation. That is all. But in another place the Constitution declares, (article 4, section 2:)

"'No person held to service or labor in *one state by the laws thereof*, escaping into another, shall, in consequence of any law or *regulation* therein, be discharged from such service or labor, but shall be delivered up on claim of the party to whom such service or labor may be due.'

"From these extracts, it would seem to be perfectly clear, that the Constitution does not create or establish; it only recognizes a class of persons held to service in the states by "*the laws thereof*," *not* by virtue of the Constitution. That clause, when fairly construed, is only an inhibition upon the free states, that they shall not pass laws to prevent the owners of slaves from reclaiming them. The argument that slavery is *recognized* by the Constitution is used as equivalent to *establishing*. The laws of the state support and maintain it, not the Constitution. It is a state institution, resting on the local law of the state, without the aid, without the support, without the maintenance of the Constitution, in any way whatever. Yet in the face of all this, it is contended, and attempted to be proved by metaphysical reasoning, that the Constitution extends beyond the states in which slavery is established; that it carries it into free territories, and guarantees it there. Can this be so? and if so, where will the power end? If the institution is one which has its foundation in the Constitution, and not one resting upon laws of the states, where is the limit to its extension? What is the next step in the application of the argument? After you have overrun your territories, what power can prevent the slaveholder from coming into the free states with his slaves? If his right is a Constitutional one; if he rests his claim there, and is correct, a state law could not affect him, because it would be in conflict with the Constitution. I can not see how this conclusion can be avoided. If the premises are correct, that result must follow. But I neither admit the premises nor the conclusion. The Constitution gives no right, it creates no right; it merely recognizes a right which is created by the laws of the state. That it is a local institution, there can be no doubt. The courts of nearly all the states have so decided. Authorities to any extent could be cited; they are familiar to all. The moment a slave goes beyond the limits of the state where slavery exists, he becomes free. It *must*, therefore, look *alone* to local laws for its support.

"I hold that the Constitution, in and of itself, by its express language, authorizes Congress to inhibit this institution in our territories. I hold that the article in the Constitution which gives to Congress the power to make all needful rules and regulations respecting its territories, includes full and absolute authority over this whole matter. What is the language of this clause of the Constitution?

"'Congress shall have power to dispose of, and make *all* needful rules and regulations respecting the territory or other property of the United States.'

"What is this grant of power?

"1st. Congress may dispose of its public domain.

"2d. It may make 'all needful rules and regulations respecting the territory or other property of the United States.'

"To dispose of, is to give, grant, or convey the public lands; but to make all needful rules and regulations, implies and carries with it full and ample power of legislation, in *all cases* where the Constitution does not otherwise prohibit. There can be no doubt as to the meaning of the terms 'rules and regulations.' The Constitution itself interprets them. A law is defined to be 'a rule of action prescribed by the supreme power in the state.' The Constitution gives Congress power to '*regulate commerce*'—to make '*rules* concerning captures'—'to make *rules* for the government and *regulation* of the land and naval forces.' It also provides that persons escaping from one state into another, shall not be discharged from service in 'consequence of any law or *regulation* therein.' In this case both terms are used—'all needful *rules* and *regulations*'—to give the widest scope to the power. But it is said that the concluding words in the clause quoted—'or other property'—limit and confine our legislation over the territory to the same as property. Grant that our territories are denominated as property, whether inhabited or not, does not the same power exist to pass all needful rules and regulations for its settlement and its final admission into the Union as a state? The power is clearly within the scope and meaning of that clause.

"The history of the manner in which that clause became a part of the Constitution, would settle the question, if there could be a reasonable doubt. In the Articles of Confederation, by which the states were united, before the Constitution was formed, no such power was found. This grant of power was therefore made in the forming of the Constitution, for the purpose of giving Congress the power. The doings of the Convention, and the declarations of Mr. Madison, are clear upon this point. But, aside from this view of the case, we have the uninterrupted use of the power by the General Government for about sixty years. Hardly a Congress has existed which has not acted upon this power, from 1787 to this time. This power has been exercised by Washington, Jefferson, Jackson, and Van Buren. The Supreme Court of the United States have settled this question. Congress has already exercised the power, and that power has been declared valid by the Supreme Court. 1 Peters' Rep., 543, Chief Justice Marshall says:

"'Whatever may be the source whence this power is derived, the possession of it is unquestionable.'

"In 5th Peters' Rep., 44, again the Court says:

"'Rules and regulations respecting the territories of the United States, necessarily include complete jurisdiction.'

"Again, the power is contained in the *bill upon which we are acting*. It continues the laws of Oregon in force for three months after the meeting of the Legislature. It provides, in the Territories of California and New Mexico, that the legislative power *shall not pass any laws* on the subject of *religion or slavery*. Here we use the power in its broadest sense. We inhibit the use or exercise of *any power* on either of said subjects, and some others.

"Could there be any doubt still remaining, and if we had no grant of power in the Constitution at all, there would yet be another source from which we must gather it. If the Constitution was silent, as it is not, yet under that power which we can acquire, we could most certainly govern. It matters little where you find the power to acquire; if you do acquire, you must have the power to govern. The first is the major, the second is the minor proposition. It would not be good sense to contend that we have a power to acquire public domain, and yet could not pass needful rules and regulations for its government. The case, when stated, is its own best argument. The sovereignty to acquire must contain the lesser power to govern. These are briefly the reasons which force conviction upon my mind. Casuists have been known to deny their own existence, and satisfactorily to prove it to their own minds. That may be a plausible and a practical doctrine, when contrasted with the one that we have no power to govern our territories. It is 'too late,' at the noon of the nineteenth century, to deny that right, or for us to avoid the duty of acting.

"Having the power to act, what is the responsible duty which I feel imposed upon me? (for I speak for none other.) It is, that I should exert all the power which the Constitution gives to exclude the institution of slavery from our territories now free, because it is a social, moral, and political evil. That such is its character, needs no argument to prove. They are conceded facts —supported by the declarations and admonitions of the best and wisest men of the South—

"'In thoughts that breathe, and words that burn.

"I would resist the introduction of that institution in justice to a superior race of men—men who are capable of a higher state of social and political refinement. I would institute such governments as are best calculated to advance the true interests of our own Caucasian race, and not degrade the dignity of labor by fastening upon it the incubus of slavery. I would resist it, because I would not invoke or use the name of Democracy to strike down, as with the iron mace of a despot, the principles of social equality and freedom. I would not profane the sacred name of Freedom, while using it, to impose a tyranny upon the minds or persons of men. Jefferson has said, that 'God has no attribute which can take sides with us in such a cause.' The eloquent Pinckney has de-

30

clared, 'That the earth itself, which teems with profusion under the cultivating hand of the free-born laborer, shrinks into barrenness from the contaminating sweat of the slave.' Sir, my course is a plain one, and clear from all doubt. Our position is unquestionable. We stand in defense of free soil, and resist aggressive slavery. And we demand enactments for the protection of free soil against this aggression. We will not disturb that institution, but we will stand in defense of the freedom of our soil as right in principle and beneficial to free white labor in all parts of our common country.

"I have expressed the hope that we might have met upon a common ground upon the settlement of this question—a question which has agitated so much the public mind; and more did I hope for it when I listened to the patriotic breathings of the message of the President on this subject; when I listened to the language he used in his message, when he submitted the treaty of peace with Mexico to us, and called our attention to this matter now before us for our ultimate decision. When I heard that language read by the Secretary, and recalled the history of the events to which he had invited our attention, I had hoped that the spirit of the fathers of the republic had not altogether departed, that the language of the Declaration of Independence had not become obsolete. I had hoped that we would come up, and, in the language of the President, in a spirit of forbearance and of patriotism, have settled the question in a way which would have secured the approbation of the country.

"Allow me to read from the President's message:

"'In organizing governments over these territories, fraught with such vast advantages to every portion of our Union, I invoke that spirit of concession, conciliation, and compromise in your deliberations, in which the Constitution was framed, in which it should be administered, and which is so indispensable to preserve and perpetuate the harmony and union of the states. We should never forget that this union of confederated states was established and cemented by kindred blood, and by the common toils, sufferings, dangers, and triumphs of all its parts, and has been the ever-augmenting source of our national greatness and of all our blessings.'

"This is the ground upon which we should have met and decided the question. It is in this spirit of liberal and elevated patriotism that I had hoped that this question would have been settled, and that it would not have been merged in a mere question of power or of local or sectional character. I had hoped that we would have been guided by the lights of experience."

MR. DAVIS, of Mississippi.—"I would ask the senator, if he will allow me, whether he, as the representative of the people of Maine, is now ready, or has at any time been ready, to vote for the Missouri Compromise line being extended until it terminates in the Pacific?"

MR. HAMLIN.—"I frankly answer, no. Because the spirit of the Missouri Compromise was not the spirit which marked the wisdom of the framers of the Constitution. I would not vote to extend an arbitrary line, which permits the extension of the institution of slavery over any portion of the continent."

MR. CLAYTON.—"Did not the senator vote for the Missouri Compromise upon the annexation of Texas?"

MR. HAMLIN.—"I did not."

MR. CLAYTON.—"He voted for the annexation of Texas, did he not?"

MR. HAMLIN.—"I was in favor of the annexation of Texas, but I did not vote for the resolutions for the annexation of Texas which passed the House, nor did I vote for the Missouri Compromise contained in the resolutions. A senator from Illinois, (Mr. Douglas,) then a member of the House, offered the Compromise there. It was adopted, but I voted against its adoption, and against the resolutions after it was incorporated into them. The resolutions came to the Senate, and the distinguished senator from Missouri (Mr. Benton) offered another and distinct resolution to accomplish the annexation of Texas. Mr. Hamlin said such was his recollection, and he would inquire of the senator of Missouri whether he offered the alternate resolution?"

Mr. Benton.—"It is of very little importance who offered the amendment.

Mr. Hamlin.—"Yes, it is of very little importance who offered it. All knew that it originated with that distinguished senator. For that resolution I voted; and deeply is it to be regretted that the annexation had not been accomplished as that resolution provided. The treasure of the country would have been saved, and the lives of our citizens preserved. We should have had no Mexican war. I did not then vote for the Missouri Compromise, and I would not vote for it to-day. I would vote for no arbitrary line, even if it took the southern boundary of New Mexico and California, running to the coast of the Pacific. I would vote for no rigid fixed line, whether upon a direct parallel of latitude or winding, because it would lead to the very difficulties which Mr. Jefferson, in his letter recognizing the Missouri Compromise in 1820, alluded to with so much force, when he said that it would create sectional parties—that it would strike upon the ear 'like a fire-bell at night.' But this line of 36° 30′, running to the Pacific, has other and insuperable objections, besides those already named. The superiority of our race and political institutions, with the events of the past, teach us, with unerring certainty, that our government is destined to extend over this country. Establish this line, and you doom the whole of the continent south to the curse of slavery, when it shall become a part of our Union. You establish it on a section of country over which free labor can not pass. That will be the inevitable result of such a line. Can it be doubted that such is the design?"

MR. CLAYTON.—"The senator speaks of compromise; will he tell us what compromise he alludes to?"

MR. HAMLIN.—"I am coming to that, and should have done so if I had not been diverted by these interrogatories. In the language of the President's message, I would have our deliberations consummated in 'that spirit of concession, conciliation, and compromise in which the Constitution was framed.' Then we would have no difficulty in the settlement of this question. What is the history of the times cotemporaneous with the formation of that instrument? The Constitution was adopted by the Convention, September 17, 1787. Virginia, in the spirit of wisdom and patriotism worthy of her ancient fame, had ceded to the General Government all her lands lying northwest of the Ohio river, and being all the lands lying within the limits of the Union. On the thirteenth day of July, 1787, and while the Convention was in session to form a Constitution, Virginia entered into a compact with the States, and established what is known as the ordinance of '87, forever excluding slavery from all that country. Thomas Jefferson, the patriot, statesman, and sage, was the originator of the principle in that ordinance which excluded slavery from that territory. Nay, it went further; it abolished slavery there and made it free soil. I think, too, that the history of these times will satisfy all, that this noble and patriotic act was designed to aid in the formation of the

Constitution by acting upon the Convention. In the same spirit of restriction, too, did that Convention authorize Congress to inhibit the importation of slaves into the United States after the year 1808. This is the history of those times—this is the spirit of *conciliation* and *compromise* that mark those days; let us adopt it now, and our work is done. We need not go so far in the rule which we will adopt. The ordinance was an act of abolition. I would not abolish slavery in the states, and, so help me God, I would not abolish freedom in our territories. Let us have nothing of abolition, either north or south, nor fix lines which shall divide a country without regard to its character or construction—which shall create sectional parties, the worst and most to be deplored of all. But let the character of the country be determined and settled as it shall be on its acquisition. If free, so let it remain, and so let it be preserved. If slave territory, so then let it continue without our action. When we look at former acquisitions, it would seem that the South should not object to this manner of compromise. From our former acquisitions, seven slave states have been added to this Union, and three more of the largest class provided for, to be carved out of Texas. One free state only has been added from these acquisitions. Justice to the North demands this course in a settlement of this question. Here is a compromise upon which all can meet, and one which can not create these sectional divisions which all must deprecate. If I have a desire in my heart above all others, it is that this vexed question shall be settled—that it shall be taken from the vortex of political conflicts, and the people quieted. Adhere to the ancient landmarks, conform to the settled usage of the country, and such will be the happy result. So much upon our power and duty to act.

"The bill before us is objectionable in its provisions, as well as in the manner in which it is presented. It comes in a triangular shape, with Oregon as the base, and California and New Mexico for its side lines. Oregon has no connection with the other territories, and why, then, are they chained and thus connected together? Why not let each stand by itself? Why make the one depend upon the fate of the other? I can see no sufficient reason. For years the people of Oregon have been demanding a government, and bill after bill has passed the other House, but as often as they have reached this body they have been either permitted to sleep 'the sleep that knows no waking,' or they have been defeated by those who now claim to be the most vigilant sentinels. During this session, and within a few weeks past, Congress has been admonished, in a message from the President, that savage hordes were committing depredations upon the whites, and the bill was not passed. The bill was before the Senate, and in accordance with the prayer of the people of Oregon, it contained a section inhibiting slavery from the territory. It was the general impression that that section could not be stricken out. A motion was made to recommit to a committee of eight, which was carried, and the bill comes back to us chained to the other territories, and with that section in the bill restricting slavery in Oregon so modified that it secures freedom for three months only after the first Territorial Legislature shall meet. This bill is called by some a compromise; all that I can see which entitles it to that name, is, that it does provide that the laws in Oregon which exclude slavery shall remain in force for three months. A compromise, indeed!"

Mr. Clayton.—"If the senator will allow me, it may not be inappropriate to make an explanation upon this point concerning which an inquiry has been made. Section 12 provides that the laws now existing in the Territory of Oregon shall remain as they are until three months after the first meeting of the Legislature of the Territory. The senator from Maine understands, of course—I take it for granted that is his doctrine—that the Legislature of Oregon will have the power upon the subject of slavery. Gentlemen who argue as he does, argue that the Territorial Legislature has full power over this subject. Now, take the sixth section in connection with the twelfth. The sixth section provides that the legislative power of the Territory shall extend to all rightful subjects of legislation, consistent with the Constitution and the provisions of this act. The gentleman holds that the Legislature can, consistently with the provisions of the Constitution, legislate on the subject of slavery. If it can do this, it will do it. If it can not do this consistently with the Constitution, it ought not to do it. Now, take the twelfth and sixth sections together, and the whole will be, I think, plain to the mind of any one. I do not see how gentlemen, advocating the opinions which are advocated by the gentleman from Maine, can object to this provision of the bill."

MR. HAMLIN.—"From the explanation which the honorable chairman of the committee has given, I apprehend that I did not misunderstand the scope and meaning of the twelfth section of this bill, and if the gentleman had listened to the conclusion which I drew from that section, taken in connection with the sixth, he would have had no occasion to interrupt me. I repeat, then, that the compromise of this bill is one which concedes that the fundamental law now existing in the Territory of Oregon shall remain in force for three months, *and for only three months.* That is the only concession which I can find in the bill, and if for that it is to be taken as a compromise bill, why then let it be called such. The twelfth section concedes that the laws of the Territory shall remain in force for three months after the Territorial Government shall have met. They will then cease and be no longer in force, unless the Territorial Government shall see fit to re-enact them, and send them here for the approval of Congress. Now, if it were intended as a compromise, why repeal all the laws of the Territory? Why was the law regarding the exclusion of slavery not permitted to remain in force until the Territorial Legislature should see fit to change it? Why abrogate, and then compel them to re-enact their laws? Sir, it is not worth the name of compromise. This is the fundamental objection. It repeals all the laws of the Territory after three months, and the seventeenth section provides that—

"'All laws passed by the Legislative Assembly shall be submitted to the Congress of the United States, and if disapproved, shall be null and of no effect;'

thus making the legislative acts of Oregon depend on our approval or disapproval. Is it not, then, literally true, that this bill concedes the free principle to Oregon for only three months, after which it must depend upon action here? So I understand it.

"There is, to my mind, another and most peculiar feature in this bill, rendering it most inconsistent in its character. It creates for Oregon a territorial government, and gives it a Legislature elected by the people thereof. It is a government in which the people participate. Every

"'Free white male inhabitant above the age of twenty-one years, who shall have been a resident of said Territory at the time of the passage of this act, shall be entitled to vote at the first election.'

"And it gives the Legislature power over all rightful subjects of legislation. In California and New Mexico this bill deprives the people of all power, and of any participation in the government over them. It creates an odious oligarchy over that people of the most objectionable kind. It sets up a government, not with the consent and participation of the people, but rather in defiance of their just rights.

"'SECT. 26. The legislative power of said Territory, shall, until Congress shall otherwise provide, be vested in the Governor, Secretary, and Judges of the Supreme Court, who, or a majority of them, shall have power to pass any law for the administration of justice in said Territory, which shall not be repugnant to this act, or inconsistent with the laws and Constitution of the United States. But no law shall be passed interfering with the primary disposal of the soil, respecting an establishment of religion, or respecting slavery; and no tax shall be imposed upon the property of the United States, nor shall the lands or other property of non-residents be taxed higher than the lands or other property of residents. All the laws shall be submitted to the Congress of the United States, and, if disapproved, shall be null and void.'

"What good reason there may be for intrusting full power and sovereignty to the people of Oregon, while you wholly deny it to California, I do not understand. Why adopt one system for Oregon, and another for California? Is it said that the people of California are not yet suited to participate in a free government or in the enactments of laws? If such even were the fact, why *wholly* exclude them from all rights? But Senators know, that at this day there are some five or six thousand American citizens there, and they are ruthlessly excluded. Is their capacity for free government to be mistrusted? Is it not rather from the fact that they would set up a free government indeed, that they are deprived of all power? I know there is a mixed population in California, and so it is in Oregon; but the same limitations and restrictions which apply in one case can be applied in the other. The right of voting has been confined in Oregon to the "free white inhabitants." The same limitation may apply to California. No sound distinction can be drawn in these cases, yet a republican government is established in one case, and an oligarchy in the others. These people were but a short time since the subjects of a foreign power, and sound policy would dictate that we should not set up a despotism over them. Is it not better to authorize our own people to participate in this government, and allow the free white Castilian race the same power? Is it not sound policy as well as correct in principle? Will it not fraternize them with our people and our Government? On the other hand, without power in the local laws by which they are governed, will they not be alien to our Union, and unfraternal to our people? It must not be forgotten that all laws which would be passed in California, as in Oregon, would be subject to the approval or disapproval by Congress. This system is wholly repugnant to our form of government. It is in violation of that fundamental principle which recognizes the 'consent of the governed,' as the basis of government. We are told that such is the early form of our territorial governments. Be it so. It is not the form of later years. If it were, the application should be uniform, not applied to the free white population of one territory and not to another.

The settlement of the question of slavery by this bill, it is said, is to be determined by the Supreme Court. I think, if that be the case, this is the first instance in the history of legislation where a question purely of a political character has been transferred to the judiciary. It is avoiding what necessarily belongs to us to determine. Is this the part of wisdom, or manly dignity and firmness, to avoid the settlement of a question which is political, and which belongs to us? I think not. We are told that the Supreme Court of the United States can determine whether slavery will exist there or not, if this bill shall pass. That by the twenty-second section of this bill, a right to appeal is granted from the Supreme Court of the territories to the Supreme Court of the United States. Suppose it to be so. What would the right of appeal be worth practically? Suppose slavery steals in there, as it will, how can the slave avail himself of this right of appeal? Who is to aid him, in the first instance, to obtain his writ of habeas corpus, on which to try the question of his right to freedom? And if he should get that process and take the first step, how could he appeal? Who would be his surety? and, at the distance of three thousand miles from Washington, by what means could he reach the court? This right of appeal, if it existed by law, could have no practical effect whatever. It leaves all unsettled, in fact, while two lines in a law we may pass, by simply inhibiting the institution, will settle all. But, sir, the bill, in fact, does not grant even a right to appeal in a case of this kind. Though the right of appeal in certain cases is granted, it does not include this case.

"The bill establishes 'a Supreme Court, District Court, and Probate Courts.' The bill also provides that—

"'Writs of error and appeals from the final decisions of said Supreme Court shall be allowed, and may be taken to the Supreme

Judicial Court of the United States, in the same manner and under the same regulations as from the Circuit Court of the United States.'

"To understand correctly what are the rights of appeal granted in this bill, it becomes necessary to see in what cases, and in what manner, writs of error and appeals are granted from the Circuit Courts to the Supreme Judicial Court of the United States. Then we can learn whether there is, in fact, anything practical in this right of appeal. This bill does not determine, in words, how appeals shall be had, but refers to existing laws granting writs of error and appeals. What are those laws? Section 22, chapter 20, United States Laws, regulates the manner of granting appeals from the Circuit Court to the Supreme Judicial Court of the United States. It says:

"'Final judgments and decrees, in civil actions and suits in equity, in Circuit Courts, brought there by original process, or removed there from the courts of the several states, and removed there by appeal from a District Court, *where the matter in dispute exceeds the sum or value of two thousand dollars, exclusive of costs,* may be re-examined and reversed or affirmed in the Supreme Court.'

"The right of appeal, then, is given only when the property exceeds in value two thousand dollars. As that would be greater than the value of a person who might sue out his writ of habeas corpus, no right of appeal would exist.

"But, on this point, we are not left to the doubtful or uncertain construction of a statute, although the language of that statute is, to my mind, clear and positive. The Supreme Judicial Court of the United States, our highest legal tribunal, have settled and adjudicated that question. It meets this case precisely. The case to which I refer is one involving the right of appeal from the decision of the Circuit Court to the Supreme Court, on the process of the habeas corpus. Barry *vs.* Mercein *et. al.*, 5 Howard's Rep., 103. This case was decided at January term, 1847:

"'This court has no appellate power in a case where the Circuit Court refused to grant a writ of habeas corpus, prayed for by a father to take his infant child out of the custody of its mother.'

"'The judgment of a Circuit Court can be reversed *only* where the matter in dispute exceeds the sum or value of *two thousand dollars*. It must have a known and certain value, which can be proved and calculated in the ordinary business transactions.'

"So the Court has decided this case. No right of appeal could lie. If it did, every man knows that it would be utterly useless as a practical matter. It would not, and could not reach the case of a person held to service—no right of trial can exist beyond the limits of the Territory by this bill. It does not meet the case. But even if it did apply to this case, it would be practically useless. If it could apply to *one case*, it would be powerless in thousands. It is all delusive. *It does not allow an appeal at all.*

"How, then, stands the case? You establish a government in California, a governor and secretary are appointed by the President, and three judges, who are not removable, and to them you commit the legislative power of the Territory; you deny them the power to legislate at all upon the subjects of religion or slavery! even if every person in the Territory should desire to exclude the latter. You deprive the people of the right to act at all—you refuse to act here, and one-half of the Senate nearly denying the power. Is not this virtually building up a wall around that Territory, which will and must serve as a protection to this institution? What is the origin of slavery? It is never created by law; it steals into territory, and then claims a law to recognize it. The senator from Virginia (Mr. Mason) says:

"'There never was a law in Virginia creating slavery, and I doubt if there has been such a law in any of the Southern States.'

"Such is the fact. There is no law creating it. It exists by brute force, in the violation of the rights of everything human or Divine. Were we called upon, could we justify it if we thus surrender up this vast country—these great principles of human freedom, and exclude from it the free white labor of the whole land? That this bill will do it, there can be no doubt, as it restricts that power which alone could prevent it. It inhibits all power in the territory from preventing the lawless spread of slavery. That inhibition will prove a guarantee. Or, certain it is, that while you thus prevent the use of all power to exclude slavery from the territory, it would be as certain as the decree of fate, that it would steal in, as it has, into all the territories, and then claiming vested rights, it would demand and obtain laws securing and recognizing it. Such has been its history in every state where it now exists; such will be the result here if this bill shall become a law.

"The senator from Delaware gave us the extent of the area included in those territories north of the parallel of 36° 30′. I was unable to get the precise amount; but if I am right in my recollection, the aggregate of territory north of that parallel was about one million five hundred thousand square miles."

MR. CLAYTON.—"One million six hundred thousand square miles."

MR. HAMLIN.—"And that south of that parallel

the area was about three hundred thousand square miles."

Mr. Clayton.—" Two hundred and sixty-two thousand square miles."

Mr. Hamlin.—" Now, sir, we have not the Missouri Compromise before us for discussion. What was the object of the gentleman, then, in presenting that table of figures? Why did not the gentleman, in connection with it, present other facts and figures for our consideration? Why did he not state, that in our free states the population is about twelve millions, and in the slave states about eight millions? Why did he not present another element—the relative proportion of territory between the free and the slave states? I have not made an exact calculation on that point, but I believe that the proportion is about as nine to four, the free states having an area of less than four and a half millions of square miles, and that the slave states embrace an area of more than nine millions of square miles, twice as great as that of the free states. Why did not the gentleman from Delaware go still further into the statistical view of the subject, and show that even with every inch of territory down to the southern limit of California and New Mexico, somewhere between the years eighteen hundred and sixty and eighteen hundred and seventy, under the operation of the laws which have heretofore governed our increase, the population of the free states would be more circumscribed, more to the square mile, than that of the slave states?"

Mr. Clayton.—" The honorable senator has so repeatedly called upon me, that I must again answer. As chairman of the committee, I stated its proceedings. I stated that the Missouri Compromise was proposed; that Northern gentlemen voted against it, and Southern gentlemen for it; and that, if adopted, the effect of it would have been to give one million six hundred thousand square miles to the North, and two hundred and sixty-two thousand square miles to the South."

Mr. Hamlin.—"I do not object to the gentleman's statement, but I merely expressed the opinion that it would be much more pertinent to the occasion, had it been accompanied by some of those interesting statistics to which I alluded.

"There are other objections to the bill to which I would gladly allude, but I have already detained the Senate longer than I designed or anticipated. Looking to the lights of other days—the patriots of other times—the eloquent warnings which we have had from our Washington, Madison, our Jefferson, our Mason, ay, and from our own Pinckney, too, and all that long list of patriotic men of the South who have adorned this Union, who have pointed out the evils that would come upon us by perpetuating and extending this institution, I owe it to the constituents whom I represent, to our posterity, to all the toiling millions who are seeking an asylum in our land, to embrace this opportunity of opposing, with unshaken firmness, any attempt to introduce or permit this institution to flow into territory now free. Let these vast and fertile regions be preserved for the cultivation of free labor and free men, so well calculated to advance the arts of civilization. Do this, and the teeming and busy millions of future ages shall bless our acts with grateful hearts."

On the 12th of June, 1856, Mr. Hamlin relinquished his position as chairman of the Committee on Commerce, and his allegiance with the party with which he had so long been connected, declaring his reasons for this ac tion in a speech which created a profound sensation in the Senate and the country. Mr. Hamlin said:

"Mr. President, I rise for a purpose purely personal, such as I have never before risen for in the Senate. I desire to explain some matters personal to myself and to my own future course in public life,

SEVERAL SENATORS.—"Go on."

MR. HAMLIN.—"I ask the Senate to excuse me from further service as chairman of the Committee on Commerce. I do so because I feel that my relations hereafter will be of such a character as to render it proper that I should no longer hold that position. I owe this act to the dominant majority in the Senate. When I cease to harmonize with the majority, or tests are applied by that party with which I have acted to which I can not submit, I feel that I ought no longer to hold that respectable position. I propose to state briefly the reasons which have brought me to that conclusion.

"During nine years of service in the Senate, I have preferred rather to be a working than a talking member, and so I have been almost a silent one. On the subjects which have so much agitated the country, Senators know that I have rarely uttered a word. I love my country more than I love my party. I love my country above my love for any interest that can too deeply agitate or disturb its harmony. I saw, in all the exciting scenes and debates through which we have passed, no particular good that would result from my active intermingling in them. My heart has often been full, and the impulses of that heart have often been felt upon my lips, but I have repressed them there.

"Sir, I hold that the repeal of the Missouri Compromise was a gross moral and political wrong, unequaled in the annals of the legislation of this country, and hardly equaled in the annals of any other free country. Still, sir, with a desire to promote harmony, and concord, and brotherly feeling, I was a quiet man under all the exciting debates which led to that fatal result. I believed it wrong then; I can see that wrong lying broadcast all around us now. As a wrong, I opposed that measure, not indeed by my voice, but with consistent, and steady, and uniform votes. I so resisted it in obedience to the dictates of my own judgment. I did it also cheerfully, in compliance with the instructions of the Legislature of Maine, which were passed by a vote almost unanimous. In the House of Representatives of Maine, consisting of one hundred and fifty-one members, only six, I think, dissented; and in the Senate, consisting of thirty-one members, only one member non-concurred.

"But the Missouri restriction was abrogated. The portentous evils that were predicted have followed, and are yet following, along in its train. It was done, sir, in violation of the pledges of that party with which I have always acted, and with which I have always voted. It was done in violation of solemn pledges of the President of the United States, made in his inaugural address. Still, sir, I was disposed to suffer the wrong, until I should see that no evil results were flowing from it. We were told by almost every senator who addressed us upon that occasion, that no evil results would follow; that no practical difference in the settlement of the country, and the character of the future state, would take place, whether the act were done or not. I have waited calmly and patiently to see the fulfillment of that prediction; and I am grieved, sir, to say now, that they have at least been mistaken in their predictions and promises. They all have signally failed.

"That senators might have voted for that measure under the belief then expressed, and the predictions to which I have alluded, I can well understand. But how senators can now defend that measure amid all its evils, which are overwhelming the land, if not threatening it with a conflagration, is what I do not comprehend. The whole of the disturbed state of the country has its rise in, and is attributable to, that act alone, nothing else. It lies at the foundation of all our misfortunes and commotions. There would have been no incursions by Missouri borderers into Kansas, either to establish slavery or control elections. There would have been no necessity, either, for others to have gone there partially to aid in preserving the country in its then condition. All would have been peace there. Had it not been done, that repose and quiet which pervaded the public mind then, would hold it in tranquillity to-day. Instead of startling events we should have quiet and peace within our borders, and that fraternal feeling which ought to animate the citizens of every part of the Union toward those of all other sections.

"Sir, the events that are taking place around us are indeed startling. They challenge the public mind and appeal to the public judgment; they thrill the public nerve as electricity imparts a tremulous motion to the telegraphic wire. It is a period when all good men should unite in applying the proper remedy to secure peace and harmony to the country. Is this to be done by any of us, by remaining associated with those who have been instrumental in producing these results, and who now justify them? I do not see my duty lying in that direction.

"I have, while temporarily acquiescing, stated here and at home, everywhere, uniformly, that when the tests of those measures were applied to me as one of party fidelity, I would sunder them as flax is sundered at the touch of fire. I do it now.

"The occasion involves a question of moral duty; and self-respect allows me no other line of duty but to follow the dictates of my own judgment and the impulses of my own heart. A just man may cheerfully submit to many enforced humiliations, but a self-degraded man has ceased to be worthy to be deemed a man at all.

"Sir, what has the recent Democratic Convention at Cincinnati done? It has indorsed the measure I have condemned, and has sanctioned its destructive and ruinous effects. It has done more, vastly more. That principle or policy of territorial sovereignty which once had, and which I suppose now has, its advocates within these walls, is stricken down; and there is an absolute denial of it in the resolution of the Convention, if I can draw right conclusions—a denial equally to Congress, and even to the people of the territories, of the right to settle the question of slavery therein. On the contrary, the Convention has actually incorporated into the platform of the Democratic party that doctrine which, only a few years ago, met nothing but ridicule and contempt, here and elsewhere, namely: that the flag of the Federal Union, under the Constitution of the United States, carries slavery wherever it floats. If this baleful principle be true, then that national ode which inspires us always as on a battle-field should be rewritten by Drake, and should read thus:

"'Forever float that standard sheet;
Where breathes the foe but falls before us,
With SLAVERY's soil beneath our feet,
And SLAVERY's banner streaming o'er us?'

"Now, sir, what is the precise condition in which this

matter is left by the Cincinnati Convention? I do not design to trespass many moments on the Senate; but allow me to read and offer a very few comments upon some portions of the Democratic platform. The first resolution that treats upon the subject is in these words— I read just so much of it as is applicable to my present remarks:

"'That Congress has no power under the Constitution to interfere with or control the domestic institutions of the several states, and that all such states are the sole and proper judges of everything appertaining to their own affairs not prohibited by the Constitution.'

"I take it that this language, thus far, is language which meets a willing and ready response from every senator here; certainly it does from me. But in the following resolution I find these words:

"'*Resolved*, That the foregoing proposition covers, and was intended to embrace, the whole subject of slavery agitation in Congress.'

"The first resolution which I read was adopted years ago in Democratic conventions. The second resolution which I read was adopted in subsequent years, when a different state of things had arisen, and it became necessary to apply an abstract proposition relating to the states to the territories. Hence the adoption of the language contained in the second resolution which I have read.

"Now, sir, I deny the position thus assumed by the Cincinnati Convention. In the language of the Senator from Kentucky, (Mr. Crittenden,) so ably and so appropriately used, on Tuesday last, I hold that the entire and unqualified sovereignty of the territories is in Congress.

That is my judgment; but this resolution brings the territories precisely within the same limitations which are applied to the states in the resolution which I first read. The two taken together deny to Congress any power of legislation in the territories.

"Follow on, and let us see what remains. Adopted as a part of the present platform, and as necessary to a new state of things, and to meet an emergency now existing, the Convention says:

"'The American Democracy recognize and adopt the principles contained in the organic laws establishing the Territories of Kansas and Nebraska, as embodying the only sound and safe solution of the slavery question, upon which the great national idea of the people of this whole country can repose, in its determined conservatism of the Union—non-interference by Congress with slavery in states and territories.'

Then follows the last resolution:

"'*Resolved*, That we recognize the right of the people of all the territories, including Kansas and Nebraska, acting through the fairly expressed will of the majority of actual residents, and whenever the number of their inhabitants justifies it, to form a Constitution with or without domestic slavery, and be admitted into the Union upon terms of perfect equality with the other States.'

"Take all these resolutions together, and the deduction which we must necessarily draw from them is a denial to Congress of any power whatever to legislate upon the subject of slavery. The last resolution denies to the people of the territory any power over that subject, save when they shall have a sufficient number to form a Constitution and become a state, and also denies that Congress has any power over the subject; and so the resolutions hold that this power is at least in abeyance while the territory is in a territorial condition. That is the only conclusion which you can draw from these resolutions. Alas! for short-lived territorial sovereignty. It came to its death in the house of its friends; it was buried by the same hands which had given it baptism!

"But, sir, I did not rise for the purpose of discussing these resolutions, but only to read them, and state the action which I propose to take in view of them. I may—I probably shall—take some subsequent occasion, when I shall endeavor to present to the Senate and the country a fair account of what is the true issue presented to the people for their consideration and decision.

"My object now is to show only that the Cincinnati Convention has indorsed and approved of the repeal of the Missouri Compromise, from which so many evils have already flowed; from which, I fear, more and worse evils must yet be anticipated. It would, of course, be expected that the presidential nominee of that Convention would accept, cordially and cheerfully, the platform prepared for him by his party friends. No person can object to that. There is no equivocation on his part about the matter. I beg leave to read a short extract from a speech of that gentleman, made at his own home, within the last few days. In reply to the Keystone Club, which paid him a visit there, Mr. Buchanan said:

"'Gentlemen, two weeks since I should have made you a longer speech, but now I have been placed on a platform of which I most heartily approve, and that can speak for me. Being the representative of the great Democratic party, and not simply James Buchanan, I must square my conduct according to the platform of the party, and insert no new plank, nor take one from it.'

"These events leave to me only one unpleasant duty,

which is to declare here that I can maintain political associations with no party that insists upon such doctrines; that I can support no man for President who avows and recognizes them; and that the little of that power with which God has endowed me shall be employed to battle manfully, firmly, and consistently for his defeat, demanded as it is by the highest interests of the country which owns all my allegiance."

On the 9th and 10th of March, 1858, Mr. Hamlin made a long and powerful speech on the bill for the admission of Kansas into the Union as a state. In that speech, he replied to Senator Hammond, of South Carolina, who had reflected upon the character of the laboring classes at the North. He said:

"I was remarking that the senator from South Carolina had mistaken the character of our laboring men—I speak of those who are 'hireling manual laborers,' for that is his expression, in its modified form. I think the senator has fallen into an error in his estimate of the character of our laborers, and it may have arisen from a variety of causes. Our government was indeed an experiment. It was established for the purpose of testing the capacity of man for self-government. Anterior to that period of time, during which governments had existed which were called free, there had been none which had founded their institutions upon the principles upon which ours were proposed to be based. Under the freest governments that had ever existed, there were prerogatives and rights secured to power, and laws creating privileged classes; but it was the object and intention of the founders of our government to do away with such a state of things, which had existed theretofore in every government in the world. Ours was to be a government resting on the consent of the governed. That was the object. We sought to take away the prerogatives which gathered around the governing power, and to establish a government among us that should elevate man intellectually and politically to that sphere and to that position to which he was justly entitled.

"When the senator from South Carolina undertakes to draw imaginary distinctions between classes of laborers, he goes back to the old, the worn, the rotten, and the discarded systems of ages that have long since passed. I tell that senator what is true, that we draw no imaginary distinctions between our different classes of laborers—none whatever. 'Manual laborers!' Well, sir, who are the manual laborers of the North, that are degraded and placed beside the slave of the South by the senator from South Carolina? Who are our manual laborers? Sir, all classes in our community are manual laborers; and, to a greater or less extent, they are hireling manual laborers. They constitute, I affirm, a majority of our community—those who labor for compensation. I do not know, I confess I can not understand, that distinction which allows a man to make a contract for the service of his brains, but denies him the right to make a contract for the service of his hands. There is no distinction whatever between them. We draw none; we make none. Who are that class of citizens in our community who are its hirelings? That is the term. I do not know whether he designs it as opprobrious; but that is the term with which he designates our laborers of the North. This is modern democracy!

"Who are our 'hireling manual laborers' of the North? Sir, I can tell that senator that they are not the mud-sills of our community. They are the men who clear away our forests. They are the men who make the green hill-side blossom. They are the men who build our ships, and who navigate them. They are the men who build our towns, and who inhabit them. They are the men who constitute the great mass of our community. Sir, they are not only the pillars that support our government, but they are the capitals that adorn the very pillars. They are not to be classed with the slave. Our laboring men have homes; they have wives; they have little ones, dependent on them for support and maintenance; and they are just so many incentives and so much stimulus to action. The laboring man, with us, knows for whom he toils; and when he toils he knows that he is to return to that home where comfort and pleasure and all the domestic associations cluster around the social hearthstone. Northern laborers are 'hirelings,' and are to be classed with the negro slave!

"Besides that, the men who labor in our community are the men whom we clothe with power. They are the men who exercise the prerogatives of the State. They are the men who, after having been clothed with power there, are sent abroad to represent us elsewhere. They do our legislation at home. They support the State. They are the State. They are men—high-minded men. They read; they watch you in these halls every day; and through all our community the doings of this branch, and of the other, are as well understood, and perhaps even better, than we understand them ourselves. I affirm that, throughout our community, the proceedings of Congress are more extensively and accurately read than even by ourselves. These are the men who are to be classed by the side of the slave! I think it is true that, in about every three generations at most, the wheel entirely performs its revolution. You rarely find a fortune continuing beyond three generations in this country, in the same family.

"That class of our community, constituting a very large

majority, has been designated here as hireling laborers, white slaves! Why, sir, does labor imply slavery? Because they toil—because they pursue a course which enables them to support their wives and their families, even if it be by daily manual labor, does that necessarily imply servitude? Far from it. I affirm that the great portion of our laborers at the North own their homes, and they labor to adorn them. They own their own homes, and if you will visit them you will find in nearly all of them a portion, at least, of the literature of the times, which shows that they read; you will find there evidences to satisfy you beyond all doubt that they are intelligent, and that they are in truth and in fact precisely what I have described them to be—the pillars of the State, the State itself, and the very ornaments and capitals that adorn the columns. With them the acquisition of knowledge is not a crime."

Speaking of the attempt to force a constitution on the people of the Territory of Kansas, he uses this vigorous language:

"Mr. President, this is all to be done under the 'forms of law.' I have heard this phrase 'forms of law,' until it has become painful to my ear. Forms of law! Will you tell me of the worst despotism that ever existed, that did not rest upon forms of law? Will you tell me of the wickedest act that has ever been perpetrated by any government, that has not been done under the forms of law? We sit not here, sir, in the capacity of a court to adjudicate and to construe the laws that have been made; we are here for the purpose of exercising our power upon broader principles of equity than those which belong to courts; but still all courts which administer laws are clothed with equity powers. All courts are clothed with equity powers to prevent a greater wrong.

"'It is a common saying, and a true,
That strictest law is oft the highest wrong.'

"Forms of law! Why, let us rather see to it that the substance of the law is executed and justice done.

"We are clothed with equity powers beyond those which obtain in a court; and we are making laws; we are not administering them. We ought, at the mere suggestion of wrong to these people, to go to the very basis and ascertain whether we are about to perpetrate a wrong and force upon them a government which is not their own. But, sir, instead of that, we are here day after day with petty juggling and pettifogging, claiming to proceed under the forms of law, forgetting the substance. What is the substance? What is the right? What care I here making laws for what may be a form. What is the substance? What is the great equity of the case? and as a legislator it is my duty to apply myself to that. What is right? what is just? Let that be done, and all will be well.

"Forms of law! God knows there is nothing but form in it. Forms of law! Long years ago the mother country undertook to oppress these colonies by forms of law, but not as unjustly as we have ruled the people of Kansas; and she persecuted that great and noble patriot, John Hampden, under the forms of law, and for his love of liberty. There is one other act which has been perpetrated under the forms of law, to which I will allude, and then I shall have done.

"Under the forms of law despotism is created. Under the forms of law, all the wrongs of which the mind of man can conceive have been perpetrated. Under the forms of law, and in the name of liberty, liberty itself has been stricken down. In the name and under the forms of law, the Son of man was arraigned and stretched upon the cross. Under the forms of law, you are about to do an act here, unequaled in turpitude by anything that has been recorded in all the progress of time, save that event to which I have just alluded. In all history, save the crucifixion of Christ, there is no act that will stand upon the record of its pages in after time of equal turpitude with this act. The purpose of it is to extend human slavery; and I may well inquire,—

"'Is this the day for us to sow
The soil of a virgin empire with slavery's seeds of woe;
To feed with our fresh life-blood the Old World's cast-off crime,
Dropped like some monstrous early birth from the tired lap of Time?'

We give two extracts from the speech delivered by Mr. Hamlin in the House, January 12, 1846, on the Oregon question. The first is a most eloquent vindication of the people of the North. Mr. Hamlin said:

"There was another remark to which he wished to allude. Too often within these walls, in the discussion of various measures, had he heard taunts and reproaches, either directly or by implication, cast upon various sections of this Union; and when they had been directed to that section where it was his pride and his pleasure to reside, he had felt them thrill along his nerves, like an electric shock, and the impulses of his heart had been upon his lips to hurl them back again. But time and reflection had chastened these feelings, and he passed them by in sorrow that they should come from the lips of any individual on this floor; and while it was his glory and his pride to be an inhabitant of that section whose motives were so often questioned here, he had a single word to say in behalf of that people. He had no objections to interpose here in defense of what may have been the errors or wickedness of her politicians, but in behalf of her citizens he had a word to say. He believed them to be as patriotic as any other class of citizens to be found in our Union. They had exhibited their patriotism and their valor on many a well-fought field. Their bones had bleached on many a Northern hill, and the barren sands of the South had drunk in their best blood. Sir," said Mr. Hamlin, "I point with pride to the North, and invite you there to witness a system which has grown up with us, and which is our ornament. I point you to our system of free labor; I point you to our common schools—to our churches with their spires pointing toward heaven —and I glory in them. They are the monuments that belong to a people who have the true spirit of citizens of a free government. These things were the glory of the North, and Mr. Hamlin gloried in them. They were bloodless moral monuments which marked the advancing progress of a free people. But I stop not there; I ask you to go with me throughout this whole broad nation: and I point you to her—I point you to the whole Union as a monument of political grandeur, towering toward the heavens, upon which the friend of freedom, wherever upon our globe he may be, may gaze; around whose highest summit the sunlight of glory forever shines, and at whose base a free people reposes, and, I trust, forever will repose. So much for New England, my home; so much for the Union, my country."

The second shows the comprehensive views which Mr. Hamlin had upon commercial questions at that early period in his Congressional career, and the prophetic wisdom with which he foresaw the mighty empire which was to be founded on the shores of the Pacific:

Mr. Hamlin next proceeded to the consideration of this question in a commercial point of view. Oregon was ours; it belongs to us; and the question of title he had no disposition here to examine. It had been thoroughly, ably examined by those who are in authority, and the result has been presented to the American republic. He had no disposition to go into that examination. He should be well satisfied to rest himself on him who, at least, might be considered the Achilles of this question, in the position that our title was better than that of England. It was more; it was a perfect title. This being our territory, then, by laws and rules established by Great Britain herself, let them examine carefully into its importance in a commercial point of view. They were told, on another occasion, within these walls, that it was necessary to extend our public domain in the Southwest, for the purpose of securing to our country a monopoly of the cotton-growing interest; and the argument was as broad as our Union; it came home to the feelings, to the interests, and to the principles of action of the representatives from every section of our country. Let them now weigh by the same rules, the rules established on that occasion, the commercial considerations involved in this question. The Northern and the Middle states are essentially manufacturing states—the Northern states particularly; they are situated in a high latitude, under a forbidding climate, and yet they have the industry of their citizens, the water-power, and the facilities given them by nature to render them a manufacturing people. The South—the "sunny South"—may grow the staple produce of that country; and the West may be the granary not only of our own country, but, give it an outlet, the granary of the world. Then, he said, in a commercial point of view, this matter came home to the feelings and the interests of every citizen of every section of our widely extended country. The North must necessarily be the manufacturing section of this Union; let them have an outlet; let there be an easy mode of transportation and communication to the far West, and we would become the manufacturers almost of the world. The Northern and the Middle states must be that portion of our Union which will supply not only India but China, and all the Eastern portions of the world, with their manufactured articles. But he stopped not here. The matter came home equally to the interests of the South; because for the supply of those manufactured articles the South would be called upon for their staple, for increased production of that staple, which, in its manufactured form, is thus destined to find its way to the markets of the East. It was a question in which the West had no right to assume a particular interest. It was a question which came home equally to the North, the South, the East, and the West. It was a great national question, co-extensive with our Union. Why, we were already opening our markets in the East; we have already established our treaty stipulations with China; we have already sent our cotton and manufactured goods into the Eastern empire. Last year more than six millions of American manufactures were sent to the Eastern continent; and of that amount more than four millions of dollars is believed to have been of cotton goods. We have opened the Chinese market; and in opening that market, with the advance which commerce will give in that distant portion of the globe to civilization, to refinement, and to Christianity, we have opened a market which will call for untold millions of the manufactured articles of the Northern and Middle states—manufactured from this staple of the South.

Besides, the commerce of the North was deeply interested in her whaling ships. That ocean is now covered with nearly 700 ships, and half a hundred smaller vessels, manned by more than 20,000 of our citizens, and sending home, as the fruits of their labor, more than three millions of oil annually.

Mr. Hamlin proceeded to enlarge upon the value and extent of the commerce which would grow up between the East Indies and our Pacific country, if we had possession of Oregon. The trade between the United States and East Indies was already very important. But it would be vastly increased when we should find a route for that trade overland to the Pacific, and across that ocean to India. Wherever commerce went, there the lights of civilization and Christianity would soon be found. Wherever the people of the East have become enlightened by commercial intercourse with us, she would consume a vast quantity of our products, while they would supply us liberally with theirs. Who could tell what uncounted millions of manufactured goods from the United States would be marketed in the East Indies? Commerce was, therefore, deeply interested in preserving the integrity of our domain. He would gladly pursue this subject further if time was allowed, and show that this question was one that concerned the commerce of the whole country, and that the whole people of the United States were interested in it. But he was limited in time, and he could not pursue the subject in all its details.

He thus closes:

"While gentlemen talked of war, which only existed in the visions of old men, or the dreams of young ones —while this bugbear was held up, we were losing the opportunity to secure for ourselves and our children this most important and valuable country. What now would arise, was only an inference on the part of these gentlemen. They had not shown how it would arise. They had not shown us the *modus operandi*. But we well knew that the British pretensions would be strengthened by our eternal delay. The longer we delayed the notice, the more arrogant would the British pretensions become. One point more. Our old men, the gentleman from Virginia says, see visions, our young men dream dreams. He was not old, and he could not see visions; and the dreams he left to the gentleman from Virginia. Let those who dreamed imagine that a war will arise from our assertion of our rights; he did not believe it. But without the aid of visions he saw a populous and enterprising state on the slope of the Pacific, with manufactures, and commerce, and navigation. The waters rushing down to the Pacific would turn thousands of wheels and spindles. Our people would move to that region, and carry with them all their arts and skill in all the various branches of manufactures which we have established in this region. In due time they will supply a large portion of America, as well as Asia, with their fabrics.

"It would not be long before our settlements would extend down to the Mexican boundary. He appealed to gentlemen from the South to come up to the rescue, and avail themselves of this fair opportunity to obtain Oregon. He asked their attention to the position we occupied before the American people and the world in regard to this subject, and assured them that for us there was no retreat from the responsibility of this act, without incurring the just reproach of the people of the United States, and, indeed, of the whole world. The Executive had presented his views to Congress, and had recommended to us the passage of the measure now before us. He had asked for our early action upon it. The stale cry of war ought not to prevent us from discharging this duty; and if we should falter in performing it, we should be branded as unfaithful to our trust. The Executive had laid before us a statement of our just claims, showing that they had a solid and stable basis. The whole world would be convinced of their truth and justice; and would an American Congress be found slow to defend and assert them? He (Mr. Hamlin) would appeal again to the South, and to the spirit of their fathers—of Sumter, Marion, and Pinckney—and call upon them to come up to this duty of defending our soil. Should fear of consequences prevent us from vindicating our rights from foreign aggression? Should the horrors of war deter them from pursuing their line of duty? Will they not come up to the struggle, if need be, and, like 'reapers, descend to the harvest of death.' True, the South has peculiar interests that would be hazarded in a war; but has not the whole Atlantic border a deep stake in the continuance of peace? We, sir, in the Northeast have an extensive commerce. Our ships are found in every sea; and we have cities on the sea-board exposed to the assaults of an enemy. But, sir, we are willing to hazard everything in the defense of our country, and to lay all our wealth as an offering on the altar of the public safety. But who can believe, sir, that England will go to war because we do an act that we are entitled to do by treaty stipulations? This was too absurd an idea to be, for a moment, entertained by any one.

"But there was another view of the subject. He did not pretend to be a wizard, nor to foretell future events; but coming events sometimes cast their shadows before them. Judging of the future by the past, he would say that the moral force of our institutions would spread themselves over every portion of this continent. Their progress was as certain as destiny. He could not be mistaken in the idea that our flag was destined to shed its luster over every hill and plain on the Pacific slope, and on every stream that mingles with the Pacific. What would monarchical institutions do—what would tyrants do in this age of improvement—this age of steam and of lightning? The mariner's compass, the steam-engine, the printing press, with the aid of electricity, which has annihilated space, have made the world like the ear of Dionysius. The voice of freedom in our halls of worship, in our temples, and the knowledge of our schools may be heard in distant lands, and will be echoed back. Let there be no holding back, no folding of arms in quiet; but let us rather, in a calm and dignified manner, meet the crisis in a way worthy of our country, and as American statesmen.

"'And the gun of our nation's natal day,
At the rise and set of sun,
Shall boom from the far Northeast, away
To the vales of Oregon;
And ships on the sea-shore luff and tack,
And send the peal of triumph back.'"

We do not propose to refer at length to Mr. Hamlin's numerous business speeches, as the interest in such efforts passes away with the occasion. We refer to two elaborate speeches of his on the fisheries, made in the Senate, as illustrative of the great research which he is able to bring to bear upon historical or practical questions.

In a speech delivered in the Senate on the 4th of May, 1858, Mr. Hamlin defended the system of fishing bounties against the attacks made upon it by Mr. Clay, of Alabama. He said:

"Mr. President, the relations which the fisheries have borne in every country to the commercial and naval prosperity of that country, I think, are intimate and important. They are measured by no narrow vision; they are circumscribed by no local position; and I think, if the senator from Alabama (Mr. Clay) had risen above the mere locality of the fisheries, and had proceeded to make an investigation of the subject upon a broader principle, he might have come to a different conclusion; at least he might have divested himself of that bitterness which was witnessed in the sneer upon his face, if not in the language which he uttered, when he said that the taking of cod was a momentous concern. The mere act of taking cod may be objectionable, if the senator pleases, to that sneer; but when measured by other considerations that justly and properly belong to it, and when viewed in an enlightened sense—in that sense which belongs to an American statesman and to an American senator—it is worthy of anything else but the sneer of any senator. The fisheries are local. The Ruler of the world has made them so. The waters of the far North are the fields in which the fish are taken, and it would be natural to suppose that the people residing near to those fields are employed in that pursuit. Though they are local, they are, nevertheless, in their importance, national. So the fields in which the sugar-cane is cultivated are peculiar to that State which is represented by the senator who sits beside me, (Mr. Benjamin;) and I affirm here to-day, that while you pay a bounty to the fishermen for national purposes, as I shall endeavor to establish, you pay a bounty, by your system of revenue laws, to the planters and growers of sugar-cane in Louisiana. You may say that the one is based upon revenue, and for revenue purposes. My answer is, that the other is for a purpose as national and as broad; and that is, of training seamen for the naval service.

"In every country which has existed from the formation of the world to the present time, the relations between the fisheries and the commerce and the naval power of the country have been intimate and direct. Indeed, sir, there is no country on the face of the globe that has been marked and distinguished for its naval or its commercial supremacy, that has not had a corps of fishermen from which to support both of these institutions. From the days of Scripture times, from the day when Sidon was founded, which was the city of fish, down to the present moment, there has been no nation that has not relied for its commercial and its naval prosperity upon its fisheries as nurseries for seamen, to supply both its commerce and its navy."

After showing, by copious illustrations, the importance attached to the fisheries by the first statesmen of the land, before, during, and subsequent to the Revolutionary war, he says:

"But, sir, I want to show you what was the part which these fishermen bore, not only in the Revolutionary war, but in the war of 1812. I invite your attention to the very important part which they contributed, and I think no class contributed more—I had almost said that all other classes had not contributed as much—to produce that happy result which was produced in either case, as these fishermen who happened to reside in a locality. If you can educate seamen cheaper in any other way, I am for abolishing the fishing bounties. I am for sustaining these fishing bounties only upon the ground that it is the cheapest mode by which you can educate men upon whom you must rely in the emergency of war. Can you do it cheaper in any other way? Then do it. I am not advocating bounties to any class of citizens, be they who they may, unless it be of national importance, for a national purpose, and be the most economical mode of effecting the object. I believe that the contribution of two or three hundred thousand dollars a year—the average is about two hundred and five thousand dollars—will continually keep in reserve a vast corps of seamen, upon whom you can rely, in time of war, better than any other class of men, a class upon whom you must call in that emergency. If, however, there is any alternative proposition, if there is any other way in which seamen can be more cheaply and economically furnished to your navy, then I am not in favor of this. I am not in favor of bounties. I am only in favor of them in this case because there is a necessity for them, from the nature of the business, which requires aid to keep it alive; and to keep it alive is the only way in which you can get the force that is requisite and necessary.

"Now, I come to the important part which this corps of fishermen bore in the struggle of the Revolutionary war. They were few in number then, compared to what they are now, but they were important. There was no branch of the service that did more honorable and gallant service than they. There was no part of the service that aided more in bringing about the happy negotiations which ended in peace and in our independence. It is recorded in the history of the times, and of it there can be no serious question, that more than fifty thousand tons of British shipping were captured in 1777 by these New England fishermen. Curwin, of Salem, a loyalist, who fled to England, states, in his journal, that from May, 1776, to February, 1778, Lloyd's Coffee-house list shows that American privateers, one hundred and seventy-three in number, captured seven hundred and thirty-three British vessels, with their cargoes, worth more than twenty-five million dollars; and they counted millions of dollars by a higher standard in that day than we do now. Other authorities, entitled to confidence, show that, during the war, full two hundred thousand tons of shipping were taken by rebel privateers. We had no navy. In all the naval service of the Revolutionary war, we had to depend mainly upon the privateer service,—that was composed almost exclusively of the fishermen. So efficient were they, that underwriters demanded, and there were paid, premiums of from thirty to fifty per cent. The mercantile interest of England clamored for peace. The fishermen were abroad upon every water; and the lagoons of the Mediterranean never swarmed with men more efficiently engaged in catching fish, than did the privateersmen of New England swarm the ocean in capturing British vessels, in the war of the Revolution.

"I wish to read an authority in relation to their services in the Revolutionary war, and it is the authority of that old patriot and statesman, Henry Knox, who shared with Washington so much of the glories, and suffered so many of the hardships of the war. He speaks with a feeling heart of the services of these men in that day. Knox, himself a member of the Massachusetts Legislature, long after peace had been declared, in speaking of these fishermen, gives them not only that proud position to which they were entitled upon the ocean, but, if possible, still higher credit for the services they had performed upon the land. In speaking of the time when Washington was obliged to cross the Delaware on his bridge of boats, he said:

"'Sir, I wish the members of this body knew the people of Marblehead as well as I do. I could wish that they had stood on the banks of the Delaware river in 1777, in that bitter night when the Commander-in-chief had drawn up his little army to cross it, and had seen the powerful current bearing onward the floating masses of ice which threatened destruction to whosoever should venture upon its bosom. I wish that when this occurrence threatened to defeat the enterprise, they could have heard that distinguished warrior demand, "Who will lead us on?" and seen men of Marblehead, and Marblehead alone, stand forward to lead the army along the perilous path to unfading glories and honors in the achievements of Trenton. There, sir, went the fishermen of Marblehead, alike at home upon land and water, alike ardent, patriotic, and unflinching, whenever they unfurled the flag of the country.'

"But, sir, these gallant, patriotic men were not less serviceable in the war of 1812 than in the war of the Revolution. I have a letter from that gallant old man who did such distinguished service for his country, Commodore Stewart. I addressed him a note some time since, asking his opinion of the value of these fishermen, on whom the Senator from Alabama seems to place so low an estimate. That senator said:

"'The mere inspection of a smack and a square-rigged ship will show that the former is no school on which to learn how to manage the latter. The contrast is as great as between a log-cabin and the labyrinth of Crete; and the cod fisherman would scarcely be more at fault in the labyrinth than in the ship.'

"That is the opinion of the senator from Alabama. I will read the opinion of Commodore Stewart."

Mr. Hale.—"He is 'green.'" (Laughter.)

Mr. Hamlin.—"Commodore Stewart may be in a green old age. God grant that many days may yet be spared to him, for the gallant service that he has done our common country. I have also a letter from the oldest active commodore in your navy, that I propose to read. The senator from Alabama says he has talked with naval officers, who have given him the opinion which leads him to this conclusion. I wish he would give us their names. I should like to see that naval officer who ever fought a naval battle with New England fishermen, who would come into the Senate and decry their patriotism, their valor, and their services. I think the senator has talked with men who never saw such service.

"But, sir, let me read this letter, so full of fact, so pregnant with meaning, from that gallant old commodore. I will not read it all. He goes on to describe acts of personal heroism of individual members of his crew, who were ready to go down amid the coral and sea-weed in defense of a common flag and of common rights. I will read only—for it is all that is important—the conclusion which he arrived at, as to those men who, according to the senator, are so lost on naval vessels. He commanded that noble old ship, the Constitution, through the prowess of which there has been spread and gathered more of glory to the American navy than any other vessel; and he speaks of the crew of New England fishermen under his command in this wise:

"'They were all enlisted in Boston, Marblehead, Salem, and Portsmouth, from whence, I believe, it is well known that most of the sea-faring men, belonging thereto, come from the New England fisheries.

"'In all my sea service, I have never seen, on board of a ship of war,' (lost in the labyrinth of Crete! says the senator from Alabama,) 'such a splendid crew for expert seamanship, discipline, sobriety, orderly and determined bearing, as well as singleness of purpose for glory and the honor of their flag, than that one of the "Constitution." It may not be inappropriate to repeat here the remark of the first Napoleon, on board the "Bellerophon," when reviewing her marines: "What could not be done with an army of such men?" I can only surmise what might be done in ships of war, with such crews?'

"Now, the opinion of the senator from Alabama does not concur with Commodore Stewart. The senator from Alabama, on such authorities as he has consulted, thinks they would be lost on a man-of-war. The commodore says, further:

"'In conclusion, I may say, in the words of the Sultan of Seringapatam to the Governor-General of India: "How can I say more," in behalf of so noble a crew of New Englanders?'

"I have a letter here from your oldest active commodore of the navy, who was an officer on board this very Constitution, a noble and a gallant man, who has done gallant service for his country, and who is entitled to its thanks—a letter hardly less significant than that which I have read from Commodore Stewart. What does he say of this class of men, who are out of place, who are not educated, who do not know what belong to their duties, because they have only been fishermen? I addressed him three interrogatories, the scope of which the Senate will understand by the answers he has submitted. He says:

"'To the first, I say, without hesitation, that during the war of 1812, and at all times since I have been in the navy, we have thought ourselves fortunate when we could obtain American fishermen for the public service, for which we consider no class of men better adapted.'

"The senator from Alabama told us they were not fit for naval service. Commodore Shubrick thinks otherwise. Commodore Shubrick and Commodore Stewart have had a little experience in this matter. Both of them have commanded crews of these very men, and they know something about them. Commodore Shubrick continues:

"'To the second, I say, that during the war of 1812, and for some years previous, great pains were taken to exclude foreigners from the navy; and I am of opinion that, particularly during the last year, a majority were Americans.'

"That was in answer to a question as to who constituted the naval crews at that time. I regret that the Chairman of the Committee on Naval Affairs is not present; but I shall state some information derived from him on this point. That interrogatory was propounded for the very reason that I understand, as a matter beyond all doubt, that two-thirds at least, probably three-fourths, of every crew that treads the decks of every vessel in our navy, is constituted of foreigners—not a very safe class of men to intrust the interests of your country and the integrity of your flag to, in the trying times of war. It may do in piping times of peace, but it had better not be so then. Wise policy, elevated statesmanship, that shall rise above the catching of a cod or the locality of the interest, would dictate that both in our commercial and in our naval marine the integrity of our flag should be intrusted to American hands and American hearts. Sir, it is a miserable, it is a local, it is a provincial view of the question, that limits it down to that narrow point.

To the third interrogatory which I put to the Commodore, he says:

"'To the third, I say, that any policy by the Government which will tend to provide, during peace, for the exigencies of war, "is wise," and none would be more so than to nurture the body of American seamen who are trained in the fisheries.'

"Now, sir, I think these two letters are very good authority, coming from gallant old Stewart and Shubrick, who stand now at the head of your active naval list, both of whom have seen much more than any other men in your naval service, of the merits of this very class of men. Why, sir, in the war of 1812, you could hardly man a frigate without these very same fishermen. According to the authority of John Quincy Adams, who examined this question with great care, and I repeat almost in his own words, all of the glory and all of the renown that were won by your little and gallant navy in the war of 1812, were won by the prowess of American fishermen. They struck for freedom with a freeman's arm. In every battle that was fought upon the ocean, and upon the lakes, they manned your ships, they constituted your crews. They shed all the luster and renown upon your little navy, with the aid of gallant officers, that was shed upon it; and now, at this late day, because they happened to be situated in a particular locality, and, I fear, in obedience to a provincial, sectional, Southern press, they are to be stricken down.

"I will read a single authority more in relation to the service which these men performed, because it is from a man conversant with that service, who lived amid these seamen. Daniel Webster said, in 1852, what is historically true, in addressing some of them:

"'There are among you some who, perhaps, have been on the Grand Banks for forty successive years. There they have hung on to the ropes, in storm and wreck. The most important consequences are involved in this matter. Our fisheries have been the very nurseries of our navy. If our flag-ships have met and conquered the enemy on the sea, the fisheries are at the bottom of it. The fisheries were the seeds from which these glorious triumphs were born and sprung.'

"During the war of 1812, we captured from the British more than two thousand three hundred sail of vessels, mounting more than eight thousand guns; fifty-six men-of-war, mounting nearly nine hundred guns, and took in all about thirty thousand prisoners of war. Of the captures in the privateer service, the greatest number was by these fishermen.

"Now, sir, I want to invite the attention of the Senate to the manner in which other nations (because we may draw some light from their practice) have regarded the fisheries as auxiliaries to commercial and naval power. The senator from Alabama tells us that the bounties which have been conferred by Holland, by England, and by France, upon their fisheries, have proved a failure. I do not quote his language, but I think I state his idea. I understand no such thing; and I think the history of the matter proves no such thing.

"From the days of the commercial prosperity of Venice down to the present time, every nation which has been distinguished for its commerce and naval power, it will be found, has not only devoted its energies to this branch of industry, but it has relied implicitly upon it as a great source from which its navy and its commerce were to be sustained. When Venice was mistress of the Adriatic; when she commanded absolutely the Mediterranean, and almost the whole of Europe; when she was indeed the first commercial power in all Europe, and it is said by some writers, equal to all Europe, she had a corps of fishermen, with which to supply her commerce and her navy along her coasts and bays. They covered the lagoons; they swarmed the Mediterranean; and her argosies were found in every port along the British coast. Her vessels visited every port in the Mediterranean, and every coast in Europe. Her maritime commerce was probably not much inferior to all the rest of Christendom. Such was Venice in the day of her greatest commercial prosperity; and that prosperity was, in a great degree, attributable to the enterprise of her seamen, who had been trained and educated in the school of her fisheries. They were hardy, industrious, and energetic, and they went wherever commerce could find an avenue.

"Holland, also, furnished a remarkable illustration of the importance of the fisheries in connection with commerce. It is an old maxim—for it has grown into a maxim—that Amsterdam was built on fishes' bones; and when Van Tromp swept the British seas with a broom at his masthead, he supplied his vessels with a corps of those herring fishermen. A dispatch on the causes of its commercial prosperity, prepared with great care by the direction of the Stadtholder, places the fisheries in the first class of causes as contributing to the advancement of the republic in its unexampled prosperity. Such was beyond all doubt the fact. Go to Spain, sir, and, in the day of her prosperity, when she fitted out her armada, and when she had colonial possessions that employed her fisheries, she was greatest in commerce, she was greatest in commercial prosperity, and she was greatest in her naval power. Go to France; and what do you find? I will show that they regard this very class of fishermen as constituting a portion of the naval service. In 1851, Mr. Ancet, in relation to the fisheries, made the following report to the National Assembly in France:

"'It is not, therefore, a commercial law that we have the honor to propose to the Assembly, but rather a maritime law—a law conceived for the advancement of the naval power of this country.

"'No other school can compare with this in preparing them (seamen) so well, and in numbers so important, for the service of the navy.

"'It may be said of this fishery, that if it prepares fewer men for the sea, it forms better sailors—the *élite* of the navy.

"'The preservation of the great fisheries assumes a degree of importance more serious, when they are viewed as being in fact the nursery of our military marine.'

"In another place, in the same report, he continues, speaking of Great Britain:

"'The loss of her most magnificent colonies has occasioned irreparable injury to the commercial marine, which is an essential element of the naval power. * * *

"'In order to preserve them, (the fisheries,) we must continue the encouragements they have received, even at periods when a commercial and colonial prosperity, infinitely superior to that now existing, multiplied our shipping, and created abundance of seamen. It is on our fisheries that at this day repose all the most serious hopes of our maritime enlistments.'

"Again he says:

"Without aid, the cod fisheries could not exist. They furnish more than a third of our seamen, and by far the best portion of them. There is no cheaper, better, or more useful school for the formation of seamen for the navy, and none is more capable of extension and development.'

"Let me read from a report made to the British Parliament, in 1846, by Mr. MacGregor:

"In speaking of the fisheries, De Witt says:

"'That the English navy became formidable by the discovery of the inexpressibly rich fishing bank of Newfoundland. * * *

34

"'And, from 1618, the fisheries were carried on by England, and became of great national consideration.

"'Before the conquest of Cape Breton, by these alone France became formidable to all Europe.'

"There was a period of time when France came nearly equalling England in her commercial power, and that was when she held control of the fisheries. Mr. MacGregor continues:

"'It was a maxim with the French Government, that their American fisheries were of more national value, in regard to navigation and power, than the gold mines of Mexico could have been, if the latter were possessed by France.'

"He says, further:

'"It is very remarkable that, in our treaties with France, the fisheries of North America were made a stipulation of extraordinary importance. The Minister of that power considered the value of those fisheries, not so much in a commercial point of view, but as essential in providing their navy with that physical strength which would enable them to cope with other nations.

"The policy of the French, from their first planting colonies in North America, insists particularly on training seamen by means of these fisheries. In conducting their cod fishery, one-third, or at least one-quarter of the men employed in it were 'green men,' or men who were never at sea before; and by this trade they bred from four thousand to six thousand seamen annually.'

"This is the view which they take of the importance of these men in France and in England to-day; and an enlightened view of the subject ought to lead us to treat them as of equal importance. They are so in fact. In 1841, when war was apprehended by France, M. Thiers called in the services of the fishermen; and M. Rodet afterward remarked, 'Without the resources which were found in the sailors engaged in the fisheries, the expedition to Algiers could not have taken place.' In reply to the assertion of the senator from Alabama, as to the effect of the bounties on the commerce of England, I will quote an authority of great weight, Mr. Sabine's able work upon the fishery:

"'It is certain, that, down to the time of Elizabeth, the foreign trade of England was in the control of German merchants, and that there had been no employment for many or for large ships of the realm. British navigation increased with the growth of the fisheries. Without the fleets maintained at Iceland and Newfoundland, there would have been neither ships nor seamen to execute the plan for the colonization of New England, and of other parts of the continent, during the reigns of James and Charles.'

"I have already stated the view which was taken of this matter in our early history. It is true, as the senator from Alabama stated, that Fisher Ames did say, in the House of Representatives, that the taking of cod is a very momentous concern. I quote the words; and when I quote them, I do not confine my idea to the mere mechanical act of taking fish, but I look at its commercial relation; at its naval relation; I look at the prosperity of the country, and its connection with that prosperity. Fisher Ames said, in the same connection:

"'It forms a nursery for seamen, and this will be the source from which we are to derive maritime importance.'

"Mr. Gerry said in the same debate:

"'I will not reiterate the arguments respecting the fisheries; it is well known to be the best nursery for seamen.'

"Jefferson, as Secretary of State, in his report, in 1791, uses this language:

"'We have two nurseries for forming seamen. 1. Our coasting trade, already on a safe footing. 2. Our fisheries, which, in spite of natural advantages, give us just cause of anxiety.'

"After reviewing the condition of the fisheries, their necessities and importance, Mr. Jefferson said, in 1791:

"'It will rest, therefore, with the Legislature, to decide whether prohibition should not be opposed to prohibition, and high duty to high duty, on the fish of other nations; whether any, and which, of the naval and other duties may be remitted, or an equivalent given to fishermen, in the form of drawback or bounties.'

"Mr. Jefferson uses this language in his message of December 16, 1802:

"'To cultivate peace, and maintain commerce and navigation in all their lawful enterprises; to foster our fisheries and nurseries of navigation, and for the nurture of man * * * are the landmarks by which we are to guide ourselves in all our proceedings.'

"The importance of these fisheries to-day is well worthy of attention."

Mr. Hamlin made the following effective answer to the remark of the senator from Alabama, that the bounty law is unequal:

"The senator from Alabama may tell me truly that his State does not enjoy the advantages of the bounty law. Granted. The law which regulates the rates of postages and collects the revenue, for the purpose of paying for the transmission of mails, is no more and no less a general law than this in relation to fisheries; and, if there be force in the senator's argument, while it may not apply in as strong a degree in point of fact, it applies precisely with the same force to the post office laws. The Northern States pay more than the expenses of their mails, and contribute that amount to the support of mails in the South. In 1850, the total postage collected in the Southern States was $1,042,809.24, and the expense of transportation, $1,496,356.50; while, in the Northern States, the postage collected was $2,975,852.19, and the expense of transportation, $1,427,822.63. In 1855, the total postage collected in the Southern States was $1,553,198; cost of transportation, $2,385,953; while in the Northern States the postage was $4,670,725, and the transportation, $2,608,295. In 1857, the receipts were at the South, $1,672,856.78, and the cost of the service, $2,329,299; while in the North the receipts were $5,498,303.12, and the cost of service $4,095,267. In 1855, Maine contributed $151.358 to the Post Office revenues, and cost $82,218; while Alabama cost $226,-816, and contributed $104,514.

"I make no complaint of this; but I only use it as an illustration, for the purpose of showing that any general law, in its application, may draw from one section of the country a portion of the revenue to carry out the system in another. The senator's own State shows a deficiency in the post office revenue of about one hundred and twenty thousand dollars annually; and I contribute very cheerfully, whether it be by direct appropriation or in any other way, to supply the deficit, in order to carry out a general system. The post office law is no more general, no more applicable to all, than this other law. In the one case, the fisheries happen to be local, although connected with the commerce and navy of the country, and they are in their importance as national as though they spread all along the coast.

"Another word, sir. I have taken some pains to examine, from a paper which has been very kindly presented to me by a friend who has resided on the Pacific coast, the fisheries in those waters, and I have arrived at the conclusion that precisely the same state of things which exist on that coast exist on the Atlantic coast; and I have not a doubt that, for the purpose of raising a corps of seamen there, the application of this law is as wise for the Pacific coast as for the coast of the Atlantic. Nor have I a doubt that, when they come to examine it carefully, they will find it as necessary there as it is here, as wise there as it is here, and wise in both instances."

All who read the extracts which we have given, will see that fearless and decided as Mr. Hamlin has been in the utterance of his individual opinions, patriotism has always governed him more than partisanship. Devoted to his own state and people as few men have been, he has never been local or sectional. He has faithfully discharged all his duties as a public man, and will be prepared to meet the exalted responsibilities which may devolve upon him. He will doubtless prove the wise and trusted counselor of the chief magistrate of the Union, and will stand faithfully at his side a defender of "the rights of all the States, and Territories, and people of the Nation, the inviolability of the Constitution, and the perpetual union, harmony, and prosperity of all."

THE END.

www.ingramcontent.com/pod-product-compliance
Lightning Source LLC
LaVergne TN
LVHW020105110826
845151LV00001B/65

* 9 7 8 1 4 2 5 5 4 4 6 6 9 *